METROPOLITAN PHILARET OF NEW YORK

ZEALOUS CONFESSOR FOR THE FAITH

METROPOLITAN PHILARET OF NEW YORK

Zealous Confessor for the Faith

Edited by
Subdeacon Nektarios Harrison, M.A.

Uncut Mountain Press

METROPOLITAN PHILARET OF NEW YORK
Zealous Confessor for the Faith
© 2022
Uncut Mountain Press

uncutmountainpress.com

This volume was Blessed by His Grace + Bishop LUKE of Syracuse, Abbot of Holy Trinity Monastery & Rector of Holy Trinity Seminary, Jordanville, New York.

All Materials & Photos from the *Eastern American Diocese of the Russian Orthodox Church Outside of Russia* are used with permission. "Republication of materials for the glory of God is permitted. Official Website of the Eastern American Diocese ROCOR, eadiocese.org." http://archive.eadiocese.org/.

All Materials from the *Orthodox Life* are copyrighted by Holy Trinity Monastery, Jordanville, New York and used with permission and with the explicit Blessing of His Grace +Bishop LUKE (Murianka) of Syracuse, Abbot of Holy Trinity Monastery.

All Materials from the *Orthodox Word* are copyrighted by the St. Herman of Alaska Brotherhood, Platina, California and used with Permission and the Blessing of Fr Damascene (Christensen), Abbot of St. Herman of Alaska Monastery.

All Materials from the *Orthodox Heritage* are used with permission from the Greek Orthodox Christian Brotherhood of Saint Poimen.

All Materials from the *Orthodox Christian Information Center* can be found at the permanently archived website www.orthodoxinfo.com

Cover Artwork: George Weis
Special thanks to volunteer translators Fr. Zechariah Lynch & Matushka, Marilyn Swezey, and Simeon Nachev.

Scriptural quotations are primarily taken from the King James Version.

Metropolitan Philaret of New York: Zealous Confessor for the Faith—1st ed.
Researcher and Editor: Subdeacon Nektarios Harrison, M.A..
Assistant Editor: Maria Spanos

ISBN: 978-1-63941-018-7

I. Orthodox Christianity
II. Russian Orthodox Church

Dedicated To

This volume is dedicated to the Holy Hierarchs of the Russian Orthodox Church Outside of Russia, my wife Tamara and my dear friends Maria, Father Deacon Joseph, Reader Joseph and their families.

CONTENTS

Publisher's Note   11

By Archpriest Peter Alban Heers, D.Th.

Editor's Preface   13

By Subdeacon Nektarios Harrison, M.A.

Preface   15

By His Grace + Bishop LUKE (Murianka) of Syracuse &
Abbot of Holy Trinity Monastery, Jordanville, New York

Life of Metropolitan Philaret   17

Eastern American Diocese Biography of Metropolitan
Philaret **17**

A Short Biography on the Late Metropolitan Philaret
(Orthodox Life, 1985) **21**

New Primate of the Russian Orthodox Church Abroad **24**

The Enthronement of Metropolitan Philaret **26**

The Repose and Funeral Service of Metropolitan Philaret,
First-Hierarch of the Russian Orthodox Church Abroad **37**

Sermon at the Burial of His Eminence The Most Reverend
Philaret First-Hierarch of the Russian Orthodox Church
Abroad by Archbishop Vitaly of Montreal & Canada **42**

Eulogy on the Late Metropolitan Philaret from the Hermitage
of Our Lady of Kursk **43**

Protopresbyter Alexander Kiselev's Eulogy at the Funeral
of Metropolitan Philaret **46**

Our Living Links with the Holy Fathers: Metropolitan
Philaret of New York **48**

Homilies 55

Paschal Epistle of the Primate of the Russian Orthodox Church Outside of Russia (1969) **55**

Christmas Message of the President of the Synod of Bishops of the Russian Orthodox Church Outside of Russia (1970) **57**

Paschal Homily (1982) **59**

On Handing the Hierarchal Staff to His Grace, Bishop Hilarion of Manhattan **62**

On the Canonization of our Holy and God-Bearing Father Saint Herman of Alaska **65**

Epistle on the Glorification of St. Xenia of St. Petersburg **70**

On Blessed Father Herman to the Orthodox Christians in Australia **73**

He Who Believeth and is Baptized Shall Be Saved **74**

Refresher for a Russian Orthodox Pastor **76**

Epistle to Titus **78**

Discussion with a Youth Group about the Vespers Service **81**

On St. Nicholas the Wonderworker **86**

The Necessity of Fulfilling the Church's Commandments **88**

Every Christian Must Bear His Cross **90**

Christ is the Conqueror of the World **93**

A Sermon on the Fourth Sunday of Great Lent **96**

Homily During the Canonization of the Russian New-Martyrs **98**

Writings 103

The First Sorrowful Epistle (July 27, 1969) **103**

The Second Sorrowful Epistle (First Sunday in Lent, 1972) **117**

The Third Sorrowful Epistle: On The Thyateira Confession (December 19, 1975) **136**

The Triumph of Orthodoxy **142**

A Conversation of His Eminence Metropolitan Philaret with Students of Holy Trinity Theological Seminary in Jordanville, New York **144**

Address Before the Memorial Service for Vladyka John **157**

On Archbishop Saint John of San Francisco **159**

Will The Heterodox Be Saved? **161**

Concerning the Old Ritual **164**

Declaration To the Bishops, Clergy and Laity Assembly at St. Tikhon's Monastery **167**

An Epistle to All the Faithful Children of the Russian Orthodox Church Abroad Concerning the Approaching Glorification of the New-Martyrs of Russia **173**

The Catacomb Church: Epistle to Orthodox Bishops and all Who Hold Dear the Fate of the Russian Church **179**

First Statement on the American Metropolia (OCA) **186**

Letters   **189**

An Open Letter to His Eminence Archbishop Iakovos (Koukouzis) **189**

In Defense of Orthodoxy: Epistle to Metropolitan Ireney **194**

The Announcement of the Extraordinary Joint Conference of the Sacred Community of the Holy Mount Athos & An Epistle Response to Mount Athos by Metropolitan Philaret and Bishop Gregory of ROCOR **198**

To Patriarch Athenagoras of Constantinople on the Lifting of Anathemas from 1054 against the Latin Papists (1965); A Statement by the Head of the Free Russian Church on the Orthodox Relation to the Church of Rome **205**

Paschal Letter to Patriarch Athenagoras of Constantinople (1968) **210**

ROCOR Encyclicals and Synodal Epistles Under Metropolitan Philaret   **217**

Epistle of the Sobor of Bishops of the Russian Orthodox Church Abroad to the Faithful (1964) **217**

Archpastoral Encyclical of the Synod of Bishops of the Russian Orthodox Church Outside of Russia to the Orthodox Russian People in Diaspora **221**

Epistle of the Council of Bishops of the Russian Orthodox Church Abroad to the Russian People (1978) **227**

Epistle to the Flock of the Russian Church Abroad, Beloved of God **232**

Encyclical Letter of the Council of Bishops of the Russian Orthodox Church Outside Russia (1983) **237**

An Encyclical Letter of the Chairman of the Council of Bishops of the Russian Orthodox Church Outside Russia (1983) **247**

Resolution of the Council of Bishops of the Russian Orthodox Church Abroad on the Reception of Heretics Strictly by Baptism (1971) **255**

The Russian Orthodox Church Outside of Russia's Anathema Against Ecumenism (1983) **257**

Appendix A   259

Ecumenical Doxology with Archbishop Iakovos, Sunday, January 26, 1969

Appendix B   267

A brief word from Metropolitan Philaret on the Soviet church

Bibliography   271

The future Metropolitan Hilarion (then newly elected Bishop Hilarion)
with Metropolitan Philaret

PUBLISHER'S NOTE

We are eternally grateful to God that our small Press has been greatly blessed to offer to the Saint-loving flock of Christ the life, witness and writings of our Father among the saints, Metropolitan Philaret of New York, First Hierarch of the Russian Orthodox Church Outside of Russia.

This book fulfills the main mission of our Press: to connect contemporary Christians to the latest and most brilliant flowers in the paradise of the Church. As one incorrupt not only in life and faith but also in body after his repose, Blessed Father Philaret has both the veneration of the faithful on earth and the miraculous testimony of heaven to confirm the boldness he now has before God. Oh, how much we need such an example in our day! How blessed we are to now have it readily accessible!

We are indebted to our brother in Christ, Subdeacon Nektarios, a devoted servant of Christ's Church and zealous disciple of the saints, who, with undivided attention and patient perseverance, labored diligently to collect, organize and present all that the great hierarch offered and God blessed. We pray that the Holy Hierarch will reward him now and forever for his sacrificial love on behalf of the brethren.

Dearest to Christ, the Lord has not, and will not, leave us bereft of eye-witnesses of the Word in our generation and those to come—even in the days of Antichrist. This book is a confirmation of His faithfulness and, also, a call to all to synergy, to cooperation, to imitation of Christ in and through His saints. May this present volume inspire us all to follow and imitate our Holy Father Philaret in his love and devotion to Christ and Holy Orthodoxy in spite of the ever-growing tide of apostasy. His joy is full and, next to him, ours too. This cannot be taken away by anyone or anything in this world!

O Holy Hierarch and Confessor of Christ, Blessed Philaret, pray to God for us!

— Archpriest Peter Alban Heers, D.Th.

EDITOR'S PREFACE

My first introduction to Holy Orthodoxy in 2004 was through a zealous priest named Hieromonk Averky (Moreno) from Holy Trinity Monastery in Jordanville, New York. This Hieromonk who later would become my long-distance Spiritual Father instilled in me at a young age the traditional Orthodox Ethos and a great love for the Russian Orthodox Church Abroad. It was this chain of events that planted the seeds that would later become this book of collected writings from one of the great First-Hierarchs of the Russian Church Abroad; the Blessed Metropolitan Philaret (Voznesensky).

In his time, the words of Blessed Metropolitan Philaret of New York, Chief Hierarch of the Russian Orthodox Church Outside of Russia, distinctly resounded with clarity and righteousness, upholding the Orthodox truth. His words in this volume continue to have ever more meaning in the current times of increasing apostasy: "untainted by political considerations or calculations of any kind... [his voice] is like the Holy Fathers of ancient times, who placed purity of Orthodoxy above all else and he stands in the midst of today's confused religious world as a solitary champion of Orthodoxy in the spirit of the Ecumenical Councils."[1]

Although Vladyka Philaret reposed in November of 1985 his timeless writings and outspoken message of adhering to "the faith which was once delivered unto the saints" is more important today than ever before. In our age of post-patristic apostasy where Ortho-

---

1 Brotherhood of Saint Herman of Alaska, "Our Living Links with the Holy Fathers: Metropolitan Philaret of New York," *Orthodox Word* 12, no.1 (January-February 1976): 3-5.

dox Christian hierarchs and clergy around the world are adopting the soul-destroying heresies of modernism and ecumenism at a staggering rate, we can always seek truth, spiritual edification and archpastoral guidance in the letters, homilies, writings and encyclicals of our First-Hierarch and Father among the saints, Metropolitan Philaret of New York.

Blessed Father Philaret, Pray to God for us!

Subdeacon Nektarios Harrison, M.A.
Russian Orthodox Church Outside of Russia
Researcher & Editor

PREFACE

In these days of general apostasy in the Christian world, even among the Orthodox, the life of Metropolitan Philaret of New York and Eastern America of the Russian Orthodox Church Abroad is a breath of fresh air in the sea of a great weakening of true faith. Metropolitan Philaret was chosen as First-Hierarch much in the same way as the sainted Patriarch Tikhon of Moscow and All Russia had been elected. It was providential as he led the Church Abroad through many contemporary temptations afflicting the Church in general, such as Ecumenism and Modernism. Vladyka Philaret was a gifted sermonizer and speaker. His many sermons helped guide his spiritual children in maintaining the true faith. Even on the eve of his repose in 1985, he left in his typewriter his last words of advice: "Keep that which you have been given."

His epistles were a warning to his fellow hierarchs in other local churches to abstain from the tendency towards Ecumenism in a false spirit of love and also were a guide to those who sought to remain steadfast despite the inclinations of a wicked age towards the "wide path." Without judging anyone, the Holy Hierarch reminded all the Orthodox of the ageless path to salvation as taught by the Holy Fathers. May his writings and his very life inspire us to remain true to our holy faith. His holy incorrupt relics are a testament to the truth that he represented and still does through books such as this.

+ **LUKE**
Bishop of Syracuse
Abbot of Holy Trinity Monastery,
Rector of Holy Trinity Seminary, Jordanville, New York
Holy and Wonderworking Unmercenaries Cosmas & Damian
July 14/1, 2022

THE LIFE OF
METROPOLITAN PHILARET

Eastern American Diocese Biography of
Metropolitan Philaret[2]

Metropolitan Philaret was born George Nikolaevich Voznesensky in Kursk on March 22, 1903. His mother, Lidia Vasilievna, died when George was only 18 years old, while his father, soon thereafter accepting monastic tonsure under the name Dimitry, became an archbishop. In 1947, his father was repatriated to the USSR, where he died shortly thereafter. Metropolitan Philaret's family moved to Blagoveshchensk, on the Amur River in 1909. In 1920, he completed the eighth-grade gymnasia. Moving with his family to Harbin, he entered the Russo-Chinese Polytechnic Institute and graduated as an electromechanical engineer in 1927. In 1931, he completed the pastoral theology courses, soon thereafter renamed the Theology Department, at the University of St. Vladimir. He would later become a professor of New Testament, Pastoral Theology, and Homiletic studies at the same. In 1930, he was ordained to the diaconate and in 1931 was tonsured a monk under the name Philaret. A year later, he was ordained a Hieromonk, in 1933 — elevated to the rank

---

2 "Biography of Metropolitan Philaret (Voznesensky)," Official Website of the Eastern American Diocese of the Russian Orthodox Church Outside of Russia, accessed July 8th, 2017, http://archive.eadiocese.org/History/metphilaret.en.htm

Met. Philaret (George) as a Layman

of hegumen, and in 1937 — to the rank of archimandrite. One of Vladyka's university colleagues recalled, "Archimandrite Philaret did great work advancing Church activities and pastoral homiletics.

Worshippers would seek to attend whatever church he was serving in. He was beloved by every class of Harbin's Orthodox population. The name of Archimandrite Philaret was renowned even beyond the confines of the Harbin Diocese. He was kind, and accessible to all who approached him and that was a great many people. People who went to him knew that they would receive proper advice, as well as comfort and help. Archimandrite Philaret was very strict with himself; he was known as a true ascetic. Our kindhearted Vladyka also had a very rare kind of memory. When one would meet him, he would express great interest in every facet of one's life; he felt no need to remind anyone of his own needs or difficulties, but would develop any topic of conversation, and was ready to answer any question."

When Soviet forces occupied Manchuria, Archimandrite Philaret decisively refused to accept a Soviet passport. When a newspaper reporter came to interview him, asking what he thought of "the wise decision on the part of the Soviet government to offer the Russian population of Harbin the chance to reestablish the citizenship of their homeland," he heard the following courageous response: "I do not consider accepting Soviet citizenship possible, and will not do so, until such time as I will not have confirmed by the facts, and 100% without a doubt, that the persecution of religion, antireligious propaganda, and attacks on servants of the Church have ceased entirely, and that the Church, which did not 'secede,' but was banished by the government, has once more taken its rightful place."

Until the end of his days in China, Archimandrite Philaret never accepted Soviet citizenship, despite the danger inherent in taking such a position. Another time, Archimandrite Philaret was disciplined for his boldness. Once, having discovered a church newsletter in which Lenin was counted among the geniuses and benefactors of mankind, Archimandrite Philaret expressed his indignation in a sermon, which received widespread notoriety. His fearless denunciations of the *theomachist*[3] Communists inspired a particular hatred within them, and they decided to burn Archimandrite Philaret alive, lighting his monastic cell on fire. But the Lord preserved His chosen one, although with severe burns, Vladyka escaped the fiery trap alive.

Eastern American Diocese - Восточно-Американская епархия
eadiocese.org

Met. Philaret in his 20s

At all times working to defend his flock, he, in his own words, "never sullied my lips and my prayer with prayers for the servants of Antichrist," despite multiple threats. Additionally, Archimandrite Philaret also exchanged correspondence with the head of the Russian Church Abroad, Metropolitan Anastassy, ignoring the dangers implicit in doing so.

The Synod of Bishops tried long and hard to receive a visa for him to exit China and judging by available archived correspondence, almost every diocese of the Church Abroad hoped to get him for itself. Only in 1962 was the Synod of Bishops able to get Archimandrite Philaret to Hong Kong, from whence he was able to quickly get to Brisbane. A large portion of his former parishioners had gathered in Australia, and upon his arrival there, with a great many signatures, they petitioned the Synod to appoint him bishop of that city. The petition was enthusiastically supported by

---

3 Theomachist: A person who resists the divine will of God.

the already ailing Archbishop Savva, and in 1963 Archimandrite Philaret, to the joy of his former flock, became Bishop of Brisbane.

At the Council of Bishops in 1964, at which Metropolitan Anastassy announced his retirement, Bishop Philaret, having arrived in place of his ruling Bishop, Archbishop Savva, was elected First-Hierarch. The Council determined him to be the new Hierarch of the Russian Church Abroad, a burden he carried for 21 years. As it happened, almost in the middle of the period of his rule, the Third All-Diasporan Council was summoned. Our faithful immediately recall the four great glorifications of God-pleasers: Righteous St. John of Kronstadt, Venerable St. Herman of Alaska, Blessed St. Xenia of St. Petersburg, and the Holy New-Martyrs and Confessors of Russia.

Our First-Hierarch appealed more than once with enlightening letters to the heads of other Churches, many of whom heeded his call. Vladyka was a remarkable preacher. Deep faith, fiery prayer, kindness and benevolence, concern for the continued, undisturbed spiritual peace and steadfast defense and confession of Truth—these were the primary characteristics of our First-Hierarch, Metropolitan Philaret.

Vladyka reposed in the Lord on November 21, 1985, on the day of the Archangel Michael. His convictions were clearly expressed in his will. In the published Spiritual Testament, the Metropolitan said the following:

Hold that fast which thou hast! (Rev. 3:11).

These words, taken from the sacred Book of the Apocalypse, have a particular significance in our time, in our greatly sorrowful, evil, temptation-filled days. They remind us of that priceless spiritual wealth that we possess, as children of the Orthodox Church. Yes, we are rich. This spiritual wealth is that which the Holy Church possesses, and it is offered to all her faithful children. The teaching of the Faith, of our marvelous, salvific Orthodox Faith; the countless living examples of the lives of people who have lived according to the Faith, according to those lofty principles and rules that the Church offers us. Those who have attained that spiritual purity and exaltedness that is called holiness; the beauty and majesty of our Orthodox Divine services and a living participation in them through faith and prayer; the plenitude of the grace-filled spiritual life that is open to each and every one, and, crowning it all, the unity of the children of the Church in that love of which the Savior said: By this shall all men know that ye are My disciples, if ye have love one to another (John 13:35).

+ Metropolitan Philaret

A Short Biography on the Late Met. Philaret[4]

His Eminence, Metropolitan Philaret, whose secular name was George Nicholaevich Voznesensky, was born in Kursk on March 22, 1903 (O.S.). His mother, Lydia Vasilievna, reposed when he was eighteen, and his father subsequently took the monastic tonsure, receiving the name Dimitry, was consecrated a Bishop, and was repatriated (from Manchuria) to the U.S.S.R., where he reposed in 1947. In 1909, the family of Metropolitan Philaret moved to Blagoveshchensk, on the Amur River, where young George completed his studies at an eighth-grade secondary school. Emigrating with his family to Harbin, Manchuria, he enrolled in the Russo-Chinese Polytechnic Institute and was graduated from it in 1927 with a degree in electromechanical engineering. In 1931 he completed pastoral courses in theology at the St. Vladimir Institute in Harbin. Later, he was to serve there as an instructor in New Testament, Pastoral Theology, and Homiletics. Ordained to the diaconate in 1930, in 1931 he received the monastic tonsure with the new name Philaret; that same year he was ordained to the rank of hieromonk. In 1933 Father Philaret was elevated to the rank of abbot (hegumen), and in 1937 to the rank of archimandrite.

One of Vladyka Philaret's colleagues at the Institute remembers:
"Father Archimandrite Philaret undertook the great, celestial, and pastoral activity of teaching. The faithful

---

4 Holy Trinity Monastery, "A Short Biography of the Late Metropolitan Philaret," *Orthodox Life* 35, no. 6 (November-December 1985): 3-5.

would pack the church in which he was serving. All levels of Harbin's Orthodox populace loved him. The name of Archimandrite Philaret was widely known even beyond the boundaries of the Diocese of Harbin. He was kind and accessible to everyone who turned to him; and there were many who did. Going to him, they knew they would receive good advice, that they would find consolation and help. Father Archimandrite Philaret was quite strict with himself; he was well-known as a true ascetic. And what a rare memory our good, kind Vladyka possessed! When we met him, he showed great interest in all aspects of our life. He didn't have to be reminded of our needs or difficulties; he had already developed with us the theme of our conversation, and gave ready answers."

After Manchuria was occupied by the Soviet forces, difficult days began in Harbin. Deceived by false information on the state of the Church in Russia, the aged Metropolitan Melety acknowledged the authority of the Patriarchate of Moscow over himself and his clergy. Among the clergy was Archimandrite Philaret. However, he adamantly refused to accept a Soviet passport. When interviewed by a newspaper reporter who asked how he viewed "the wise step of the Soviet government which is offering the populace of Harbin the opportunity to be reinstated as citizens of their native land," Archimandrite Philaret gave the following bold reply, "I do not consider it possible to accept, nor will I accept, Soviet citizenship, until such time as I am really convinced, beyond a shadow of a doubt, one hundred percent, that the persecution of religion, antireligious propaganda, and the hunting down of the ministers of the Church has ceased entirely, and the Church, which did not separate, but was driven from the country, has resumed the position befitting it there."

Archimandrite Philaret thus, until the end of his residence in China, refused to accept Soviet citizenship, despite all the danger attendant upon such a position. On another occasion, Archimandrite Philaret was subjected to persecution for his boldness. Having become acquainted with an issue of the Journal of the Moscow Patriarchate, in which Lenin's name appeared in a list of the foremost benefactors of the human race, Archimandrite Philaret expressed his indignation in a sermon which became widely known.

His fearless denunciation of the godless Communists incited their particular rage, and they decided to burn Archimandrite Philaret alive, setting fire to his cell. But the Lord preserved His chosen one. Although badly burned, he escaped from the fiery trap alive. Protecting his flock in every way possible, he, as he himself put it, "never defiled (his) lips or his prayer with prayer for the servants of Antichrist," despite repeated threats. Furthermore, over the course of several years, Archimandrite Philaret communicated with Metropolitan Anastassy, the head of the Russian Orthodox Church Abroad, through various channels, despite the danger which this entailed.

The Synod of Bishops long and persistently endeavored to obtain an exit visa for him, and, judging by the correspondence preserved in the archives, nearly every diocese of the Church hoped to obtain him for itself. Only in 1962 was the Synod of Bishops successful in securing the release of Archimandrite Philaret to Hong Kong, from which he departed almost immediately for Brisbane, Australia. A significant number of Father Philaret's former parishioners had settled in Australia, and soon after his arrival there a petition was submitted to the Synod, over many signatures, requesting that Archimandrite Philaret be consecrated Bishop for Brisbane.

At the Council of Bishops of 1964, at which Metropolitan Anastassy retired, Bishop Philaret, a vicar Bishop who had come to the council with Archbishop Savva, his ruling Bishop, was elected First-Hierarch. He held that position for twenty-one years. Nearly midway through his tenure as First-Hierarch, the Third Pan-Diaspora Council was convoked. Especially memorable for our faithful are the four canonizations of saints which were celebrated within the past twenty years: St. John of Kronstadt, St. Herman of Alaska, St. Xenia the Blessed of Petersburg, and the New-Martyrs and Confessors of Russia. Our First-Hierarch repeatedly appealed to the heads of other Churches in admonitory letters, and several hierarchs heeded his voice. Vladyka Metropolitan was an excellent preacher.

A profound faith, ardent prayer, kindness and benevolence, care that spiritual peace not be violated, and steadfast confession of the Truth, were the characteristic traits of our departed First-Hierarch, Vladyka Metropolitan Philaret.

The New Primate of the
Russian Orthodox Church Abroad[5]

The newly-elected Metropolitan Philaret was born George Nicolaevich Voznesensky in Kursk, Russia on March 22, 1903. His father, a priest, was later a Bishop of the Russian Orthodox Church Abroad, His Grace Dimitry of Hailar, China, and lived in Harbin, Manchuria. Metropolitan Philaret lived with his father's family in Blagoveshchensk, Russia from 1909, where he completed his secondary school education. In 1920 he arrived in Harbin, where he graduated from the Russo-Chinese Polytechnical Institute with the diploma of electromechanical engineer. In 1931 he completed a course of pastoral theology in Harbin. A year prior to this, on May 5/18, he was ordained deacon, while on Dec. 22/Jan. 4, 1931, he entered the priesthood. A few days after this he became a monk and was given the name of Philaret. In 1937 he was raised to the grade of archimandrite, performing various duties in the Harbin diocese.

After the occupation of Manchuria by Soviet troops, Harbin fell upon troubled and difficult times. Having been deceived by false information about the position of the Church in the USSR, the very old Metropolitan Meletius recognized the authority of the Moscow Patriarchate over himself and his clergy. Now, while Archimandrite Philaret was a member of the clergy at that time, he absolutely refused to accept Soviet citizenship. When, in an interview by a newspaper reporter, he was asked how he regarded "the wise move of the Soviet Government in offering the Russian population of Harbin the right, once again, of becoming citizens of their native land", the reporter received the following bold reply: "I do not consider it possible to accept soviet citizenship, nor will

---

5 Holy Trinity Russian Orthodox Monastery, "New Primate of the Russian Orthodox Church Abroad," *Orthodox Life* 87, no. 3 (May-June 1964): 15-17.

I accept it, until such time as I am one hundred per cent convinced — by facts and beyond any shadow of doubt — that the persecution of religion, anti-religious propaganda and baiting of the Church's servants have ceased completely; when the Church, which is not merely "separated" but has in fact been banished from the State, once again takes Her rightful position within it." And His Eminence never did take out Soviet papers throughout the many years of his stay under communist rule in China, despite the grave danger in which such a stand placed him.

Archimandrite Philaret

On another occasion Archimandrite Philaret was subjected to certain disciplinary measures for his outspokenness. Having read in an issue of the Moscow Patriarchate's Journal the name of Lenin included in a list of geniuses and benefactors of the human race, Archimandrite Philaret expressed his indignation openly in a sermon from his pulpit which became widely known. In spite of frequent warnings and threats, Archimandrite Philaret repeatedly urged his flock to refrain from all pro-Soviet declarations and demonstrations. In his own words, he "never defiled his mouth and his prayers by praying for Antichrist's servants." At the same time, in the course of quite a number of years, he had kept in touch with His Eminence, Metropolitan Anastassy by various means, disregarding the real danger connected with these activities.

The Holy Synod had been taking all possible measures to get Archimandrite Philaret out of China since 1953. Visas to various [countries] were obtained for him repeatedly, but no advantage was taken of them. Sometimes this would be owing to the fact that he refused to leave his flock to the mercy of fate; at others, the communists would not issue an exit permit. And so His Eminence remained in a position which he himself described as that of a hunted rabbit being pursued by a pack of hounds. His Eminence Metropolitan Anastassy always wanted to have Archimandrite Philaret with him in New York, but yielded to Archbishop Savva's insistent pleas to retain him as his suffragan Bishop in Brisbane. Exactly a year ago Archimandrite Philaret was ordained Bishop of Brisbane, Australia. His labors there led to the fruitful development of many of the Church's activities.

The Enthronement of Metropolitan Philaret[6]

The enthronement of Metropolitan Philaret, which took place on Saturday and Sunday, May 17/30 — 18/31, developed into an unprecedented solemn feast which left a deep and abiding impression upon all. To a degree perhaps never before experienced by such a multitude, participants in this feast felt themselves engulfed by the grace-endowing and holy mystery of the Church. Of great influence was the fact that the entire service, both on Saturday and on Sunday was, so to say, spiritually imbued with the coming act of elevation to the head of the Church of the new metropolitan.

It was Dimitry Alexandrov, graduate of Holy Trinity Orthodox Seminary and firm worshipper of the Russian Church's ancient traditions, who was fortunate enough to come upon the original text of the enthroning ceremony which was used in old Moscow. Thus, by the Grace of God, our humble Church in Exile was, so to speak, especially called upon to feel Herself — even in her present humble and exiled-induced appearance — the very same Russian Orthodox Church of old, and that specifically by finding Herself today beyond the boundaries of Her beloved native land. In the continuing act of enthronisation, the consciousness in the faith of BEING THE CHURCH received incarnation.

All experienced quite an exceptional lifting of the spirit when at the end of the First Hour the whole Church was suddenly plunged into the sea of lights, the Royal Gates swung open and Metropolitan Philaret emerged, arrayed in the usual Bishop's violet

---

6 Holy Trinity Russian Orthodox Monastery, "The Enthronement of Metropolitan Philaret," *Orthodox Life* 87, no. 3 (May-June 1964): 6-15.

mantle and a black cowl with its diamond cross. All the Bishops disposed themselves in a semi-circle on either side of him. The metropolitan's blue mantle was brought out by Archbishop John; Archbishop Alexander carried the metropolitan's white cowl on a salver. (Both the mantle and cowl had just then been consecrated in the altar by Metropolitan Anastassy). The subdeacons removed the Bishop's mantle from Metropolitan Philaret's shoulders and Archbishop John handed him the metropolitan's mantle. "Axios." — was his cry. "Axios" — was the cry of all the Bishops and clergy. "Axios" — thundered the two choirs in succession. The impression was that these words were coming from the breasts of all those present, who had approached close to each other right up to the ambo. Archbishop Alexander presents the white cowl on the platter to the new metropolitan. And again "axios" is proclaimed in the same order as before, making it seem as if immeasurably more was being done before here than the normal elevation to the high order of metropolitan. The subsequent congratulations of the new metropolitan and the receipt of his blessing by all was conducted in an uncommonly warm atmosphere. All spoke of the great miracle that had been worked upon us by the Lord. Many wept from happiness and emotion.

One cannot help mentioning the blessed effect of Easter hymns which continued to sound throughout the service. Our spiritual joy took on a special tint which transformed everything we experienced into a second Easter. If the Church had been sufficiently filled during vespers on Saturday night, then it was literally packed right from the beginning of Divine Services on Sunday morning for Divine Liturgy. Worshippers stood close to each other right up to the ambo.

At 10:00 a.m. the new metropolitan was welcomed as he arrived in church. All the Bishops with their [croziers] and clergy arranged themselves on either side of the church entrance. The metropolitan is escorted into the church by the two senior prelates — Archbishops John and Alexander. After the entrance prayers and the singing of "Ton despotin" the same archbishops lead His Eminence to the cathedra in the center of the Church. "Axios" — proclaim Arch-

Eastern American Diocese - Восточно-Американская епархия eadiocese.org

Axios at the Enthronement of Metropolitan Philaret

bishops John and Alexander, followed by the Bishops and clergy and finally by the choir. The new metropolitan blesses the people on all four sides around him. The arrayment of the metropolitan begins. The mitre is brought out by the two senior clergyman — Archimandrite Panteleimon and Protopresbyter George Grabbe. The usual service begins. The Divine Liturgy flows on in triumphant and holy solemnity, peculiar to services conducted by a multitude of Bishops — there are sixteen prelates! But the solemnity is far from being a surface one; prayers rise to God from all hearts with a fervor perhaps never reached in this hallowed place of worship. The Church, here and now, is living a full life, fusing all into one holy entity. In such a spiritual state, physical fatigue is not felt, and the overcrowding itself is felt as an outward sign of the inner spiritual closeness. An endurance appears which will afterwards surprise many as they look back upon this solemn day. Wonderful are Thy works, O Lord!

Metropolitan Philaret delivers a sermon. There is simplicity in all his words and actions there is nothing artificial about him. "Be, and not merely appear to be" — this testament of his famous namesake seems to be incarnated in His Eminence. "Why, he is a born metropolitan!" — could later be heard from many. And the fact that there was not the merest trace of anything superficial in this simplicity forced one to not only admire the new metropolitan, but to become imbued with a feeling of deep personal affection for him. Unassumingly, calmly, naturally and with confident simplicity was each expected movement executed and each word delivered by him and this only increased the ineffable majesty of what was taking place. For it was not only that the youngest among the Bishops was being suddenly elevated to the highest position which was significant, but this very [height] received a new meaning, opening up for us perspectives which only yesterday seemed to have been antiquated.

Metropolitan Philaret delivered a sermon on the subject of the day's Gospel reading. In retelling with perfect accuracy, Christ's conversation with the woman from Samaria at Jacob's well, His Eminence underlined the extreme theological depth of this conversation, especially the unprecedented circumstantiality with which Our Lord replied to the woman's questions. He had never spoken so openly even with His disciples! And finally — those clear and great words of the Messiah, which also had not yet been heard by His disciples:

"I that speak unto thee am he!"

At this point the preacher turns his attention directly upon his listeners.

To whom is Our Lord speaking in this manner? Is it not to a wanton and sinful woman? Would we not have condemned her immediately, having recognized her as being depraved and morally worthless? Our Lord and God is here teaching us a lesson: not to despise even the most terrible sinners. For this follows from the first and most important commandment, love — which does not condemn anyone, but is forbearing and compassionate.

But there is yet an even greater lesson here. Admittedly, the life of the woman from Samaria was burdened with passions and great sins; her heart was not alien to what?

KNOWLEDGE OF GOD! That is why Our Lord was able to reveal Himself as the Messiah specifically to her! The preacher then reminds his listeners of the publican Zacchaeus; treated with contempt by all as a morally worthless individual. In him, too, Our Lord saw a spark of goodness, thus converting it into a roaring flame. To all their environment, both the woman from Samaria and the publican were fallen souls, all around them could see nothing else in them. Our Lord noticed this spark in them and how brightly did he make it burn! This woman from Samaria — did she not become the first preacher of Christ?

Let us not, then, condemn anyone. Let us try to discover a spark of goodness at least in each and every one. Can there be such a person who would lack even this measure? For this to be true, a human being must become a veritable demon! Let us regard each other with love, for love does not condemn anyone; it regards everyone with forbearance and compassion. And may the Lord of all be with us. Amen. At the end of the service — another memorable event, without which that spiritual happiness and fervent hope which were increasingly enveloping everyone, could not have reached fulfillment. The beatific "staretz", the new metropolitan, all the Bishops and clergy — all move out of the altar to the center of the church. Archbishop John brings out the Panagia on a salver. Metropolitan Philaret makes an address to Metropolitan Anastassy. He reminds him of how mindful were all the members of the Sobor of Bishops to the Holy Father's word of farewell. He reminds him how earnestly the Sobor had begged His Lordship not to carry out his decision to step down. The Lord Metropolitan had remained adamant, and the Sobor had bowed before this decision. A successor was elected. But Metropolitan Anastassy continues to be, spiritually and morally, the head and the father of all. "All of us are your spiritual children. And the Sobor of Bishops has instructed me to place upon you, together with the title of Beatific, a second Panagia. I ask you to submit to the will of the whole Sobor and to accept this expression of our filial love toward Your Beatitude."

"Axios!" — exclaims Metropolitan Philaret, and this echoed in turn by the Bishops and the clergy, and by the choirs. The fulness of joy has been attained. The wise and beatific father remains close to the new Primate. His Beatitude has not retired into seclusion. His wise leadership has merely taken on a new form, now leaning upon the filial loyalty of the new head of our Church. The Te Deum is sung with a new prayerful exhilaration. At the end of the Te Deum, Archbishop John hands Metropolitan Philaret his crozier, while Archbishop Alexander loudly repeats (mutatis mutandis) the very words which, many centuries ago, were heard by new metropolitans in old Moscow:

"The Almighty and Life-endowing Holy Trinity, Immeasurable Dominion and Indivisible Kingdom, is granting you this great throne of prelates, the Metropolis and Primacy in the Russian Church Abroad, by the act of election by your brothers, Russian Orthodox Bishops. And now, Lord and brother, take this crozier of pastorship and ascend the throne of the holy primacy in the name of Our Lord Jesus Christ, and beseech His Most Pure Mother on behalf of all Orthodox Christendom and those Russian people in exile who have been placed in your charge, and tend them like a good shepherd, and may the Lord God grant you the health and life for many years."

The choir sings, "Ispolla etti despota." Metropolitan Philaret replies, "May the Almighty and All-containing Right Hand of the Most High protect and strengthen all of you. May He grant peace and contentment to His Holy Church and deliverance to our native land. And to you my brothers, prelates of the Russian Church Abroad, to all the Russian people presently in exile and to all Orthodox Christians, may He grant health and life for many years." The choirs again sing "many years."

The enthronisation ceremony has come to its end. All surge forward toward Metropolitan Anastassy to receive his blessing. The fear of his early departure is so great that, people push and jostle each other to get near. Many are fortunate enough to receive the blessings of both metropolitans. The love of all who have gathered is directed toward both; to the well-known and personally close to all, beatific father-metropolitan, [and] to the new ruling head who, prior to this, was known to hardly anyone, but who, literally within the short space of a few hours, became just as close and just as dear. This makes the flood of congratulations a natural conclusion to the blessed emotions experienced during this great and solemn feast. A full hour went by for all to express their warm feelings to the new metropolitan.

The two metropolitans, Bishops and clergy unite with some of the laity at a reception held in the refectory, where many have an opportunity to express their feelings. Archbishop Averky, on behalf of Holy Trinity Monastery, presented Metropolitan Philaret with an icon of Our Lady of Pochaev, and in a brief welcoming address, begged the new Primate's prayers and paternal attention for the monastery, with its printing office and seminary, so that it may continue to fruitfully develop and strengthen its activities in the service of the Russian Church Abroad. Metropolitan Anastassy was the last to speak. With tender emotion he speaks of the grace Our Lord had sent. In the midst of unprecedented trials and tribulations, something also unprecedented arose, which elevated the youngest among us to the position of head overall. His Beatitude called upon everyone to rejoice in the firm belief that this event's beneficent effects would be felt even by following generations.

We must beseech God to further strengthen and increase the many noble qualities which Metropolitan Philaret, in his humility, refused to recognise in himself. Virtually glowing with happiness, Metropolitan Anastassy repeats these thoughts in various forms, as if to implant them firmly in the hearts of his listeners. In conclusion, he recalls how Metropolitan Philaret had always been joyful by nature, even in his school days; how he had been a comfort to all who knew him. His soul, ever sound, had always sought to be united with others in sound joyfulness, which he had the ability to transmit to others as no one else could. His Beatitude felt a deep satisfaction now over the fact that all members of the Church had immediately accepted Metropolitan Philaret as a shepherd after their own heart. May the good Lord not take him away from us! May our hearts rejoice in the Lord! Let us pray to Him so that now, when there is so little happiness on earth, He may preserve our Church in happiness. May the risen God defeat His enemies. Christ is Risen!

A public assembly was arranged for 6:00 p.m. in a nearby building belonging to the Presbyterian church. The huge hall was crowded. The Sobor of Bishops, headed by the two metropolitans, sat at the speaker's table. At the center of attention was of course, Metropolitan Philaret, the first to speak. After a few introductory remarks, His Eminence felt it incumbent upon him to direct particular attention of his listeners to the sad state of neglect of the Gospel in our time. It would appear self-evident that everyone had to be familiar with the Gospels, yet in fact what do we find? Whenever some specialist, such as a physicist or a mathematician, picks up a book dealing with his field, he is immediately able to find what he wants in it. While, we Orthodox, whenever some of us have to find something in the Gospels — do we not find ourselves helplessly lost in the Holy Book? Do we not find it a stranger to us? And yet it is only there that we will find an answer to all our problems, and nowhere else will we be able to obtain an answer. Let us turn to the Holy Book with the questions puzzling us.

In the Gospel according to St. John we will find recounted Our Lord's conversation with Pilate. The Roman governor asked Our Lord, "Art thou the King of the Jews?" Jesus answered him, "Sayest thou this thing of thyself, or did others tell it thee of me?" Pilate answered, "Am I a Jew? Thine own nation and the chief priests have delivered thee unto me. What hast thou done?"

And what did Our Saviour reply to this? "My Kingdom is not of this world." Here you have the clear and exact answer to the problem which is worrying all of us and which easily becomes a dividing issue. May the Church serve political ends? Of course not! This does not mean, however, that the Church should remain indifferent to what is happening around her. To provide an example,

His Eminence quite naturally referred to what was experienced in the Far East.

Some high dignitaries of the Soviet Church appeared there one day. They made public speeches and were excellent orators. Many were charmed and delighted by their sermons. Not so the present speaker: on him they had an opposite effect. Things in no way deserving of praise were presented in glowing colors and any criticism was forbidden. St Gregory Nazianzen says that by silence is the truth often betrayed. Did not Metropolitan Philip accuse Ivan the Terrible? Was that interference in politics? No! Philip had spoken out as a loyal subject. He was not meddling in politics, but illuminating what was going on around him with the bright rays of the Gospel's eternal truth.

Do we not, then, receive a clear indication in the Gospels as to the Church's attitude towards politics? His Eminence returns to Christ's conversation with Pilate. Pilate said unto him, "Art thou a king then?" Jesus answered, "Thou sayest that I am a king. To this end was I born, and for this cause came I into the world, that I should bear witness unto the truth. Every one that is of the truth heareth my voice." "What is truth?" replies Pilate and leaves. Truth Incarnate stood before Pilate, yet he turns away from Her, attempting to justify this action with his scornful question. Once again, is it not directly to us that exact indication is given of the Gospel's attitude towards what is today at the center of the world's attention? Ecumenism!

What is its mission, toward the realization of which it is attracting everyone? To search for the Truth! It is alleged that fragments of this Truth are to be found everywhere and that it merely remains to bring these segments together for the fullness of Truth to be revealed! How could our Church possibly agree to such a thing? By so doing She would only be delivering the Truth up to abuse and ridicule. No, our Holy Church has not committed, nor will She ever commit, this crime. Let all around us seek after the Truth, let them unite in the name of this task. The Orthodox Church is not a party to this quest; She has no need to look for the Truth — She possesses Her in full measure.

Metropolitan Philaret returns to the Far East in his recollections. There the Church had been preserved unimpaired. Only the vaguest rumours were heard of Western disagreements. The terrible trials arose with the coming of the Japanese. Great courage was displayed by the frail and ailing Metropolitan Meletius when the Japanese began to demand obeisance from all before their goddess Amaterasu. Even worse trials arose with the name of this task. The Orthodox Church is not a party to Far Eastern Church's absorption by the Moscow Patriarchate, but pointed out a number of mitigating circumstances behind the tragedy. This made him all the more [grateful] to our Church in Exile for Her continued loyalty to Orthodoxy. And all of us must likewise become completely imbued with this feeling of gratitude. It is only the Russian Church Abroad which today continues to openly denounce godlessness. Her way is that of the Cross, but it is also the road to salvation. And here too, the Gospels will serve as our guide — so long as we firmly remember that there is only one purpose in the Church's existence, to prepare souls for eternity.

A number of other speakers followed, and all were heard with undivided attention by the vast auditorium. All were imbued with the one spirit. And the heart felt expressions of good will were equally warm as the speakers addressed themselves to His Beatitude, Metropolitan Anastassy, and to his successor who was now being honoured. There was no loss felt because both metropolitans were regarded as one in the public eye. This conception was fully justified in the closing addresses of the two Metropolitans. The meeting was coming to a close. Of deep significance was Metropolitan Philaret's reply to the many welcoming addresses he had received. Having thanked all for their kind words, he cast his mind into the future. It was unknown to us. But do not all of us see what is happening in the world?

Attempts are being made to reconcile the irreconcilable; everything is being dumped into one pile, for what purpose? For the sake of material welfare and prosperity! Everyone keeps talking about peace — but will Our Lord grant peace to the wicked? We can only expect things to get worse in the future. Great trials and

tribulations await us. High spiritual qualities, great courage and an unshakable faith will be required of all of us in order to withstand. And all these — to the highest degree — will be demanded, first of all, from the head of the Church. He will have to possess the combined virtues of Sts. Basil the Great, Gregory Nazianzen and John Chrysostom. His Eminence is unable to discover the barest trace of these gifts within himself. But he does not lose courage, prayer can do anything! Through the prayers of many even the weakest receive the strength of the Holy Spirit. He implores all to remember him in their daily prayers.

The final note was sounded in the gentle words of His Beatitude, Metropolitan Anastassy. Let there be darkness ahead; his radiant and joyful outlook remained unclouded. The Lord had heard our prayers. Our Lord had not abandoned His Church and had given us great comfort at the very time when we were in the direst need of it. We all manifestly experienced His grace. Our new head has brought us not only love, but strength of the Holy Spirit as well. Let us take his words close to heart [and] let us pray the Lord to grant us all that spiritual strength without which a rebirth is impossible. May the Lord multiply His life-giving strength in His Church — He alone works miracles! He alone has the power to restore Holy Russia!

Many good wishes we have heard here today, emanating from the fullness of heart. But all these wishes come to but one thing, without which we will show ourselves powerless of doing anything truly good. We must be reborn in the Holy Spirit and unite in Him. For Satan himself has now appeared in the world. Terrible times are approaching. Only the grace of God can help us, and we have every reason to firmly believe we will receive His assistance. This day is a famous and historical day. Our Lord has manifestly extended His help to us. All around us the very depths of hell are rapidly destroying all the foundations of the world. But the Lord is our strength. What can we ourselves do? Our strength is not in us, but in God. And He is with us. Let us pray to the Lord not to abandon us also in the days to come and to crush the head of the serpent with His power. Christ is Risen! Thus ended this truly "historical and famous day," opening up a new era in the history of our Church in Exile.

The Repose and Funeral Service of Metropolitan Philaret, First-Hierarch of the Russian Orthodox Church Abroad[7]

Vladyka Metropolitan Philaret had been ailing for quite some time and in August of 1985, had undergone minor surgery. After the operation, his physicians assured both Vladyka Metropolitan and the Secretary of the Synod that his health would hold for another five years. However, their hopes were not justified, and about a month before Vladyka's repose he began to decline. Mastering himself, he nonetheless attended the liturgy in church on a nearly daily basis, and on feast days, even if he was not able to serve, he still vested in his mantle and preached the sermon, seated on the ambo.

Sunday, November 10th, was the last day he appeared in the Synodal cathedral. Vladyka was no longer able to serve by himself, but stood in his customary place near the right kleros. That day, His Grace, Bishop Gregory served. For those who were close to Vladyka and had known him for a long time, it was obvious that it took a tremendous effort for him to stand up to return the bow of the serving hierarch. That day, Vladyka received Communion in the altar, and afterwards, having vested in mantle and omophorion, delivered his last sermon.

---

7 Holy Trinity Monastery, "The Repose and Funeral Service of Metropolitan Philaret First-Hierarch of the Russian Orthodox Church Abroad," *Orthodox Life* 35, no. 6 (November-December 1985): 5-9.

At about 4:00 A.M., on Monday, Vladyka summoned his spiritual father, His Grace, Bishop Gregory, to hear his confession and to receive Communion. Vladyka Metropolitan was very apologetic for disturbing him at such an early hour, and Bishop Gregory noticed the intense suffering the Metropolitan was experiencing. Vladyka's personal physician, when summoned, said that an operation was essential, but warned that it would be complicated and serious. Search then began for a vacant room in a hospital, and on Thursday, 8/21 November, Vladyka was to be admitted prior to this surgery. But the Lord judged otherwise. On the morning of the feast of the Archangel Michael, Vladyka reposed peacefully in his sleep.

Vladyka's cell attendant, discovering that he was no longer breathing, hurriedly called His Grace, Bishop Gregory, and then proceeded to call in the doctor and an ambulance. The paramedics' attempts to revive Vladyka Metropolitan did not meet with success. While they were laboring over the lifeless body of the Metropolitan, Archimandrite Gelassy began the reading of the canon for the departure of the soul. Vladyka's dining room, adjacent to his cell, rapidly filled with agitated parishioners, among whom the sad news had spread with the speed of lightning.

The departed First-Hierarch had always had an aversion to the hospital environment, and to medical treatment in general. Submitting only when absolutely necessary, he reluctantly gave his permission for medical examination and a few tests. With his physical condition already weakened by loss of blood, it was doubtful that he would have survived such a serious operation. In sending him a peaceful end in his sleep, in his own bedroom, the Lord delivered him from the hands of the coroner's office personnel. Vladyka was clothed and vested by the hands of his own clergy and placed by them in the coffin brought in for that purpose.

News of the repose of the Metropolitan spread with such rapidity that the receptionist and the chancery of the Synod could barely cope with the incessant calls. Nearly thirty priests and more than a hundred people attended the first panikhida, held that evening at 7:00 P.M. His Grace, Archbishop Vitaly, the Deputy President of the Synod, arrived from Canada for the panikhida, which he

concelebrated with their Graces, Bishop Gregory of Washington
and Florida, and Bishop Hilarion of Manhattan. Bishop Gregory
delivered the sermon at that panikhida. He emphasized that the
name of Metropolitan Philaret would go down in the history of the
Russian Orthodox Church Abroad as that of a hierarch who presided over four canonizations of saints. Despite his mild character,
Vladyka at times had to stand for his own opinion, as was notice-
able in the question of several of the names of the New-Martyrs of
Russia. Vladyka knew well and loved the divine services, and was
a great man of prayer, in which he serves as an example for us all.

Right up to the day of the burial, the panikhidas, which were
served morning and evening, invariably brought together many
clergymen and laymen, who hastened to bow down before the
body of their First-Hierarch. The all-night vigil on Saturday was
preceded by an amply attended panikhida served by Archbishops
Vitaly of Canada, Anthony of San Francisco, Laurus of Syracuse
and Holy Trinity, as well as Bishops Constantine of Richmond
and Great Britain, Gregory of Washington and Florida, Alypy of
Cleveland, and Hilarion of Manhattan. The vigil began with the
chanting of the introductory psalm to a setting composed by the
late First-Hierarch. Almost twenty priests, eight protodeacons and
deacons, and a multitude of acolytes, went forth at the polyeleos.
There were a great many people in church as well.

The whole while, from the first hour after the repose of Metropolitan Philaret until his burial, the Holy Gospel was read over his
coffin without interruption, except during the divine services and
panikhidas. On the following day, Sunday, the liturgy began in the
Synodal cathedral at 10:30 A.M. The choir, under the direction
of Alexander B. Ledkovsky, made a special effort to perform all
the compositions of the late Metropolitan with which they were
acquainted, at the liturgy.

The liturgy was concelebrated by their Graces: Archbishops
Vitaly of Montreal and Canada, Anthony of Western [America]
and San Francisco, Laurus of Syracuse and Holy Trinity, Bishops
Gregory of Washington and Florida, Alypy of Cleveland, and
Hilarion of Manhattan. Archbishop Seraphim of Chicago, Detroit

Metropolitan Philaret's Funeral (November 1985)

and the Midwest, and Bishop Constantine of Richmond and Great Britain, remained in the altar. Thirty priests, five protodeacons and four deacons, with a great many acolytes, also served. During the liturgy, the flock, grieved by the repose of their archpastor, was unexpectedly gladdened by the arrival in the church of the myrrh-streaming Iveron Icon, which remained for the length of the funeral services. The liturgy concluded at 1:20 P.M., and the funeral began immediately afterwards. More priests, from nearby parishes, arrived, so that there were forty-six priests and nine deacons, plus acolytes of all ages, in the middle of the Church. The Cathedral was, as at Pascha, full to overflowing.

During the communion of the clergy, a beautiful sermon was delivered by Protopresbyter John Legky. A second sermon was given by Fr. Alexander Kiselev in the middle of the funeral service, and towards the end, His Eminence, Archbishop Vitaly delivered a brief sermon, also reading the spiritual testament to the flock which had been found among Metropolitan Philaret's papers just after his repose. This statement was signed by Vladyka Metropolitan, probably three days before his repose, and reinserted into the typewriter. Photocopies of this page were distributed to all who attended the funeral.

Solemn and magnificent, without any significant omissions, the funeral produced a sense of compunction among those attending. Especially moving was the moment when the clergy lifted the coffin of the Metropolitan upon their shoulders and bore it to the ambo, and thence, during the chanting of the Eirmos: "A helper and protector," carried it around the inner walls of the Church and set it back in the center of the Church, allowing everyone an opportunity to bid farewell to the departed. This leave taking ended at about 7:00 P.M., and the coffin was borne out into the courtyard of the Synod, to be placed in a hearse for transportation to Holy Trinity Monastery, Jordanville, New York, where the interment was to take place.

The Burial took place in the monastery on the following day, Monday. At 9:30 the Liturgy began, after which a panikhida was celebrated by all of the above-mentioned hierarchs, thirty priests, and seven deacons. The choir of the monastery chanted with compunction. After the liturgy, His Eminence Archbishop Anthony of San Francisco delivered a eulogy, and Archbishop Laurus spoke after the panikhida. There also the church was filled with people who had travelled from New York, as well as parishioners of the Diocese of Syracuse. A large group of Greeks arrived from Canada to bid farewell to their departed First-Hierarch.

At the conclusion of the panikhida, the clergy again shouldered the coffin and bore it around the church, and then to the Church of the Dormition in the cemetery, when a litia was served and the coffin placed in a niche in the crypt under the church. A group of those who honor the late Metropolitan intend to erect a fitting chapel near the Holy Trinity Cathedral, where the remains of the First-Hierarch will ultimately be interred. The Synod of Bishops received a number of expressions of sympathy from the heads of several Orthodox Churches, as well as from prominent lay persons and organizations, several of whom gave donations to the Synod of Bishops "in lieu of flowers."

Vladyka Metropolitan Philaret achieved worldwide fame for his "Sorrowful Epistles," addressed to all the Orthodox Bishops of the world, in which he warned them of the danger of ecumenism. With

his repose an important page in the history of the Russian Orthodox Church Abroad has been turned. His repose was reported in
The New York Times (twice), The [N.Y.] Daily News, News Day,
and in numerous newspapers throughout the nation which received
the information through the Associated Press News Service. A short
announcement was telecast over New York's Channel 7 television
station (the ABC television network), and broadcast over the radio.

Sermon at the Burial of His Eminence the Most Reverend Philaret First-Hierarch of the Russian Orthodox Church Abroad by Archbishop Vitaly of Montreal & Canada[8]

A great page has been turned in the history of the Russian
Orthodox Church Abroad. An entire chapter of it has come to an
end. The candle of our First-Hierarch's life has been extinguished.
The mouth which proclaimed the pure, inviolate confession of the
Orthodox Faith has been closed. When word of his repose spread
throughout the whole world, the Orthodox world was startled, for
the voice of the conscience of the Orthodox Church had fallen silent. In accordance with the unfathomable ways of the Providence
of God, our First-Hierarch was destined to lead our Church to the
very threshold of the Apocalypse, when in the thick darkness of
our life, against the somber purple background of time's horizon,
ominous flashes of the beginning of the end are visible. He stood
still, like a lighthouse, and with the light of his righteous words he
clove the darkness of the night which increasingly enshrouds us all
around: yet his tender soul already began to grow faint because
of the appearance of approaching trials. The torments of his
soul were soon transmitted to his already weakened body, and he
became utterly exhausted. Then the all-merciful Lord, seeing the

---

8 Holy Trinity Monastery, "Sermon at the Burial of His Eminence The Most
Reverend Philaret First-Hierarch of the Russian Orthodox Church Abroad by
Archbishop Vitaly of Montreal & Canada," *Orthodox Life* 35, no. 6 (Novem-
ber-December 1985): 10-11.

inner sufferings of His servant, sent His angel, who, while he was asleep, made His repose peaceful, serene, and painless.

And now, O our First-Hierarch, when you stand before the throne of God and bow down before the One God Who is worshipped in the Holy Trinity, the Father, the Son, and the Holy Spirit— pray with your glorious predecessors, Metropolitans Anthony and Anastassy, for the suffering Church of Russia, for her militant forces on earth, the ship of which is entering a sea of stormy weather and the contrary winds of men's passions. Pray to the Lord, that we who remain in the vale of trials may walk the same path which was traced for us by the great Apostle of the Gentiles for the life of Christ's Church and Her faithful children, when he wrote in His Epistle to the Corinthians so tersely and so powerfully "by honour and dishonour, by evil report and good report; as deceivers, and yet true; as unknown, and yet well known; as dying, and, behold, we live; as chastened, and not killed; as sorrowful, yet ever rejoicing; as poor, yet making many rich; as having nothing, and yet possessing all things" (2 Corinthians 6:8-10).

Such a path did our First-Hierarch tread; in such conditions does our entire good and faithful clergy live, the whole faithful flock of our Church. Help us, O Lord, to travel this glorious path of witness until the end, that we also may hear the sweet voice of our Saviour say: "Good and faithful servant thou hast been faithful over a few things; enter thou into the joy of thy Lord" (Matthew 25:21).

Eulogy on the Late Metropolitan Philaret from the Hermitage of Our Lady of Kursk[9]

Friends and Well Wishers of Our Lady of Kursk Hermitage:

A man's wisdom will lighten his countenance...
(Ecclesiastes 8:1 LXX)

As you all must know, our Vladyka Metropolitan (Philaret) left us to join the angels on the Feast of Angels. Having been appointed

9 Holy Trinity Monastery, "Eulogy on the Late Metropolitan Philaret from the Hermitage of Our Lady of Kursk," *Orthodox Life* 35, no. 6 (November-December 1985): 21-22.

by Vladyka to be starosta these seven years in Mahopac, I have
had some occasion to know him. My relationship with him was
quite formal. I did not know him with that effortless ease and
intimacy with which so many others knew him, yet I thoroughly
enjoyed the quiet and regal presence of this gentle and angelic man.
His 'presence' was the keynote of what seemed most singular and
extraordinary to me, something wordless, intensely dignified, and
conscious, that penetrated to the very bones of those present. Great
silence and time were main springs of his person, his very words
were enclosed in silence, silence was at the heart of them, they arose
out of silence. He seemed to wait there behind the silence, to wait
there for you, for everyone — so as to greet them — in a holy place.
He waited for us all, even the whole Church, and condemned no
man, neither did he despise any. Those who were foolish and naked
he protected because he hated mockery.

He waited there in full consciousness, no man fooled or tricked
him — he, an undeceived but generous witness. He waited there behind the silence of his words and smiles, behind the joyful, intensely
personal celebrations of those he loved most effortlessly, behind the
delicate and shy pauses when we stood in our own foolishness and
triviality before him. He waited for us all in silent reverence, with
the greatest respect and attention. Never to break, nor despoil, nor
wound — that in silence and in secret our hearts might arise in
us and recall us again to the True Love. He knew full well that
wisdom and love and the redemption of a Christian soul cannot be
legislated or coerced.

He gave "time" to men with the same extravagant generosity
that his own saint gave goods when he had been upon the earth.
These gifts of "time" would suspend a human life in hope a little
longer, were more valuable than gold to so many. He bought for so
many a few more days, months, or years in which a soul might be
recalled, unbruised, in kindness to his Christ. In the angelic presence of his own person he gave freedom to men, whereby another
might judge them, if any — but not he — a freedom that might
perhaps allow some shame and sanity to emerge from the deepest
recesses of the heart, and the heart to be broken from within by the

Lord Himself. This is a great and wonderful freedom; this is a gift which leads to the hope of salvation!

He lay in state in the Synod Cathedral those several days, magnificent still, with that same unbroken presence. The simplest child understood under whose shadow it had stood, swollen little faces appeared everywhere throughout the services. An experience of terrible vacancy and loss was on the faces of so many. Only the spiritual beauty and power of requiem services could assuage such grief. In the words of a great Russian writer of the last century, describing an eternal "Russian monk," our Vladyka was long known for having "kept the image of Christ fair and undefiled, in the purity of God's truth, from the times of the Fathers of old, the Apostles and the Martyrs." Our Vladyka exhorted us in his last testament "to hold fast and keep clean before God that which our Holy Church has given us from the beginning."

Others will write historical descriptions of Vladyka; we wished only to say a "word" about him here in Mahopac. Our rector, Archpriest Konstantin Fedoroff, spiritual son of Vladyka, who has the greatest depth of love and gratitude for him, is certain that Vladyka has not left us — and never will. He exhorts everyone to keep and hold the spiritual content of Vladyka's injunctions, that only the greatest spiritual goods can come to us through Vladyka's prayers. We also pray that Christ will be once again swaddled in the spiritual stables of our own hearts on the coming Christmas. ETERNAL MEMORY!

Simeon Richard, Starosta

I share the thoughts of the starosta and wish you all spiritual joy.
Archpriest Konstantin Fedoroff
Acting Rector, Hermitage of Our Lady of Kursk

Protopresbyter Alexander Kiselev's Eulogy at the Funeral of Metropolitan Philaret[10]

In the name of the Father and the Son and the Holy Spirit!

Today we escort the third Metropolitan of our Orthodox Russian Church Abroad to the eternal life. It is not now time for us to make some kind of comparisons between these three hierarchs. I will allow myself in my allotted time a short word on the spiritual character of our reposed Metropolitan Philaret — that is, how he seemed to me to be. I think that the words of the Savior, spoken at one time to children, "Of such is the Kingdom of Heaven" (Matthew 19:14), apply to him fully. Our Metropolitan had those particular character traits that are particular to those people who preserved them from their childhood – preserved that openness, that kindness, that tenderness, that, which favorably disposes one man to another. Vladyka possessed these traits in great measure, and this was felt foremost by the children and youth beloved by him. And so Vladyka lies in his coffin. He departs for a life inhabited by the righteous.

Vladyka, with these especially gentle traits of his, led what one might consider a very difficult life, combining these traits with those of a man standing at the head of the Church. And I would like to straightway speak my mind, and say that we are all guilty in his struggles. We all, who in one way or another relied on him, multiplied his already difficult duties, particularly strenuously coupled with his gentle and, in the best sense of the word, virginal characteristics, the sustainment of which for adults is often less than simple. We are all guilty of this. Those who transgressed and those who did not stop the transgressors, and those who thought their business was to come to Church from time to time and considered themselves Orthodox, let alone Orthodox members of the Russian Orthodox Church Abroad, as something special in Orthodoxy.

---

10 "Protopresbyter Alexander Kiselev's Eulogy at the Funeral of Metropolitan Philaret," Official Website of the Eastern American Diocese of the Russian Orthodox Church Outside of Russia, accessed July 8th, 2017, http://archive.eadiocese.org/History/metphilaret/eulogy.en.htm

All of us, in one way or another, are guilty of not helping him, quite the opposite, we complicated the already difficult ways of Church life, that Church life which cannot be separated from all of the terrors of this world that occur around us. It is impossible that all of this will not penetrate the Church, and in some degree it has penetrated, for everyone who lives outside of the Church, like it or not, is to some degree filled with that atmosphere in which the modern world finds itself, and upon entering the Church, brings that atmosphere into the Church. How then is it to live as the First-Hierarch of the Church in such circumstances?

And then, forgive me another candid word. The words of the Gospel come to mind, the words of the Savior, our Lord Jesus Christ, Who said once, "You have made my Father's house a den of thieves" (Matthew 21:13). Do you and I not do the same thing? Of them I am chief. We clergy, we lay people, and everyone – each in his own right – have we not sinned before the departed First-Hierarch and before our Church by our unworthy life, which carries on far from how it should, far from how we would like it?

Therefore, today it is proper for us not only to repent for our sins before the Church and Her First-Hierarch. I think this insufficient. It is insufficient to repent. We must promise, give an oath, that we will attempt to defend our Church and consequently, ourselves as well. We must defend our internal selves, in every manifestation of our lives, from that which sullies the Church, which stains the Church, which makes Her, even in the smallest way, reminiscent of the words of the Savior, which I have brought just now to your attention. For this reason we here, escorting the departed, stand in the doorway, awaiting a new head, a new First-Hierarch of the Russian Orthodox Church Outside of Russia. Whoever he may be, he will need what our departed hierarch needed. Let us give him of our help. Let us not say, this is not my responsibility, I am no priest, while the priest says, this is not my responsibility, I am no Bishop; while the Bishop says, this is not my responsibility, I am not the First-Hierarch.

Who is responsible then? One man? No matter what grace may be visited upon this man, it is beyond the strength of anyone.

It is the responsibility of the whole Holy, Catholic, and Apostolic Church, of which we are the members. Let us then not just call ourselves such, but let us right ourselves, for the sake of the Church, for the sake of our own salvation, for the sake of not calling ourselves Orthodox Christians, but being such. Let us not boast that we are better than all the other Orthodox Christians, we, the Russian Orthodox Church Outside of Russia, but let us be whom we ought to be. May the Lord God help us! Let us truly want this! Let us apply all our efforts to attaining this goal, not by our intentions alone, "with which," St. John Chrysostom notes, "even the road to hell is paved." Not by intentions alone, but with true deeds, for which our Church and Her new, future head, the First-Hierarch, will be waiting. Amen.

Our Living Links with the Holy Fathers: Metropolitan Philaret of New York[11]

AMONG THE PRIMATES of the Orthodox Churches today, there is only one from whom is always expected — and not only by members of his own Church, but by very many in a number of other Orthodox Churches as well — the clear voice of Orthodox righteousness and truth and conscience, untainted by political considerations or calculations of any kind. The voice of Metropolitan Philaret of New York, Chief Hierarch of the Russian Church Outside of Russia, is the only fully *Orthodox* voice among all the Orthodox primates. In this he is like to the Holy Fathers of ancient times, who placed purity of Orthodoxy above all else, and he stands in the midst of today's confused religious world as a solitary champion of Orthodoxy in the spirit of the Ecumenical Councils.

The chief heresy of our age, ecumenism, against which the voice of Metropolitan Philaret has been directed, is by no means an easy one to define or combat. In its "pure" form — the declaration that the Church of Christ does not exist in fact but is only now being formed

---

11 Brotherhood of Saint Herman of Alaska, "Our Living Links with the Holy Fathers: Metropolitan Philaret of New York," *Orthodox Word* 12, no. 1 (January-February 1976): 3-5.

— it is preached by very few among those who call themselves Orthodox. Most often it is manifested by anti-canonical acts, especially of communion in prayer with heretics, which reveal the absence of an awareness of what the Church of Christ is and what it means to belong to her. But no one anti-canonical act in itself is sufficient to define a heresy and therefore it is the greatness of Metropolitan Philaret at this critical hour of the Church's history that, without insisting pharisaically on any one letter

Met. Philaret with sisters of the Lesna Convent in France.

of the Church's law, and without twisting to the slightest degree the words of any ecumenist hierarch in order to "prove he's a heretic" — he has grasped the heretical, anti-Orthodox spirit behind all the ecumenist acts and pronouncements of our day and boldly warned the Orthodox hierarchs and flock about the present danger of them and their future ruinous outcome. It is most unfortunate that too few Orthodox Christians today have grasped full import of his message to the Orthodox Churches — lack of understanding that has come both from the "left" side and from the "right."

On the "left" side Metropolitan Philaret is senselessly regarded as "fanatic" and is accused of a number of extreme views which he has never expressed or held. His voice of true Orthodox moderation and sobriety is reviled and slandered by those — one must strongly suspect — whose conscience, weakened by compromise and openness to modernist renovationism, is not clean. To such ones the bold voice of Metropolitan Philaret ruins the harmony and accord by which most of the other Orthodox Churches are proceeding to their dreamed of "Eighth Ecumenical Council," at which renovationism will become the "canonical" norm and the Unia with Rome and the other Western heresies will become the official "Orthodox" position.

But no less on the "right" side is the position of Metropolitan Philaret misunderstood and even condemned. There are those who, in their "zeal not according to knowledge" (Romans 10:2), wish to make everything absolutely "simple" and "black or white." They would wish him and his Synod to declare invalid the Mysteries of New Calendarists or Communist dominated Churches, not realizing that it is not the business of the Synod to make decrees on such a sensitive and complex question, and that the church disturbances of our time are far too deep and complicated to be solved solely by breaking communion or applying anathemas, which — save in the few specific instances where they might be applicable — only make the church disturbances worse. Some few even think to solve the tragic situation of Orthodoxy today with the declaration, "We are the only pure ones left," and then abuse those who take a stand of true Orthodox moderation with a most un-Orthodox mechanistic logic ("If they have grace, why don't you join them or receive communion from them?") At various times the Russian Church Outside of Russia has avoided or discouraged communion with several other Orthodox bodies, and with one in particular (the Moscow Patriarchate) it has no communion at all, on grounds of principle; and separate hierarchs have warned against contact with the "modernist" bodies; but this is not because of any legalistic definition of the lack of grace-giving Sacraments in such bodies, but because of pastoral considerations which are respected and obeyed by all true sons of the Church without any need for a merely "logical" justification.

The Orthodox stand of Metropolitan Philaret is rooted in his experience from childhood of the age-old Orthodox way of life. His family was devout; his father (Archbishop Dimitry) knew St. John of Kronstadt and in the Diaspora was a hierarch in the Far East. In his formative years in the Far East, Metropolitan Philaret was in contact with holy men: Bishop Jonah, a wonderworker and disciple of Optina Elder Barsanuphius; the clairvoyant elders of the Kazan monastery in Harbin, Michael and Ignatius (the latter of whom he buried); Abbess Rufina, whose convent was transformed by numerous miraculously-renewed icons; and he had clearly before him the example of a number of holy hierarchs, including Metropolitan Innocent of Peking, champion of the Old Calendar, the wonderworking Bishops of Shanghai, Simon and John (Maximovitch), and Metropolitan Meletius of Harbin. His love for holy men and champions of Orthodoxy in the past is evident in the fact that he took a leading part in the publication of the Lives of "Standers for Orthodox Faith" such as Elders Ambrose and Macarius of Optina, writing in addition an excellent introduction to the Life of Elder Ambrose.

In all [of] this and in his uncompromising stand for true Orthodoxy, he is very like his namesake in 19th-century Russia, Metropolitan Philaret of Moscow, the champion of Patristic Orthodoxy against the anti-Orthodox influences coming from the West, and the protector of Optina Monastery and its elders. For over ten years now the voice of Metropolitan Philaret has resounded unwearyingly in a succession of letters of protest and warning to Orthodox hierarchs, particularly of the Patriarchate of Constantinople and in two "Sorrowful Epistles" addressed to the world-wide Orthodox episcopate. The present letter is a kind of third sorrowful epistle to all the Orthodox Bishops, occasioned by the first Orthodox-ecumenist "confession," which makes much more definite the errors which had been perhaps only "tendencies" up to now.

It should be noted that, despite the shocking lack of response by Orthodox hierarchs to his earlier "Sorrowful Epistles," the present epistle is still addressed to "the Orthodox hierarchs," "the hierarchs of God," letting them know that it is the least of their brothers who is addressing them, not in order to call them names or make a public spectacle of them, but in order to call them back to Orthodoxy before they have departed from it entirely, without any hope of return. It should also be noted that there is no trace whatever of the lightmindedness and mockery which mar some of the otherwise welcome anti-ecumenist writings of our day, especially in the English language. This is a document of the utmost seriousness, a humble yet firm entreaty to abandon a ruinous path of error, a document whose solemn tone exactly which matches the gravity of its content, proceeding from the age-old wisdom and experience of Patristic Orthodoxy in standing in the truth and opposing error.[12] May it be read and its message heeded!

---

12 See the three "Sorrowful Epistles" in the Writings section of this volume.

Above and below: The funeral of Metropolitan Philaret

Right: The incorrupt relics of Metropolitan Philaret
Courtesy of His Grace +Bishop Luke (Murianka) of Syracuse and
Archimandrite Nektarios Harding, Holy Trinity Monastery, Jordanville, NY.

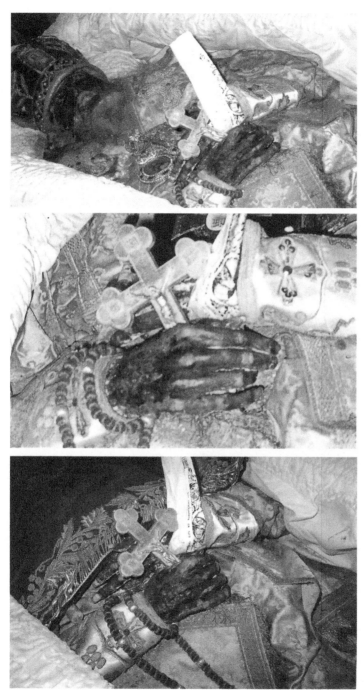

His Grace Bishop LUKE of Syracuse (left) and His Grace Bishop GEORGE
of Canberra (right) as Subdeacons to Metropolitan Philaret.
Bishop Laurus (Škurla) behind Metropolitan Philaret.

HOMILIES

Paschal Epistle of the Primate of the Russian Orthodox Church Outside of Russia (1969)[13]

Christ is Risen!

"This is the chosen and holy day, the first of Sabbaths, the Sovereign and Queen, the Feasts of Feasts, and Triumph of Triumphs." Thus sings the Holy Church in the canon of Holy Pascha, praising the Risen Lord, the Giver of life, the Conqueror of death and hell. Why is the radiant and joyful day of the Resurrection of Christ called "the Chosen day" by the holy writer of hymns St. John of Damascus, inspired by the Holy Spirit and after him the whole Church? Let us recall the 117th Psalm of the Holy Prophet and Psalmist, King David. In this Psalm he praises the Lord for His mercy and in the 24th verse speaks those words which are included in the Paschal service. This is the day which the Lord hath made; we will rejoice and be glad in it. Illumined by the Holy Spirit, the holy psalmist sees, as it were, the Resurrection of Christ already taking place; he contemplates the radiant Paschal triumph and prophetically points ahead to "the chosen and holy day." In the celebration of Holy Pascha we see the fulfillment of the psalmist's words. Triumphantly and joyfully the Holy Church celebrates the

13 Metropolitan Philaret of New York, "Paschal Epistle of the Primate of the Russian Orthodox Church Outside of Russia," *Orthodox Life*, no. 2 (March-April 1969): 3-4.

chosen and holy day of the Radiant Resurrection of Christ, turning the whole service of Holy Pascha into a continuous hymn of joy and glorification of the Risen Savior.

The Church calls us to joy, but there are different kinds of joy, and for people who are not very close to the Church, there is often that joy of which it was said of old: the sons of men have put joy to shame; for in this case they rejoice over that for which they should not rejoice, but for which they should weep — weep with tears of repentance. Rejoice in the Lord, and again I say, rejoice, wrote the great messenger of the Gospel, St. Paul, to his spiritual children of the city of Philippi. The Risen Savior Himself, having appeared to the myrrh-bearing women on their way, said to them, "Rejoice." And we know with what joy the Church services are filled on the night of the Radiant Resurrection of Christ, when constantly, and frequently repeating itself, the troparion of the feast of Pascha is sung: "Christ is risen from the dead, trampling down death by death, and on those in the tombs bestowing life." All the Paschal Service is, in essence, the unveiling of the content of this troparion, and it tells of how the Resurrection of Christ the Savior is the triumph of light over darkness, of good over evil, and of life over death. May the Lord grant us sinners also to be communicants of the radiant, Paschal joy.

Christ is Risen!

+ Metropolitan Philaret

Christmas Message of the President of the Synod of Bishops of the Russian Orthodox Church Outside of Russia[14]

Great is the mystery of godliness:
God was manifest in the flesh (1 Tim 3:16).

The radiant festal days have arrived. A long while ago, already on the eve of the Feast of the Entry into the Temple of the Most Holy Mother of God, the Church, in its solemn evening services, proclaimed the pre-festal song: "Christ is born! — Glorify Him! Christ from the heavens — Meet Him!", inviting its faithful children to prepare to meet the great feast day of the Nativity of Christ. And behold, this feast day has arrived, and the Christian world rejoices and triumphs, glorifying the God-Child, Christ the Savior, Who came onto the earth for us men and for our salvation. The Holy Gospel brings to us the good news of how, on the blessed nativity night, above the fields of Bethlehem the holy angels announced to the shepherds that Christ the Lord had come into the world — and brought onto the earth peace, God's benevolence. Fear not: for behold, I bring you good tidings of great joy, which shall be to all people.

But we also know from the Gospel that this great joy was soon obscured and replaced by great sorrow; in Bethlehem and its surrounding areas the angelic singing was replaced by the wailing of the slain infants and the weeping of the orphaned mothers, and the fields of Bethlehem were covered with the blood of innocent children. Thus it was in ancient times; this was the "great joy" obscured by great sorrow. But do we not see also in our own stormy and extremely seditious days how our festal joy is also obscured by sorrow?

Is it not of great sorrow to us, the children of the Russian Orthodox Church, to see what is now taking place in the emigration, when

---

14 Metropolitan Philaret of New York, "Christmas Message of the President of the Synod of Bishops of the Russian Orthodox Church Outside of Russia," *Orthodox Life*, no. 1 (January-February 1970): 3-4.

before our very eyes, Orthodox hierarchs, who instead of guarding themselves and their flock from the dominion of the red beast, are entering into close contacts and intercourse with hierarchs who are in the service of atheists and haters of God, and are striving to drag their flock along this fatal path?

One Orthodox Russian characterized the actions of the "American Metropolia[15]" concisely and clearly: the Metropolia is receiving its "autocephaly from the red Patriarchate. But the latter is in full subordination to the Soviet regime and besides, without its approval, cannot make one move. Consequently, the Metropolia is receiving its 'autocephaly' from the atheistic regime — from the M.V.D.[16]" What in essence can be said against this simple and irresistible logic?

We know under what, unprecedented in history, super-humanly distressing and tormenting conditions the church authority in the Soviet Union finds itself, under the yoke of the atheistic satanic regime. We know and pity those unfortunate hierarchs who fulfill the will of their evil masters, and who, not being free, cannot in any way be the true bearers of the voice of our suffering Mother Church. However, pitying them, we categorically refuse to have any kind of relationship with them. But if these unfortunate ones, who find themselves under a heavy yoke, undoubtedly deserve compassion and leniency, what can one say about those in the free world, who without oppression and compulsion, are freely and voluntarily extending a hand of intercourse to them, and through them, to the regime which dictates to them and orders them around? What a frightening temptation! What a frightening act is taking place before our eyes.

Russian Orthodox people! Let us remember the ancient apostolic call: See then that ye walk circumspectly — beware, act prudently (Ephesians 5:15). Take heed for yourselves, and again take heed! And in these radiant festal days, joyously and with thanksgiving glo-

---

15   The American Metropolia is the former name of the now Orthodox Church in America prior to receiving their "autocephaly" from the Soviet Moscow Patriarchate.

16 M.V.D. – Soviet Ministry of Internal Affairs

rifying the One Who "came down to the earth, that He might lead us up into the heavens", let us not forget in our prayers our brothers by blood and by faith, who are suffering for the faith throughout all the vast expanse of the gigantic concentration camp, called the "U.S.S.R." Let us also pray that the Lord, Who enlightens every man who comes into the world, will enlighten our spiritual eyes as well, will teach us to see His holy Truth and to serve it, and to be faithful children of His Holy Church. With what seductive and luring delusions is life now filled! May the Lord help us, save us, have mercy on us, and keep us from them by His Grace, and may He grant His peace and comfort to every faithful soul, devoted to Him, during the days of the Great and Radiant Feast!

+ Metropolitan Philaret

Paschal Epistle (1982)[17]

It is the Day of Resurrection, let us be radiant O ye people; Pascha, the Lord's Pascha: for from death to life, and earth to heaven, Christ God hath brought us, as we chant the hymn of victory.

Thus sings the Holy Church in the words of Saint John of Damascus during the festal days of Holy Pascha. The great and holy days of Passion Week, days in which the Church commemorated the saving work and sufferings of the incarnate Son of God, which he deigned to take upon Himself in His incarnation — for the sake of us men and of our salvation. All the services of Passion Week, moving and deeply edifying, are devoted to this holy remembrance. In celebrating these services, the Church as it were, follows step by step Her Lord and Savior and prayerfully, sorrowfully, and gratefully hymns each step, each moment of His redemptive sufferings in corresponding prayers, liturgical ceremonies, and performance of the mysteries.

But Passion Week has ended! Once, in our Homeland, Archbishop Innocent of Kherson, one of the splendid preachers of

---

17 Metropolitan Philaret of New York, "Paschal Epistle by Metropolitan Philaret (1982)," *Orthodox Heritage* 17, no. 03-04 (March-April 2019): 28-29.

which there were many in Russia, in his inspired sermon on the day of Great Friday, the day of the sufferings on the Cross and the death of Christ the Savior, exclaimed: Again Golgotha and the Cross! Again the Tomb and the Winding-sheet. But behold, we see that the Tomb is empty and the Winding-sheet no longer covers anyone. Christ is Risen — and taking the place of grief and sadness has come that joy that the Risen One Himself predicted to His disciples, and ye now therefore have sorrow: but I will see you again, and your heart shall rejoice, and your joy no man taketh from you (John 16:22).

This joy is the joy in the Risen Lord. He rose from the grave as the victor over Hades and death — everything is flooded by the blinding light of His glorious Resurrection, and the joy about which He predicted to his disciples has now become the inheritance of all faithful children of His Church. Christ's Church renews this joy of the Resurrection every year in the joyful days of Pascha. And the faithful children of the Church hear her good tidings, rejoice and celebrate. But not in vain do we read in the Holy Gospel the words of the Savior, Fear not, little flock (Luke 12:32).

In our time, a terrible time, a time of such falling away from all principles of faith and morality that we see now, the number of true believers is truly a little flock compared with that majority of mankind that has in fact lost the true faith and trampled on all the principles of Christian morality. Seeing what people, who have forgotten completely about Christian purity, modesty, and chastity, permit themselves and not only permit themselves, but even maintain that all the vileness and filth with which life is now filled is something legitimate, moral, and deserving of approval. Seeing this, the word is of Sacred Scripture that tells how man has joined the dumb beasts and become like unto them comes involuntarily to mind. And not only has he become like them, he has even become worse than them, for beasts do not know those abominations of which the Apostle said it is shameful even to speak — but that are now done by the sons and daughters of man who have lost their shame and conscience.

But, lest my mouth speak of human things, let us turn to the joyous feast of the Resurrection. In the Gospel reading that we heard at the Divine Liturgy on the night of Pascha are the words, *And the light shineth in darkness; and the darkness comprehended it not* (John 1:5), the Divine light shone in the darkness and the darkness could not grasp or extinguish it. In the same way, the light of Christ's Resurrection shines in the world and the darkness of human delusions cannot darken or extinguish it. The Lord Jesus Christ, speaking with the Apostles at the Mystical Supper, told them, *In the world ye shall have tribulation: but be of good cheer; I have overcome the world* (John 16:33). He was still only preparing for His podvig of redemptive and saving sufferings, but in His divine omniscience He saw this podvig as already having been accomplished and as Victor spoke of it to His Disciples, to reassure them. And in His infinite mercy and goodness, He makes all those who believe in Him participants in this victory, which is why the Apostle says: *Thanks be to God, which giveth us the victory through our Lord Jesus Christ* (1 Corinthians 15:57). And in the sacred book of the Apocalypse, we read God's promise, *He that overcometh shall inherit all things and I will be his God, and he shall be my son* (Apocalypse 21:7).

Rejoice then, Christian. And do not fall into despondency on seeing how evil is spreading in the world. Of course, it is difficult for the Christian soul to see this spread of evil, filth, falsehood, and malice. Even in his time, our great righteous one, Saint John of Kronstadt, pointed out one of the most difficult trials for a Christian is the triumph and spreading of evil and falsehood and the impossibility of stopping it. Yes, there are such periods in life. The Savior suggested this in the Garden of Gethsemane when He said to His enemies, who had come to seize Him, *this is your hour, and the power of darkness* (Luke 22:53). And they took Him. But their time passed, the power of darkness ended, the light of Christ's Resurrection shone forth, and the life conquered death, Good conquered evil, and Truth conquered falsehood.

In the joyous days of Pascha, Russian believers often recall how the great God-pleaser and wonder-worker, Saint Seraphim of

Sarov, in the course of the whole year, not just during the Paschal season, met all who came to him with the joyful greeting, my joy, Christ is Risen! The great ascetic, in his vast and laborious spiritual experience, recognized all the power and dominion of evil in the world. But he also recognized the triumphant power of the Joyous Resurrection of Christ, before which evil is powerless. And being always filled with the radiant, triumphant joy of Pascha, he shared it with those who came to him with their afflictions and sorrows, transfusing, as it were, this joy into their dejected and grieving souls.

How beautiful our Orthodox Faith is! With what a bright, unfading light it illuminates our lives, filled with sin and vanity! But all its power and light are in the Resurrection of Christ. If Christ the Savior had not risen but had remained in the tomb, life would have turned into a terrible, evil, and unbearable nightmare. But Christ's resurrection did take place and the Church summons all its faithful children to rejoice and to celebrate Christ's Resurrection. For in it we celebrate the slaying of death, the destruction of Hades, and the beginning of a new, eternal life.

Christ is Risen!

Metropolitan Philaret
Pascha 1982

On Handing the Hierarchal Staff to His Grace, Bishop Hilarion (Kapral) of Manhattan[18]

Right Reverend Bishop Hilarion, our beloved brother in Christ!

I greet you on receiving the great gift of God, the grace of the episcopacy. I greet you not only for myself personally, but on behalf of my brother archpastors, who laid their hands on you during the accomplishing of the great mystery of the priesthood, and on behalf of the archpastors who comprise our Council of Bishops and on behalf of the clergy who prayed earnestly during

---

18 Metropolitan Philaret of New York, "Speech Made by the First-Hierarch, His Eminence, Metropolitan Philaret, On Handing the Hierarchal Staff to His Grace, Bishop Hilarion of Manhattan," *Orthodox Life* 35, no. 1 (January-February 1985): 39-40.

the consecration and this mass of the faithful who stand patiently through this uncommon, lengthy service and, of course, have also prayed diligently for you.

At this time, so precious and holy for you, you would, of course, like to hear something you may remember fondly for the rest of your life. I will not speak my own words, but will cite the great proclaimer of the Christian Faith, the preeminent Apostle Paul. Once, in Ephesus, he discoursed with the Ephesian pastors, and the Book of the Acts of the Apostles has preserved his words: "Take heed, therefore, unto yourselves, and to all the flock, over which the Holy Spirit hath ordained you Bishops, to feed the Church of God, which He hath purchased with His own Blood" (Acts 20:28).

The Holy Spirit ordains a Bishop. These words of the Apostle frighten us, on the one hand; but on the other hand, they encourage us. They frighten us because it is the Holy Spirit who ordains us hierarchs, and it is to Him that we must give answer — not to men, not to the people, but to the omnipotent Lord God, the Holy Spirit. How can we not fear the dread answer we must bear? On the other hand, they give us courage, because the Holy Spirit places the one He has chosen on the eminence of the episcopal ministry, not merely to abandon him having once placed him there.

No, He will always support His faithful servant with the power of His grace. And this grace-bearing help has always been essential for those who undertake lofty service in the Church, and is so at the present time, of course, more than at any time in the past. We see what life today is turning into; we see how not only the non-Orthodox around us, but even our own flock, unfortunately, are forgetting the basic precepts of piety and morality. In particular, when you carry out your Archpastoral ministry, do not forget our dear Russian youth. Here and now conditions are exceptionally difficult, because, in accordance with the scarcely normal conditions of life which have arisen here, they have to graduate from a school of higher education without fail. They labor intensely to amass material, but the greater part of their contemporary knowledge and science is a new Tower of Babel.

At one time, in antiquity, there was a marvelous book, now forgotten, the Hexameron of Basil the Great, the discourses of that great hierarch on the six days of creation. An astonishing work! Therein the profound, independent, and creative mind of the great hierarch and thinker brought to bear many observations and deductions of a purely scientific character, which even now have not lost their strength; for contemporary science, although it has torn itself away from spiritual basics, also utilizes much of what Basil the Great once said. It is precisely a scientific treatise, beautiful and profound and at the same it is a universal hymn to the wisdom, omnipotence, and love of the Creator, God Almighty. This is what Christian science must be. But modern science either says not a word about God, or speaks negatively [of Him] in the majority of instances. Thus it is necessary to understand that our youth has to strain their every power to pass these sciences which, I repeat, for the most part are, from the Christian point of view, a contemporary Tower of Babel. Love the youth and care for them in all your future ministry.

The Lord God never forsakes one who does not forsake. He will not abandon His faithful one if His servant is really loyal to Him. May the Lord help you in your future service to preserve your loyalty to Him; then His gracious assistance and power will ever be with you. You need but have faith and a humble awareness of your own unworthiness. As the ever-memorable Fr. John of Kronstadt, the pastor of all Russia, loved to say, "I expect only bad of myself; but from the Lord I expect every benefaction and help."

May the Lord bless your future labor of Archpastoral service. Take this hierarchal staff. It is given to a high priest of God that, as the holy fathers say, it may be a support for the hierarch in his labors and ministry, and may likewise be a rod of chastisement when it proves necessary to punish obstinate errors, disloyalty, and betrayal of God. God grant that in this sense it prove possible for you to use this staff only a little or not at all, but accept it as a support for thy service, for not once, or twice, but many, many times in your life you will sense your weakness, your shortcomings and the insufficiency of your strength. And only when the Lord strengthens you will all your difficulties be happily resolved. Accept this staff and bless the people who await you.

On the Canonization of our Holy and God-bearing Father Saint Herman of Alaska[19]

OUR BELOVED FLOCK, Rejoice in the Lord always and again I say Rejoice! (Philippians 4:4). Remember with what feeling five years ago we greeted the day of the glorification of the righteous St. John of Kronstadt. The ever-memorable Metropolitan Anastassy, who had participated in the glorification of St. Herman (in 1913), in that year of 1964 had already lost his physical strength and laid aside the burden of Church administration. But the All-High who once strengthened St. Simeon the God-Receiver, on that day drew our elder and father to his Cathedral Church for divine service and a meeting with grace. But the Apostle insists. And again I say, Rejoice! Come, then, all those who ask God's mercy and His help, as the Church refer to all of us.

When we pray for this help at the All-night Vigil, as intercessors for us we call upon those who have pleased God: the Mother of God, God's angels, the Forerunner, the Apostles and so on; not being able to enumerate the whole multitude of saints, we commemorate a selected list of them. This sacred list of names is perpetually supplemented and renewed. During the past three-quarters of a century we have begun to invoke St. Seraphim and the Hierarchs Theodosius, Ioasaph, Hermogen, Pitirim, John, Sophronius, and Joseph. Finally, in these prayers has resounded the name of the righteous St. John of Kronstadt. And now, children, we join to these sacred names yet another name; that of our venerable and God-bearing Father Herman of Alaska.

The veneration of St. Herman ripened persistently in the bosom of the Russian Church. He was written about in the book Ascetics of Valaam, in the Theological Encyclopedia, in the Out-

---

19 Metropolitan Philaret of New York, "On the Canonization of our Holy and God-Bearing Father Saint Herman of Alaska," *Orthodox Word* 6, no. 3 (May-June 1970): 111-114.

line of the Russian Spiritual Mission in America, in the books of
E. Poselyanin, and, of course, in the well-known work of Bishop
Nikodim of Belgorod, who was later martyred by the Bolsheviks,
Ascetics of the Russian Land in the 18th and 19th Centuries. In
the December volume of the latter book there is a separate article
about the Elder Herman; but in order to demonstrate with what
force the consciousness of the Church set apart the ascetic labor of
the Elder, even as compared with other ascetics, let us here cite the
words of this same work, but from the February volume from the
article on the Abbot of Valaam, Nazary. Here there is an account
of the Abbot's selection of missionaries for America from among
the monks of Valaam and further on it said, "among these elect
the following especially stood out, Archimandrite Ioasaph, the head
of the mission who drowned after being elevated to the office of
Bishop — his activity, while by God's decrees it was brief, brought
about great benefit; the zealous Hieromonk Juvenal, who earned a
martyr's crown and the Monk Herman, who labored for forty-years
in apostolic self-denial manifesting gifts of clairvoyance and miracles and reposed in the fragrance of sanctity" (p. 304).

Thus was it written at the beginning of our century, but even
in the '60's of the last century, that is, thirty years after the repose
of Elder Herman, which was in 1837, the renowned Abbot of Valaam, Damascene, hearing of the veneration of Father Herman in
Alaska, commenced the gathering of information about him. The
life of the Saint is most moving. And now you who have not heard it
or read it will both hear it and read it. Herman was a contemporary
of St. Seraphim, three years older than he, and outlived him by four
years. He was the spiritual son of Abbot Nazary of Valaam, who
took part in the publication of Paisius (Velichkovsky's) Philokalia
that revelation of the art of arts, inner prayer. Thus in the Russian "Spiritual Meadow" of the second half of the 18th century
there are interwoven the names of St. Seraphim, the Elder Paisius
Velichkovsky, Abbot Nazary (who died at Sarov), and St. Herman,
with, of course, many other names which mean much to a spiritual
person.

Father Herman, coming as a youth to the Trinity-Sergius Hermitage near Petersburg, was, like St. Seraphim, granted a miraculous healing by the Mother of God. Having gone soon thereafter to wondrous Valaam, which he came to love dearly, he had experience already there, with the blessing of his elder, of the anchoretic life. Under obedience he left with the mission to America. There could not be any monastic community there, but Herman himself was the bearer of the ancient spirit of asceticism: strict fasting, a shirt for clothing, a bench for bed, a log for pillow, a board for blanket, chains; austerity toward himself, but a wonderful meekness with his neighbors. He built an orphanage for children; fearless during an epidemic, he gave himself over to caring for the contagiously ill. Around him were poverty, danger from the natives, and great affliction from his own countrymen.

The traders and foremost among them the head of the Russian colony, looked after their own profit and colonizing interests, behaving cruelly with people, in the spirit of their age. And it was here that the Elder Herman, although in his great humility he had refused the priesthood, revealed himself as the model of a true compassionate pastor, and in his own words he wished to be a "nurse" for these Aleuts and other local tribes. This gave birth to a responsive love in hearts simple but sensitive to good, and the Lord aided the Elder by the grace both of clairvoyance and of miracle-working.

The life tells of the Elder's taming of the elements of both fire and water and from his repose until the present day those who call on his name have many times received healing or other help. The life tells also about the high character of the instruction of this apparently simple monk Herman. The best living testimony to this grace-filled instruction of the Elder's was the Schema-monk Sergius, a highly educated person, who in the world was the naval officer S. N. Yanovsky and for a short time after Baranov was also the head of the Russian colonies in America. Under the sole influence of the Elder Herman this prominent Russian public figure, and his children as well, accepted monasticism. His life in itself is full of edification. The principal information about the life of St. Herman was given by him; the first graphic portrayal of the Elder belongs to his daughter-novice.

The repose of the Elder was truly in the fragrance of sanctity; he reposed having known beforehand the day of his death, having foretold the circumstances of his burial in the wilderness without people; and he departed to the Lord as if on the eve of Pascha, with candles lit at his command, with the reading of the Acts of the Apostles by his disciple. The Russian Orthodox Church Outside of Russia should naturally approach the canonization of saints without haste. Thus in spite of the "immeasurable sea of miracles" (Akathist to St. Nicholas) of which there is testimony concerning the righteous St. John of Kronstadt, our father wavered between the desire to glorify him in general and the intent to glorify him in Russia. Only at the time of the Sobor in 1964 did the fervent desire to pray to the righteous John as a glorified saint overcome all other motives.

It was difficult to proceed to the present canonization as long as the canonization of the universally renowned miracle-worker John of Kronstadt was still being postponed. But even at the Sobor of 1939 in Sremsky-Karlovtsy, during consideration of this question, Metropolitan Anastassy explained that Elder Herman was venerated in Alaska as a saint, and that the question of his canonization had already arisen in America. Then it was decided to write to Bishop Alexy of Alaska concerning the preparatory process necessary for the canonization. This was when the American Metropolia was part of our Church Abroad. In the same year at the Sobor of Bishops in America, the chairmanship of the committee for preparation of the canonization was entrusted to Archbishop Tikhon, who later laid the foundation of the new San Francisco Cathedral of the Most Holy Mother of God, the Joy of All Who Sorrow, where it has now been decreed that the glorification of the Saint be celebrated.

A special veneration for the memory of Elder Herman was held by the successor of Archbishop Tikhon, Archbishop John of Western America and San Francisco. In his cell to the present day the Elder's portrait hangs together with the icons. In San Francisco, with the blessing of the late Vladyka John, there was organized a

Brotherhood of St. Herman of Alaska, which undertook a responsible missionary and publishing activity. With a large circulation
in English, but also in Russian, the brothers have acquainted their
readers with the life and miracles of the Elder, who spiritually
nourished and gave growth to the beginnings of Orthodoxy in
America. On the feast of Sts. Sergius and Herman of Valaam and
on the day of the repose of Elder Herman there has been, from
the time of Archbishop John, a panikhida served for Elder Herman
in the printshop of the brothers and afterwards the Magnification
has been sung before his iconographic image, in anticipation and
expectation of his canonization by the Church.

At the Sobor of 1964, in connection with the glorification of
St. John of Kronstadt, we asked ourselves: and will those who are
not within the enclosure of the Russian Church Abroad canonize
the new Wonderworker? At the same time, in connection with the
preparations of the American Metropolia for the canonization of
St. Herman (concerning which there was talk even then), we said
to ourselves that no initiative in this matter would prevent our own
canonization of Elder Herman.

And so be it. This glorification of St. Herman was conceived
in the hearts of the Elder's contemporaries, the simple Aleuts
whom he tenderly loved, was carried at first in the womb of the
Homeland which we share with the Elder, and then in America,
when the American Metropolia was still with us. And when now
this Metropolia was the first to draw its conclusion, we did not in the
least hesitate to draw also our own conclusion to the veneration of
the Elder Herman and designate the same date for the glorification
as the Metropolia's. This was still before the latest church events,
over which we grieve; but of them, for the sake of the Saint's glorification, we shall not speak here. The conclusion has been drawn
to that veneration which has existed for more than a hundred years;
and it was also about a hundred years ago that the first See of the
Russian Church in America was founded, which was then in San
Francisco.

And for you, beloved, as for all who will call on the help of
St. Herman, we wish all that consolation which the meek, newly

glorified Saint of God, Herman, is powerful to solicit both now and in the future. May this glorification be grace-giving and sanctifying to each of the faithful, to the much suffering Russian people from which the Saint has come, to Alaska, and to all America, to the harsh Northwest of which St. Herman, with his fellow laborers, brought the light of Christ. Amen.

+ Metropolitan Philaret
First-Hierarch of the Russian Orthodox Church Outside of Russia

The Glorification of Blessed Xenia: Epistle of the Chief Hierarch of the Synod of the Russian Orthodox Church Outside of Russia to the God-Beloved Flock in the Diaspora[20]

NOW THE DAY has come near for which Russian Orthodox people of the Diaspora have long been preparing. For the course of sixty years they have had the spiritual joy of glorifying among the saints Father John of Kronstadt (1964), and after him St. Herman of Alaska (1970). And now has come near the third spiritual solemnity of this type: the glorification of Blessed Xenia of St. Petersburg, who is so much revered by the Orthodox Russian people both in the Diaspora and in the Russian land.

St. Symeon Metaphrastes many years ago wrote the life of St. Xenia of Rome and he began his words concerning the Holy God-Pleasers by saying that they "illumine like stars all that is under the heavens; they are visible to the inhabitants of India, and they do not hide even from the Scythians." Now, when a thousand years have passed after these words were written, we see that they refer also to our Russian Xenia of Petersburg. News of her coming glorification was already held long ago. There was talk of this at the Third All-Diaspora Council in 1974, and the Sobors of Bishops in 1974 and 1976 examined this question in more detail and

---

20 Metropolitan Philaret of New York, "The Glorification of Blessed Xenia," *Orthodox Word* 14, no. 4 (July-August 1978): 148-150 & 199.

decided to perform the glorification of Blessed Xenia as a Holy God-Pleaser. The regular Sobor of Bishops will begin on August 28/September 10 and it will end on September 11/24 with her glorification. On her gravestone is an inscription which ends with the words: "Whoever has known me, may he remember my soul for the salvation of his own soul. Amen."

And what do we know of the life and struggles of Blessed Xenia? Xenia Grigorievna was married to a court singer, Andrew Feodorovich Petrov who died quite unexpectedly and suddenly and, evidently, without the rites of the Church. His death changed, as quickly as lightning, the whole outlook and way of life of Xenia. She understood everything that was great, and disdained everything small, unnecessary, temporal. The great thing which rose up before her spiritual gaze was the eternal blessedness of those who have endured much here on earth. And therefore, there is the highest form of sanctity, when a man, in the words of the Apostle Paul, "counts all things to be loss, and counts them but refuse, that he may gain Christ and know Him, and the power of His resurrection, and the fellowship of His sufferings, becoming conformed unto His death so as to attain unto the resurrection from the dead" (Philippians 3:8-11).

From the history of the Russian Church we know of at least a few fools for Christ's sake, and they shock us by their struggle. In Moscow, for example, there was the renowned Basil, and likewise Maximus, the blessed ones; in Novgorod the blessed ones Nicholas Kachanov and Theodore; in Kiev Blessed Theophilus, who is yet uncanonized. And behold, St. Petersburg also — as the new Russian capital was called in those days — became the witness of the struggle of Blessed Xenia. Not answering to her female name, she was called by the name of her reposed husband, Andrew Feodorovich, as if emphasizing by this foolishness her desire to be an entirely new man, or to obtain by prayer the salvation of the soul of her husband who had died suddenly. By this name we are reminded of the St. Andrew who is, as it were, at the head of the choir of the blessed ones, namely St. Andrew the Fool for Christ who beheld the vision of the Protection of the Most Holy Mother of God.

From the life of this St. Andrew we know how much such strugglers endure sometimes from men, how many sufferings of evil they subject themselves to and how much there is revealed to them the unutterable mysteries of God. Blessed Xenia also walked about our Petrograd not only in rain and snow, but also in fierce frosts, almost without shoes, clothed in the oldest kind of garment. She walked about with feet swollen with cold. In the Smolensk cemetery where later she was buried, Xenia, hiding her struggle, carried bricks, taking them up at night to the top of the Church which was being built so as to furnish the builders with material and to wear out her flesh. At night she went out from the city into a field and stood there in prayer. In the city she was a source of mockery, and there were incidents when people threw dirt and stones at her. But this was only sometimes. In general, people in Petersburg were touched by her and loved her — those, that is, to whom was revealed the meaning of her voluntary belittlement and sufferings.

This meaning is the acceptance of one's cross and bearing it, following the Lord. And the fruit of suffering is the power of God accomplished in the womanly weakness of Xenia; her clairvoyance, healings, help, which occur up to now by prayer to her. People have been flocking to the Smolensk cemetery right up to now. There, over the grave of the Blessed One, a chapel was erected. Panikhidas used to be celebrated from morning to night with hope in help by the prayers of the slave of God Xenia. Now the chapel is closed up, and there, as we have been informed, there has been made, with the aim of mockery, a bust of Lenin so immense that it cannot be carried out the door. May the glorification of the Blessed One, which has now drawn near, be the answer of believing hearts to the persecution of our Faith in the city and land of Blessed Xenia. But even now notes are being written with entreaties to the saint, and these are placed as close as possible to the walls of the chapel, and even now people strive to take from there particles of earth sanctified by the nearness of Xenia.

The text of the inscription which at one time was made on the gravestone is the following: "In the name of the Father and the Son and the Holy Spirit. On this place is placed the body of the slave of God Xenia Grigorievna, the wife of the court singer, colonel by rank, Andrew Fedorovich. She was left by her husband at the age of 26, wandered for 45 years, and lived in all 71 years. She was called by the name Andrew Feodorovich. Whoever has known me, may he remember my soul for the salvation of his own soul. Amen."

And thus for 45 years Blessed Xenia performed her struggle. In this time there was manifested in her both the gift of clairvoyance and the gift which is higher than any other, love. She foresaw the death both of Tsars and of simple people; she helped people to put their lives in order, to build families, to earn their bread, to provide for their children. She helped at times with a strict appearance, but with a loving heart. Many incidents of miraculous help which occurred after the death of the Blessed One were sometimes written down but often, by reason of persecutions or carelessness, this was not done. But they have accumulated in the memory of the preservers of our piety, the believing laymen, for even now the Orthodox Russian people in some part preserves faith and piety. Believing laymen carry to the Blessed One their needs and sorrows, and our hierarchy abroad, fulfilling its service, now humbly testifies that Blessed Xenia, together with other God-Pleasers from our people is "a splendid fruit of the saving sowing" performed by the Divine Sower on Russian soil (Troparion to All Saints of Russia).

+ Metropolitan Philaret
July 14, 1978

On Blessed Father Herman to the Orthodox Christians in Australia[21]

"SUCH was our own native Ascetic of piety," writes our Metropolitan Philaret, "with many both general Orthodox and specifically Russian characteristics of this piety, who came to the wild inhabitants of Northwestern America in 1794 and reposed in the Lord on December 13th, 1837. He died having known beforehand

---

21 Metropolitan Philaret of New York, "Metropolitan Philaret on Blessed Father Herman," *Orthodox Word* 6, no. 1 (January-February 1970): 3.

the hour of his repose, while candles were burning at his command and the Acts of the Apostles were being read, as if also preparing for Pascha — but an eternal Pascha. The writer of his Life says that his face shone and the cell was filled with fragrance."

The canonization of the saints of God is nurtured into the Church's bosom gradually. The question is tested by the attitudes of our fathers and our ancestors in faith, and in this fashion there matures the Church's glorification of a saint. Before the universal church conscience of the Church Outside of Russia there stands a special circumstance: there is no exceptionally abundant literature or multitude of documentary testimony as there was concerning the righteous St. John of Kronstadt. "But," writes Metropolitan Philaret, "we have what we do have, the faith of our ever-memorable fathers and predecessors from Archbishop [later Metropolitan] Innocent to Metropolitan Anastassy and other of our hierarchs who have reposed, in the God-Pleasing labors and ascetic deeds of the Elder Herman." Holy Father Herman, Pray to God for Us!

He Who Believeth and is Baptized Shall be Saved[22]

We just heard, in the order of Sunday Gospel readings for the vigils, a reading according to the Evangelist Mark. This is the first part of the final chapter of his Gospel. In its second part are words on which I wish to focus my attention. There the Lord says to the apostles: "He who believeth and is baptized shall be saved, but he that believeth not shall be condemned." Often among believers there arise questions and concerns and what happens to those people who were not baptized and did not become Christians, not because they refused to accept the Christian faith, but because they simply never encountered Christian preaching? St. Theophan the Recluse once answered a similar question thus, "remember that there are mysteries that have not been opened unto us." In that Gospel verse

---

22 "He Who Believeth and is Baptized Shall be Saved," Official Diocese of the Eastern American Diocese ROCOR, translated by Reader Gregory Levitsky, accessed July 13, 2022, http://archive.eadiocese.org/History/metphilaret/01believeth.en.htm

it clearly states that, "he who believeth and is baptized," that is, who firmly stands on the Christian path, and is saved – "shall be saved," but "he that believeth not shall be condemned." This indicates that those who have encountered the preaching of Christianity and, instead of accepting it and becoming a Christian, reject it, or maybe even become its foe, are faced with condemnation, as the Lord clearly stated.

As far as concerns those who fall into neither category, Bishop Theophan says, "why do you so concern yourself with people who have so died, not having determined their relationship with the preaching of the Gospel? Remember that we have the Lord, the Savior, of whom the Apostle Paul said that He is the Savior of all men, especially of those that believe," that is, He it is who came to save the whole human race. Inasmuch as the fate of all humanity and the fate of each individual will be determined by the Savior of the world, your concern is in vain. The Lord, first of all, is supremely just, and secondly, is endlessly merciful! He seeks to save, not to destroy, every soul, this concerns sinners, as well. When a sinner walks in the path of sin, the Lord never ceases instructing him, sending him circumstances good and beneficial for his soul, that his soul might awake and accept the true faith.

One way or another, I repeat, the Lord seeks to save each human soul. It was for this very reason that He came. The Lord once told one of His faithful servants, "I came to save the human race and I brought it salvation, but if what I did were insufficient for even one person, I would once again come to earth and once again undertake my bloody, terrible path to the Cross, that I might save that one soul, so dear to me." We must remember that man is God's dearest creation. The Lord adorned him with His image and likeness, and when man came to walk on the path of sin, He Himself came to earth to redeem and save him. So we can be calm in the sense that the Lord will pronounce no unjust or cruel, if you will, judgment against any soul. Only if one obstinately rejects His truth, sins stubbornly, expresses no desire to abandon his sin, and remains such to the end, then he will be guilty of his own demise.

This is not unlike a man who is dying of thirst who, when drink is placed in front of him, turns away from it, and later cries that he is dying of thirst — but he turned away himself! So it is here, if one but abstains from murdering himself spiritually and remains even mildly capable of accepting the light of truth, then that soul will not perish. As one Orthodox hierarch said, "hell will welcome the offspring of hell!" — that is, those people who murdered their souls by their way of living, and for whom no other lot exists. Do you remember what the Lord said when He spoke of the Dread Judgment? He will turn to the righteous and say, "inherit the kingdom prepared for you from the foundation of the world." But when He turns with a terrible and sorrowful word to the sinners, He will say, "depart from me, ye cursed, into everlasting fire, prepared (for whom? for you? no!) for the devil and his angels!" The sufferings of hell were not prepared for you – no! For you, God's Kingdom was opened. You could have walked into it as the righteous, but you made yourselves such, that there is no fate for you but to be with the enemy of God and murderer of man — the devil. You are responsible for your demise! And so, let us remember this. The Lord is just, but He is also endlessly merciful, and if there is a chance to save any soul, even one tangled in sins, remember that He will save it, can save it, and wishes to save it! Amen.

Refresher for an Orthodox Pastor[23]

1. Having accepted the grace of ordination, bear in mind of what a gift and of what mercy the Lord has found you worthy — and what responsibility you now bear. A priest is an apostle to his flock. "I do not belong to myself, but to others," said the great Russian pastor Fr. (now St.) John of Kronstadt.

2. Scripture says, "the priest's lips should keep knowledge, and they should seek the law at his mouth, for he is the messenger of the

---

23 "Refresher for a Russian Orthodox Pastor," Official Diocese of the Eastern American Diocese ROCOR, translated by Reader Gregory Levitsky, accessed July 13, 2022, http://archive.eadiocese.org/History/metphilaret/02orthodoxpastors. en.htm

Lord of hosts." Mind these words, Orthodox pastor. You must be a herald of God's Law and the truth of God's Gospel for your flock, which will turn to you for this very thing.

3. Fear as fire negligence in the holy work of ministry, more so in your service before the Dread Altar of the Lord of Glory. "Cursed be he that doeth the work of the Lord negligently," sternly warns the Holy Bible. Be a good example of the fear of God and piety for those who co-serve with you and assist you in your service. Be gone from the holy altar all you who enter it impiously.

4. Constantly pray to the Lord for help and understanding in running parish affairs. May the Lord grant you a spirit of chastity, humble mindedness, patience, and love. One must have all of these virtues for work in a parish. Treasure the advice of older and more experienced brethren, and the wise counsel of laymen, pious and faithful to the Church. Hold fast the helm of your parish ship, but at the same time, before deciding an issue firmly and by pastoral fiat, first pursue the guidance of people who have earned your trust — although everything in the Church is decided by spiritual leaders — the pastors, it is first discussed in conciliar wisdom — in the spirit of catholicity, universal unity must imbue the parish's life and work.

5. Holding firmly, I repeat, the helm in your hands, also try to attract good, pious church people to the living work of the parish, creating one harmonious, spiritual family with your assistants. Do not forget the children. Try diligently to teach, instruct, and raise them in the spirit of the Church, always and firmly demanding this of them and their parents. May your true helper in this be your God-given partner in this life — your Matushka. In the life of parishes, there have frequently been miscommunications and conflicts due to priests' wives involving themselves in pastoral matters and the work of their husbands — this must be avoided. But at the same time, there are aspects of parish life in which a pastor's wife can be his best helper, in large part in the work of the Christian education and upbringing of the children.

6. Laboring in the parish, do not stop laboring on your own soul. One must merge with the other. The Holy Apostle Paul instructs his disciple, St. Timothy, "let no man despise thy youth; but be thou

an example of the believers, in word, in conversation, in charity, in spirit, in faith, in purity. Till I come, give attendance to reading, to exhortation, to doctrine, take heed unto thyself, and unto the doctrine, continue in them, for in doing this thou shalt both save thyself, and them that hear thee."

May the Lord be your Helper in everything. Having twice accepted the grace of ordination to the diaconate and the priesthood — forget not to pray constantly for the hierarchs who laid their hands upon you.

Epistle to Titus[24]

Titus was also one of the closest disciples of the Apostle Paul. The epistle to him is not long, but nonetheless joins the ranks of pastoral epistles. There are many parallels between it and similar instructions that we find in the Epistle to Timothy. This is understandable, as the Apostle Paul consecrated both Timothy and Titus Bishops, to be his assistants and his successors. We read this in the Epistle to Titus, "Paul, a servant of God, and an apostle of Jesus Christ, according to the faith of God's elect, and the acknowledging of the truth which is after godliness. "But what is this "God's elect?" Does this mean that the Lord chooses who must be saved and does not choose others? It appears that the Lord does not treat everyone the same. He chooses some, but not others. How can this be? Becoming one of God's elect depends entirely on God's omniscience. Man remains free, but the Lord knows in advance and foresees, in a way inconceivable to us, what path he will take. And if he chooses the righteous path, he becomes one of "God's elect." This is why the Mother of God appeared to St. Sergius and said to him (of course, he was stunned by this appearance of the Mother of God, the Queen of Heaven), "fear not, thou elect of God!" Not because this was some marked chosen one, but because the Mother of God knew St. Sergius and therefore called him thus.

---

24 "Epistle to Titus by Metropolitan Philaret," Official Diocese of the Eastern American Diocese ROCOR, translated by Reader Gregory Levitsky, accessed July 13, 2022, http://archive.eadiocese.org/History/metphilaret/03titus.en.htm

"According to the faith of God's elect, and the acknowledging of the truth which is after godliness; in hope of eternal life, which God, that cannot lie, promised before the world began." This means that the truth which is after godliness is the hope of inheriting eternal life. And that hope relies on what the Lord promised, and God cannot lie, what He said will be. "But hath in due times manifested his word through preaching, which is committed unto me according to the commandment of God our Saviour to Titus, mine own son after the common faith, grace, mercy, and peace, from God the Father and the Lord Jesus Christ our Saviour." As a father does a son, he teaches him peace and the blessing of the One God, and then abruptly turns to the matter at hand, "for this cause left I thee in Crete" — at that time, the Apostle left Timothy in Ephesus. Timothy was the Bishop of Ephesus, where he suffered, while Titus was Bishop of Crete. "For this cause left I thee in Crete, that thou shouldest set in order the things that are wanting, and ordain elders in every city, as I had appointed thee, if any be blameless, the husband of one wife, having faithful children not accused of riot or unruly."

As in the Epistle to Timothy, the Apostle maintains, how can one who cannot rule his own home rule the Church? "For a Bishop must be blameless, as the steward of God; not self-willed, not soon angry, not given to wine, no striker, not given to filthy lucre." This is reminiscent of parallel instructions to the Apostle Timothy. "But a lover of hospitality (that is, one who welcomes strangers and indulges them), a lover of good men, sober, just, holy, temperate; holding fast the faithful word as he hath been taught, that he may be able by sound doctrine both to exhort and to convince the gainsayers." Of course, if one were to accept priestly or episcopal service and not know Christian teaching as well as he should, how can he convince those who are lost, and instruct those in need of instruction?

"For there are many unruly and vain talkers and deceivers, especially they of the circumcision whose mouths must be stopped, who subvert whole houses, teaching things which they ought not, for filthy lucre's sake." Remember what we just read in the Epistle to Titus, "one of themselves, even a prophet of their own, said, the

Cretans are always liars, evil beasts, lazy gluttons." This is a rather severe assessment, no? But hence arises a famous paradox, which is used as a logical fallacy to demonstrate that a formal logical conclusion can lead to different conclusion that negates the first. That which is here said by one prophet applies to the prophet himself, who is famous as having developed the paradox.

Here is the paradox: Epimenides, himself a Cretan, says that all Cretans are liars. And, since he is a Cretan, he too is a liar. Since he is a liar, then he spoke an untruth, and that means that Cretans are not liars. Since they are not liars, then that means he spoke the truth, which means they are liars. And since he is a Cretan, then he is a liar, and so it goes. There is an exit from this formal logical loop. The exit, of course, takes the form of an old proverb, "there is an exception to every rule!" Epimenides said, "the Cretans are always liars, evil beasts, lazy gluttons," and the Apostle Paul adds, "this witness is true. Wherefore rebuke them sharply, that they may be sound in the faith; not giving heed to Jewish fables, and commandments of men, that turn from the truth. Unto the pure all things are pure."

He who is pure in soul and heart can speak on any topics, even those, it would seem, which are seductive and impure, and yet remain pure. "Unto the pure all things are pure but unto them that are defiled and unbelieving is nothing pure; but even their mind and conscience is defiled." Whoever is defiled sees impurity everywhere. Whoever is pure sees purely, but whoever is impure sees the vile in everything. "They profess that they know God; but in works they deny him, being abominable, and disobedient, and unto every good work reprobate."

The Apostle speaks of his time here, but we in our own time see the very same thing. Many people who speak of God say many pious, elegant words, but deny Him in their works. For when words are not supported by works, but rather the works part ways with the words, then it becomes clear – this man has no true, firm conviction in Christ. If he had it, then he would be faithful to that truth. This is that about which we already spoke in the last times especially, there will be many people having an appearance of piety. They will profess that they know God, they will speak holy words, but by their works they will deny Him, being abominable, and disobedient, and unto every good work reprobate. Amen.

Discussion with a Youth Group about the Vespers Service[25]

When festal Vespers are served jointly with Matins, they are called the "All-Night Vigil." Small Vespers are generally not served independently, but only on those days when the All-Night Vigil is served and is served sometime before it. Daily Vespers are more often than not, served on all weekdays. Great Vespers are served on the eve of feast days and other special days over the course of the liturgical year. Let us now do an overview of the basic Daily Vespers. Festal Vespers contain certain things that Daily Vespers do not. Small Vespers are a kind of abbreviation of Daily Vespers — much is omitted that is otherwise included in the Daily Vespers. It recently occurred to me that perhaps my memory had failed me, when I saw an audio recording of a Ledkovsky choir with the label "Bless the Lord, O my soul," composed by me, and further labeled "Psalm 104," when I know that it is Psalm 103 not 104 as written on the tape. This psalm is a long one. Therein David described God's omnipotence and wisdom in the creation of the world with bright, wonderful verses.

Those who had been to Mt. Athos, not recently, but in the good old days, spoke about how, for instance, when they were in some monastery on the eve of that monastery's patronal feast day, they would append an early Liturgy to their Vigil. This would occupy 12 to 14 hours without a break to leave the church. In addition, they told me, "Bless the Lord, O my soul," the Proemial Psalm, would be sung over the course of an hour and fifteen minutes, because a soloist (the choir's leader or director) would chant each verse, then

---

25 "Discussion with a Youth Group about the Vespers Service," Official Diocese of the Eastern American Diocese ROCOR, translated by Reader Gregory Levitsky, accessed July 13, 2022, http://archive.eadiocese.org/History/metphilaret/04vespers.en.htm

echoed by the choir. The choir leader would sing, "O Lord my God, Thou hast been magnified exceedingly," the choir would repeat, and so on. And this whole long psalm would be sung twice, once by the choir leader and again by the choir. And so, in the unhurried chant of the monastery, this would occupy an hour and fifteen minutes.

By the way, I read a history once of some pious landowners, who loved to attend church and stood through long cathedral services, once went, rather than to Mt. Athos, to the Optina Hermitage. In Optina, as in many of our monasteries, there are no long services such as those on Mt. Athos. But the services were very long, served according to the Typikon. The landowners arrived with their families, went to the Vigil and there they were grandly singing "Bless the Lord, O my soul." They stood with some difficulty until "Lord, I have cried" and then went to sleep. They slept some and then arose, decided to return to church, and arrived for the Polyeleos. They stayed for the Polyeleos, venerated the icons and returned to bed.

When the service is a daily, weekday service, then this psalm is read. It is sung at Great Vespers on a feast, otherwise it is only sung at the All-Night Vigil. The psalm is ended. Next we have the Great Litany, or the "Litany of Peace." Why is it called this? Because it speaks much of peace. The first three petitions, "In peace, let us pray to the Lord," "For the peace from above," "For the peace of the whole world." The litany is ended. According to the Typikon, during Daily Vespers, with rare exception, one kathisma is read. It is read almost nowhere. It is read in monasteries, but in churches it is almost never read, although it is indicated. After the kathisma is the Little Litany, which is an abbreviation of the Great Litany, its beginning and end. After that is the prayer sung at every Vespers service, taken from the order of the Old Testament Temple: "Lord, I have cried unto Thee, hearken unto me, hearken unto me, O Lord," the words of the psalm, followed additionally by, "Let my prayer be set forth as incense before Thee."

How do you interpret these words? What does, "Let my prayer be set forth" mean? I ask because often the words "set forth" are misunderstood or even taken for another meaning. The prayer has ended; the wording here refers to the consummation, the fulfillment, of the prayer. "Let my prayer be set forth as incense before Thee;" in other words, let my prayer be completed and offered as censing before Thee. At the same time, the great censing of the church begins. Fr. John (now Saint) of Kronstadt liked to say, when speaking about the censer, that when the censer is burning and emitting sweet fragrance, the sweet-smelling smoke rises to the sky — "such must be your prayer, and if you see the censer cold, extinguished and emitting no smoke, no sweet fragrance, that is what our prayer usually resembles." That is why we pray, "Let our prayer be set forth," let our prayer be fulfilled and arise as incense before Thee.

Little children, when they hear this, don't understand it very well. In monasteries and parishes, where the Typikon is observed more or less fully, after these verses excerpts from the psalms are read, although on feasts these are sung. Eventually we reach the verse, "Bring my soul out of prison, that I may confess Thy name." This verse is often heard at Sunday Vigils, as it marks the beginning of the singing of the resurrectional "stichera," i.e., separate prayers. The name "sticheron" remains from antiquity, when the majority of the services were composed, and the prayers were written in poetic verse. Now it is extremely rare to find stichera composed in poetic verse, but the name has stuck. Further, each sticheron is prefaced by a verse from the psalm. When there is a festal service, you can have up to ten stichera — on a daily service, six.

When serving a daily service and you have six sticheral verses, that are sung by tone. I already spoke to you about how each Sunday, each week, has its own tone — eight in total. The verses are sung according to the tone of the week. But that is only the first three, while the second three verses are dedicated to the saint of the day. Sometimes that saint has been assigned the same tone, sometimes a different one. For instance, often in monasteries, to make it easier to sing, the tone is announced, "In the sixth tone, Lord, I have cried unto Thee, hearken unto me," and then they sing. Then, for the following verses, if in the same tone, they say "In the same tone: If thou, Lord, shouldest mark iniquities, O Lord, who shall stand?" Three verses are sung in this tone, followed by the verses for the saint; then they pronounce the tone (if it is different, for instance, fifth tone) and then sing the attendant verses. Sometimes, though, it is "in the same tone." After the singing of "Lord, I have cried unto Thee...Let my prayer be set forth," the verses are sung. The final verse is almost always in honor of the Mother of God. After the verse to the Mother of God, we sing "O Gladsome Light."

I have lived 61 years on this earth, and not until I came to Australia did I hear "O Gladsome Light" read. In the hymn itself we hear "We praise (in Slavonic and some translations, "hymn" — trans.) the Father, Son, and Holy Spirit, God." I remember serving at our monastery in Lesna and saying that I was surprised that some of our churches read it instead of singing it. Every Vespers service says, "We praise (hymn – trans.) the Father, Son, and Holy Spirit," (not read), and it is even called the "Evening Hymn." In the Lesna monastery, the Typikon is strictly adhered to, and the hymn is always sung.

After the singing of "O Gladsome Light," the verse for every day, the prokeimenon, is exclaimed. After the prokeimenon is read "Vouchsafe, O Lord." This is, of course, always read, except on Pascha. During Bright week, all seven days of Pascha, "Vouchsafe, O Lord" is sung. Nothing should be read, except Holy Scripture, Epistle and Gospel. Therefore even the prefacing verses are sung. After this comes the Litany of Supplication when the Deacon or Priest concludes a petition with "let us ask of the Lord," the choir replies, "Grant this, O Lord!" One Russian hierarch noted, "when we ask something, or children ask something of their parents, they put their whole soul into that request. But often times the choir sings, 'Grant this, O Lord,' without thinking at all about how we actually want the Lord to grant it unto us, while the faithful doze in church — a very appropriate petition!"

After the Litany of Supplication, the Aposticha are chanted, which also include Psalm verses before the stichera. The verses for "Lord, I have cried" are sung after the Little Litany, while the Aposticha are sung after the Litany of Supplication. It too almost always ends in a verse in honor of the Mother of God. A prayer is then read, the words of which are taken entirely from the Gospel, "Now let Thou Thy servant depart in peace, O Master." I recall that in Harbin we would only sing this prayer once a year — on the eve of the Meeting of the Lord, at the Vigil, and on all other days we would read it. After "Now let Thou Thy servant depart" follow the prayers, "Holy God," "O Most Holy Trinity," "Our Father."

After the exclamation, "For Thine is the Kingdom" we sing the troparion to the saint whose memory we celebrate the following morning then, Glory, Both Now, and the troparion in honor of the Mother of God, called the Theotokion — the dismissal troparion. Here the (Daily) Vespers draw to a close, the Litany of Fervent Supplication is read, and then the dismissal — the final exclamation, "Christ our God, the Existing One, is blessed" we call the dismissal the priest's final exclamation, when he says that Christ is our true God, by the prayers of the saints (commemorated that day), will have mercy and save us, for He is Good and the Lover of mankind. Also, without exception, the parents of the Most Holy Theotokos — the holy and righteous Joachim and Anna — are always commemorated, as are the Holy Apostles.

These are the Daily Vespers. The Small Vespers differ from them in that many of the prayers are omitted. There is no Great Litany in the Small Vespers, no Litany of Supplication, just the Litany of Fervent Supplication at the very end. And there are many abbreviations in the prayers, and very few sticheral verses. For example, during the full festal Vespers during a Vigil, before a Sunday, the prokeimenon "The Lord is king, He is robed in majesty" is sung four times, but during Small Vespers only twice. There are instances when Vespers are served at irregular times. Then they are combined with other divine services that normally follow them; for instance, on special days during Great Lent and Holy Week. Then the Vespers are combined directly with the Liturgy, sometimes with the Liturgy of the Presanctified Gifts, sometimes with the Liturgies of St. John Chrysostom or St. Basil the Great. I would like to remind you on what days we serve the Liturgy of St. Basil the Great. Ten days a year, the Eve of Nativity, the Eve of Epiphany, on the feast of St. Basil the Great, on the five Sundays of Great Lent, on Great Thursday and Great Saturday.

On Saint Nicholas the Wonderworker[26]

People who are familiar with and know the order of our Orthodox divine services (Typikon) know that these services often utilize prokeimena. This Greek name denotes any text from the Holy Scripture that has a particularly close relationship to any given feast day. For example, when there is a feast in honor of St. Basil the Great, St. Gregory the Theologian or St. John Chrysostom, these great theologians and teachers of the faith, then the prokeimenon corresponds to their great glory, "My mouth shall speak of wisdom; and the meditation of my heart shall be of understanding." For their mouths, truly, pronounced to the world the words of divine wisdom.

Today we celebrate the feast of another great hierarch, St. Nicholas the Wonderworker, but we hear another prokeimenon, "Precious in the sight of the Lord is the death of His saints." This prokeimenon is proclaimed in honor of many great saints. But although St. Nicholas the Hierarch and Wonderworker instructed and taught his flock with inspired and grace-filled words, his principal glory does not lie therein. We know wherein lies his true glory. Holy ascetics and saints who were glorified for their works of charity and mercy are so named, "merciful." Very recently the Church glorified one such great merciful saint, Righteous Philaret the Merciful. And today She magnifies St. Nicholas, whom the Russian people likewise named in honor of his wondrous works of love and charity "Nicholas the Merciful." And [the] Russian people, seeing someone in sorrow, in misery, in infirmities, will say to him, "Pray to Nicholas the Merciful, and he will tell the All-Merciful Savior of your need."

I would like to remind you of the special glory given to St. Nicholas, above that given to other Holy God-Pleasers. It is the fact that his name is honored among pagans who know not Christianity. And there is a reason for this. There was an incident well-known to the citizens of Harbin. In Harbin there was a so-called "New Cem-

---

26 "Saint Nicholas the Wonderworker," Official Diocese of the Eastern American Diocese ROCOR, translated by Reader Gregory Levitsky, accessed July 13, 2022, http://archive.eadiocese.org/History/metphilaret/05stnicholas.en.htm

etery." It was bordered on one side by a long, tall, steep cliff. One day, some Chinese children were playing there. They were playing under some overhangs of the cliff that could easily fall. And so, while the Chinese children were playing there, suddenly a radiant elder appeared to them, who sternly told them in Chinese that they were to immediately leave this place. The frightened children ran and as soon as they had run away from that spot, a huge piece of the cliff collapsed. They would have been crushed under it, had it not been for the elder's warning. News of this spread swiftly among the Chinese, of course, and later among the Russians.

One Russian hunter, occupying himself with his favorite pastime, walked far off into the jungles of China. Weary, he entered a small Chinese village. The Chinese, a welcoming, genial people, offered him a place to rest. Entering into one of the huts, he saw nailed above the entryway an icon of St. Nicholas. He realized that, these being pagans, the icon must have somehow accidentally ended up with them, and he asked the master of the house to give him the icon. He grew upset with him and answered, "This old man is a very good man; we honor him much, because he helps us greatly."

I recall one more instance at the train station in Harbin there was a large, ornate icon of St. Nicholas, which many considered to be wonderworking. All Russian Orthodox people (excepting, perhaps, the atheists), when they traveled by train and wound up in the Harbin train station, considered it their Christian duty to pray before that icon and put up a candle. There was one incident that took place in the spring. There was an ice floe on the large, wide Songhua River. Many people had gathered at the station, and trains were passing through frequently. Suddenly they see a Chinese man run into the building, soaking wet. He ran in, threw himself before the icon, falling to his knees and began to cry aloud something in his own language. It turned out that he was thanking the holy Hierarch. What had happened? He was in a hurry and decided to risk it — he chose to cross the river by jumping across the drifting ice. The ice on the Songhua was fairly solid and thick. So there he was running and suddenly he fell into the water and found himself under the ice, drowning. But, remembering the icon and how deeply the Russians venerated it, cried out in Chinese, "Old man from the station, help me!" And he appeared on the shore, wet, but on the shore, how? He couldn't understand. He then got up and ran the whole long way to the station, fell before the icon and offered his thanks.

It is no coincidence that St. Nicholas is venerated not only by the Orthodox Christian population, but by pagans, as well. It is done unto them according to their faith! And that is why the Russian person will always turn to St. Nicholas, regardless of what he may need, because he knows and believes that many voices call out to the holy Hierarch, there in the holy, Heavenly realm, but the holy Hierarch will always hear and come to the aid of the voice of faith, the voice of hope against hope. It is no coincidence, I repeat, that the Russian people call him Nicholas the Merciful. Amen.

The Necessity of Fulfilling the Church's Commandments[27]

Very interesting times have come, beloved brethren! They are interesting because, if you were to compare our contemporary world with that which existed in Mother Russia before, then we see an almost total inverse. For instance, it is currently the Apostles' Fast. But among modern Orthodox Christians, many do not know this. Once upon a time, in Russia, Russian Orthodox people knew the Church calendar and rules very well, and ordered their lives according to how the Church tells us to live here on earth, in this temporal life. But now, I repeat, some do not know the rules of the Church. This is not just ignorance or lack of knowledge, but a certain enfeeblement, impermissible for a Christian, and even a scornful or irreverent attitude on his part toward the old, beneficial commandments of the Church.

Our Lord Jesus Christ once said that heaven and earth would sooner fade away, "Till heaven and earth pass, one jot or one tittle

---

27 "Necessity of Fulfilling the Church's Commandments," Official Diocese of the Eastern American Diocese ROCOR, translated by Reader Gregory Levitsky, accessed July 13, 2022, http://archive.eadiocese.org/History/metphilaret/06commandments.en.htm

shall in no wise pass from the Law;" that is, everything that we read in our Orthodox teachings and about which the Holy Gospel speaks will be fulfilled, but those who do not observe those teachings will be in direct disobedience to Divine Law. Let us examine how this matter was approached in olden times. We see the Church glorifying the holy Maccabean martyrs, all of the brothers, their teacher, Eleazar, and their mother. Their tormentor, the pagan king, subjected them to terrible sufferings, tortures, and torments all because they refused to eat the food forbidden to them by Mosaic Law. In other words, they refused to break the fast, refused to eat that food which was forbidden to them by the Church. And they went to their deaths.

People today are shockingly irreverent and talk of this with indifference, while true men of the faith, those who believe in God and believe God, those men look on all of those rules and commandments as something sacrosanct that must be kept. One of our ascetics in Russia was once asked why the Lord sometimes ceases to bestow invisible, divine grace-filled acts, the demonstration of God's mercy. The elder replied: "Because the people have stopped listening to the Lord God, particularly those Orthodox Russian people who do not observe the fasts." That was then, but now the situation is totally different. Then there were many Orthodox Christians, whereas now you will be hard-pressed to find any, although that applies not only to our day and age. The famous Russian writer and philosopher, the talented poet Khomiakov, a man of great spiritual life who always strived to strictly observe all of the Church's rulings and directives, came to St. Petersburg, Russia's capital. He felt as though he were in the desert, nobody kept the Church fasts — nobody! He did his work, but he also observed the fasts, and stunned everyone with his firm and steadfast approach. Today it is no easy task finding people who observe the fasts so dutifully.

Beloved, let us remember the Church's commandments — the Church never asks us to do anything that is unnecessary — never! Of what is good in life, man has a choice: he can live in one way, or in another. However, there are certain laws of the Church that every Orthodox Christian is obliged to keep and follow. One of these laws is the keeping of the fasts, when the Church calls on us to moderate ourselves during certain times of the year. Only those who observe these fasts can be called Orthodox Christians. Here we may recall the words of St. Seraphim of Sarov, who was a great faster. He said it directly, "Whosoever does not fast is not a Christian!" Whatever he may call himself, whatever he may consider himself, he is not a Christian. This is entirely natural, this stern judgment of the holy laborer; after all, what school will allow a student to stay on who ignores the school rules? What institute will keep a servant that fulfills none of its rules? The Church likewise has its own rules, its own law. I repeat, She offers us many choices to make our lifestyle, our occupation — She will bless it all, so long as the Christian undertakes it in a Christian fashion. But where She lays down her rules, there a Christian must submit without question. After all, the Church offers us all this for our own good, because obedience to the Church is one of the greatest virtues. Amen.

Every Christian Must Bear His Cross[28]

During the Divine Liturgy today we all heard what our Lord Jesus Christ said that every Christian must bear his cross, "Whoever wants to be my disciple must deny themselves and take up their cross and follow me." He Himself bore a cross His whole life; not only to Golgotha did He carry His heavy wooden Cross, on which He would soon be crucified. He carried a cross His whole life! He bore a cross in being the Son of God. The Infinite God united with human nature and, as the God-man, lived among the people, sharing their life with them. This was insufficient: He brought to earth a deposit of love and mercy. He forgave everyone, judged no one, performed countless miraculous acts of mercy, love, forgiveness, and healing. And the more He poured out this light of love amongst the people, the tighter and tighter did His embittered enemies close

---

28 "Every Christian Must Bear His Cross," Official Diocese of the Eastern American Diocese ROCOR, translated by Reader Gregory Levitsky, accessed July 13, 2022, http://archive.eadiocese.org/History/metphilaret/bearcross. en.htm

Metropolitan Philaret in Jerusalem

in around Him, hating Him with a satanic hatred, until finally they nailed Him to the Cross.

As you heard, it was commanded that a Christian can only follow Him if he takes up his cross and follows Him. As St. Theophan the Recluse taught, this most holy cross is threefold. One part of this cross is all of the hardships that a man must bear, desiring to live a pious Christian life and seeing that he is unsuccessful, because his sinful habits and habitual sins control him and subject him to themselves. Thus it is often: a man's soul is aflame, hoping for a good Christian life, but his habitual sins, all those habits that he has nurtured, inexorably pull him toward themselves. And wherever he may go, this follows him everywhere. For that reason St. Theophan himself compares the condition of a sinful person with that of a person to the back of whose shoulders has been tied a smoldering, stinking, rotting corpse. He is bound, and wherever he may run, all of this stays with him. So it is with our sinful nature "you can't escape yourself" as one Russian once said.

The second cross is comprised by the efforts of every struggle and hardship of our earthly life. This is what is so often called our CROSS — namely those sorrows, infirmities, losses, etc. But here I must point out that if man ultimately faces all of these sorrows humbly and obediently, accepting them as sent by God's providence for his own good, he will accept everything differently. So long as he grumbles, resists, and rages, his soul will never be at rest. But when he stops grumbling, humbly and obediently receiving these trials from the right hand of God, he will see that although everything around him is seemingly the same, he himself is different, he accepts all of these sorrows and difficulties calmly with a Christian conviction, that this is how it must be! Our Lord and Heavenly Father will not give you a stone instead of bread, and when he gives you sorrows, it means that you must endure it in a Christian manner.

The third part, the third cross, is, according to St. Theophan (and he is famous for his spiritual labors) the cross of those temptations that attack a man when he has overcome the allure of everyday sins, as it was with the great spiritual athletes. They were well beyond the seduction of conventional sins. Then come the force and abyss of the most dangerous temptation – the temptation of pride. And then sometimes they would falter in their struggle against these temptations of prideful thoughts. This cross is rightfully known only by those who have to carry it, as that same St. Theophan noted. But one way or the other, our duty is to bear our cross, for the Lord recognizes no other followers. Amen.

Christy is the Conqueror of the World[29]

The Holy Gospel has preserved for us the words of the Savior, which the Lord spoke to His apostles at the Mystical Supper as He bade them farewell, before going to His holy sufferings. Before Him lay the whole awful spectacle, the whole immeasurable abyss of sufferings, which we can neither comprehend nor imagine, and He said to them, "In the world ye shall have tribulation: but TAKE HEART, FOR I HAVE CONQUERED THE WORLD" (John 16:33). Not for nothing did Fr. John of Kronstadt, as he wrote in his journal, love to gaze upon the image, the icon of Christ the Giver of Life, bearing in His hands the standard of victory after His Resurrection! "What a Glorious Victor!" wrote Fr. John. "What an evil and terrible enemy has He conquered!" And the Apostle of love writes, "This is the victory that has conquered the world — our faith!" (1 John 5:4). And so the Orthodox Church triumphs in this victory of Her Orthodox faith, celebrating it on the first Sunday of Great Lent, which is named in its honor: "The Triumph of Orthodoxy." The Church, as though looking back on the path She has walked, sees that path's trials and sorrows. Persecuted from the beginning by the enemies of Christ — the Jews, then persecuted by the pagan rulers of Rome, and then battling various heresies, the Church walked a sorrowful path, but overcame and CONQUERED!

Perhaps it was not so difficult for the Church when She was subjected to bloody persecutions, for in them the true path is reinforced;

---

29 "Christ is the Conqueror of the World," Official Diocese of the Eastern American Diocese ROCOR, translated by Reader Gregory Levitsky, accessed July 13, 2022, http://archive.eadiocese.org/History/metphilaret/christconqueror.en.htm

more dangerous were the heresies that appeared, threatening to undermine the truth of Orthodoxy. The heretic Arius arose and claimed that the Son of God was not equal to God, not begotten of Him and equal to Him in nature, but only created by Him. And an Ecumenical Council was needed to condemn this heretic, and overturn this heresy. After him followed many heresies and the first heresies focused exclusively on the Most Holy Person of our Savior, our Lord Jesus Christ, and only later did they fixate on other dogmas.

And now in our time, all manner of distortion and fraud — even outright rejection — have been leveled against one of the chief dogmas of the Church — the DOGMA OF THE CHURCH. You yourselves know that in our Symbol of Faith we say, "I believe in one holy, Catholic, and Apostolic Church." Blessed is the man who abides in this Church, for the Lord gave His promise, "I will build my church and the gates of hell shall not prevail against it" (Matthew 16:18). This means that, if you are within the Church, you will reap that joyous and comforting promise, but if you are without, beware! Once St. Seraphim of Sarov said to an Old Believer who came to him and began to offer him his thoughts and opinions, "Drop your nonsense! The ship of the Church has as its Captain Christ the Savior, and as its Helmsman the Holy Spirit, and it traverses the sea of life which tosses us to and fro. And what storms must it overcome! And you think you will cross the sea of life in the little boat of your own opinions? Drop your nonsense!"

And so, a Christian, if he wishes to celebrate the Triumph of Orthodoxy as his own, as an Orthodox Christian, let him examine his Orthodoxy. Our Orthodox faith is holy, eminent, and irreproachable, for the Incarnate Son of God brought it to us from the heavens Himself, and the Church preserves it. Whether any individual follows it faithfully is a matter for his own conscience. According to his loyalty or disloyalty, let him properly celebrate the feast of the Triumph of Orthodoxy. Indeed, often a man may consider himself faithful, a loyal son of the Church, but at the same time, God knows what he harbors in his thoughts. Here I will employ an example, once in Moscow there lived a wealthy merchant, whom many, and even he himself considered nothing short of a pillar of Orthodoxy, so Orthodox was he. So much a man of the Church! Out of his own pocket, he kept a lamp always lit in the famous Iberian Chapel, and whenever anyone would praise him for it, he would say, "Yes, of course — perhaps there is something on that side after all!" Just like that, by the way! There you have your pious Orthodox Christian, who doesn't even believe in life after death. But if there is no life after death, then the Gospel is a fiction and a fallacy. And so it is with many articles of our faith, which people dispute, even those who are strong in faith, and even more those who refuse to keep the fasts.

From antiquity we know of the holy example of the Maccabean Martyrs, who refused to eat food forbidden by the rules of the Church in force at the time, and for that they suffered and became holy martyrs. But how do modern-day Orthodox Christians treat this rule? The Orthodox Church tells us specifically what days are fasting days and what we can or cannot eat, but no! Not only do they eat what they like, but they maintain that these are ancient prejudices not to be bothered with, and they consider themselves Orthodox. A man can examine his Orthodoxy as follows: when he sees that something in his life does not correlate with the teachings of the Church, then he takes care and drops it. If you will hold on and cling to that something, then the Church will not recognize you as Her own, and from there is it not far to that dreaded anathema, which will be proclaimed tomorrow, and in which NO ONE condemns anyone else, but in which the Church says, these ones are no longer ours, they are not within the aegis of our Church. And so, again I repeat, examine your Orthodoxy, you Orthodox Christian, you Russian Orthodox soul! And only if you truly believe all that our Church teaches, then the Triumph of Orthodoxy will be your own triumph, and will be for you a great feast. Amen.

A Sermon on the Fourth Sunday of Great Lent[30]

In the name of the Father, and of the Son, and of the Holy Spirit!

Many of us, certainly, know that from Christian antiquity we have received testimony of that special friendship that once existed between two of God's great saints, equal in talent, equal in spiritual elevation, and both living out equally spiritual aspirations — these were the holy hierarchs St. Basil the Great and St. Gregory the Theologian. These great hierarchs gave us the most ideal example of that friendship which Christians must have amongst themselves. But Gregory the Theologian far outlived his friend. Basil the Great reposed at a relatively young age — he was but in his fiftieth year, while Gregory the Theologian was over sixty years old at the time of his repose. But, when Gregory the Theologian spoke in memory of his friend, he noted that St. Basil, in his words, defeated one sin every day and acquired one virtue. And in this way he rose up ever higher and higher.

Nowadays we have forgotten, unfortunately, that which must be at the center of every Christian's attention, the fact that each one of us, regardless of what duties we fulfill or work we perform in the outside world, internally must always work on our own souls, trying to implant in our souls and in our hearts the seeds of virtue, and tearing out the weeds of every sin and vice. But here, of course, one must be gradual, not trying to do everything at once. Tomorrow the Church celebrates, in addition to Sunday, the memory of that great teacher of this Christian spiritual approach, St. John Climacus or St. John of the Ladder, so called because of his seminal work, "the Ladder of Divine Ascent," a work which glorified him forever in the Orthodox Church, a work which was once the most beloved reading of our pious predecessors, as well as being read by the Royal Family during their imprisonment, before their martyric deaths.

---

30 "Sermon on the Fourth Sunday of Great Lent," Official Diocese of the Eastern American Diocese ROCOR, translated by Reader Gregory Levitsky, accessed July 13, 2022, http://archive.eadiocese.org/History/metphilaret/4sungtlent.en.htm

And so the venerable saint, having himself walked this spiritual path, and having enriched himself by it first, earnestly, plainly, and clearly shows how one must go gradually from one virtue to the next, going ever higher and higher, cultivating himself spiritually. Characteristically, his "Ladder" contained an expression that the saint uses when one begins to speak of that highest of Christian virtues — Christian love; the saint humbly remarks, "He who says that God is love, and he who speaks of love, is one who has dared to speak of God Himself. This is rather dangerous, and above our station." That is how humbly the venerable saint spoke! Or recall our great and holy teacher of the spiritual life, in whose honor this marvelous church is dedicated! "Wretched Seraphim," as he called himself, was one of the greatest saints not only of Russia, but of the whole Universal Church, our venerable father Seraphim. Once a very earnest — but still young and inexperienced monk — set about his labors zealously, so to speak, though lacking the requisite experience. And so St. Seraphim said to him in a gentle, fatherly tone, "My joy, do everything gradually, little by little, and not all of a sudden. A virtue is not a pear — you can't eat it up and go grabbing for another."

And so, each of us must remember that our principal goal is to cultivate our souls in the performing of good, Christian works. But do not let this be [some] erratic outward demonstration; instead, let every man gradually cultivate himself spiritually. Spiritually experienced people know how important this is, and more importantly, this is how you find the path to the Kingdom of Heaven. For we know that "nothing that defileth" shall enter into God's Kingdom, as it says in the Holy Scriptures; and so therefore, in order to inherit God's Kingdom, Christians must improve themselves, that we might "cleanse ourselves from all filthiness of the flesh and spirit, perfecting holiness in the fear of God" (2 Corinthians 7:1), as the great Apostle Paul wrote. Amen.

Homily During the Canonization of the Russian New-Martyrs[31]

In the Name of the Father and the Son and the Holy Spirit.

My brothers, in a few minutes we will hear for the first time the magnification sung to all the new Divinely revealed God-pleasers, who are being glorified this day. We have read the list of the New-Martyrs and Confessors; remember that this is, of course, just a very small portion of all those who have suffered. We do not know and cannot know every person who suffered for Christ. Remember, that which we have read today — this is a list that is fearful. It is a list that shakes your soul because you can see with what unbelievable anger and evil possession the enemy of the human race sought to devour those who were blameless witnesses and confessors of Truth and Faith in Jesus Christ. Indeed, in our unfortunate homeland there is not even one place, it seems, and not even one corner in which the blood of the witnesses for Christ was not spilled. Therefore, I repeat, it is a fearful list. But at the same time, this their glorification is a great triumph of our Faith. A great triumph. The depths of hell, as never before in the history of the human race, have at this time risen against our homeland, our Church, and our people; yet they[32] have miscalculated because they have put their hopes in the depths of hell.

The Church feels the power of the blood of the confessors and martyrs, and through it has confirmed her victory. With the glorification of the New-Martyrs, all of us here present are also participating in their glorious triumph of the Orthodox Faith. Do not forget, in our homeland there are millions of the martyrs for the Faith. They are more than any other time period of God's Church; there has never been a time with so many martyrs. If we have read

31 "Sermon of Saint Metropolitan Philaret of ROCOR 1981," YouTube, accessed, July 29th, 2022, https://youtu.be/IBk7IA7-jCM

32 Translator Note: In using "They," Metropolitan Philaret is referring to the Atheist Soviet Persecutors.

Met. Philaret during the Canonization of the Russian New-Martyrs

the list with sorrow, it is because through it we see with what hatred they tortured the blameless defenders of faith in Christ. What is happening today is very clear to us; in ancient times there was also martyrdom and martyrs were tortured for Christ. But then it was different because the pagans did not deny Divine truth. They did not have a correct understanding because they were striving for one religious understanding and for them Christianity was a delusion. But today, the insane enemies of God and truth have revolted against God Himself, the Creator of all things.

The Church is victorious over them because the blood of the martyrs has confirmed the truth. In the Church troparion we sing that the multitude of the Holy New-Martyrs adorn the Church like fine embroidery on a priceless garment. This is the raiment in which the Russian Church is clothed. We rejoice because we are participating in this glorification, for it is God Who glorifies them, not us. He has glorified them. They are holy unto Him. He has crowned them with crowns of blessedness and eternal joy. We are now only witnesses to the fact that they are our protectors and intercessors before God. And we may pray to them fervently as to all the saints of the Church. Amen.

WRITINGS

The First Sorrowful Epistle[33]
(July 27, 1969)

To Their Holinesses and Their Beatitudes the Primates of the Holy
Orthodox Churches, The Most Reverend Metropolitans, Archbishops,
and Bishops: A Sorrowful Epistle from the Humble Philaret,
Metropolitan of the Russian Orthodox Church Outside of Russia

The Holy Fathers and Doctors of the Church have exhorted
us to keep the Truth of Orthodoxy as the apple of our eye. And
Our Lord Jesus Christ, teaching His Disciples to maintain every
jot and tittle of the Divine Law intact said, "Whosoever therefore
shall break one of these least commandments, and shall teach men
so, he shall be called the least in the kingdom of heaven" (Matthew
5:19). He sent His disciples to teach the doctrines He gave them to
all nations in a pure and unadulterated form, and that duty then
devolved upon each of us Bishops, as the successors to the Apostles.
We are also taught to do this by the dogmatic definition of the
Seventh Œcumenical Council, which says, "We keep unchanged all
the ecclesiastical traditions handed down to us, whether in writing
or by word of mouth."

And the Holy Fathers of that Council added, in their first
Canon, "the pattern for those who have received the sacerdotal

---

33 Metropolitan Philaret of New York, "A Sorrowful Epistle," *Orthodox Life*, no.
4 (July-August 1969): 3-14.

dignity is found in the testimonies and instructions laid down in the canonical constitutions, which we receiving with a glad mind sing unto the Lord God in the words of the God-inspired David saying, 'I have had as great delight in the way of Thy testimonies as in all manner of riches.' 'Thou hast commanded righteousness as Thy testimonies forever.' 'Grant me understanding and I shall live.' Now if the word of prophecy bids us keep the testimonies of God forever and to live by them, it is evident that they must abide unshaken and without change."

Every one of us solemnly promises at his consecration to abide by our Faith and to obey the canons of the Holy Fathers, vowing before God to keep Orthodoxy inviolate from the temptations and errors which creep into the Church's life. If a temptation appears in the fold of only one Orthodox Church, the remedy for it may be found in the same fold. But if a particular evil penetrates into all our Churches, it becomes a matter of concern for every single Bishop. Can any one of us be silent if he sees that many of his brethren simultaneously are walking along a path that leads them and their flock to a disastrous precipice through their unwitting loss of Orthodoxy?

Should we say in this case that humility commands us to keep silent? Should we regard it as indiscreet to lend advice to other descendants of the Holy Apostles, some of whom are occupying the most ancient and distinguished sees? But Orthodoxy believes in the equality of all Bishops, as regards grace, and distinguishes between them only as regards honour. Should we be satisfied with the fact that every Church is responsible for itself? But what if the statements which trouble the faithful are made in the name of the whole Church, and therefore also involve our name, even though we have not authorized anybody to use it? St. Gregory the Theologian once said that there are occasions "when even by silence truth can be betrayed." Should we not also be betraying the truth if, on noticing a deviation from pure Orthodoxy, we merely kept silence — always an easier and safer thing to do than speaking out?

We observe, however, that nobody in a higher position than our own is raising his voice; and this fact constrains us to speak out, lest at the Last Judgment we should be reproached for having seen the danger of Ecumenism threaten the Church, and yet not having warned her Bishops. To be sure, we have already addressed His Holiness Patriarch Athenagoras and His Eminence Archbishop Iakovos of North and South America, expressing our grief and concern over their ecumenical activities, in which the birth right of the Church has been sold for a mess of pottage in the form of the world's applause. But the position taken by the Orthodox delegates at the Assembly of the World Council of Churches at Uppsala makes the concern of the zealots of Orthodoxy even more acute, and makes it necessary for us to communicate our sorrow and confusion to all our Brother Orthodox Bishops.

We may be asked why we write about that assembly only now, nearly a year after the closing of its sessions. Our answer is that on this occasion we had no observers present, and obtained information about the assembly only from the press, the accuracy of which is not always to be relied upon. Therefore we were awaiting the official reports; and having studied them, we find it imperative to address this letter to all the Orthodox Bishops whom the Lord has appointed to take care of His Church on earth. The report on the Uppsala Assembly shocked us greatly, because from it we could see more clearly than ever how far the error of Ecumenism is winning the official approval of a number of our Churches. When the first steps were taken in the organisation of the Ecumenical Movement, many of the Orthodox Churches, following the initiative of the Patriarch of Constantinople, began to participate in its conferences. At that time such participation did not cause any worry even among the most zealous Orthodox. They thought that the Church would suffer no injury if her representatives appeared in the face of their various errors. Such a participation in interfaith conferences could be thought of as having a missionary character.

This position was still maintained to a certain extent, though not always consistently, at the Evanston Assembly of the World Council of Churches in 1954. There the Orthodox delegates openly stated that the decisions of the Assembly diverged so sharply from our teaching on the Church that they were unable in any way to join with the others in accepting them. Instead, they expressed the doctrine of the Orthodox Church in separate statements. Those statements were so plain that, in fact, they should have issued in the logical conclusion that the Orthodox ought not to remain as members of the World Council of Churches on the same basis as others. The Protestants might well have asked them, "If you disagree with our basic principles, why are you with us?" We know that in private conversations some Protestants did use to say this, but the question was not raised in the plenary sessions. Thus the Orthodox remained as members of an organisation the disparate origin of which they had just so clearly illustrated. But what do we see now?

The Pan-Orthodox Conference in Geneva in June 1968 took a different course. It expressed "the general desire of the Orthodox Church to be an organic member of the World Council of Churches and its decision to contribute in all ways to its progress, theological and otherwise, to the promotion and good development of the whole of the work of the World Council of Churches." His Holiness Patriarch Athenagoras informed the World Council of this decision in his special letter dated June 30, 1968. There were no reservations; no mention was made of any missionary aims, either in the one case or the other. We must be very clear as to what sort of religious union it is of which the Orthodox Church has been declared "an organic member," and what the dogmatic implications of such a decision are.

In 1959, in Toronto, certain basic statements were accepted by the World Council of Churches which, while more cautious than the present statements, were already not in conformity with the Orthodox doctrine of the Church. On p. 4 it was then stated that, "the member Churches of the World Council consider the relationship of other Churches to the Holy Catholic Church which the Creeds profess as a subject for mutual consideration." This statement is already unacceptable for us because the Church is spoken of not as actually existing in the world, but as some kind of abstract entity mentioned in various Creeds. However, even then on p. 3, we read, "the member Churches recognize that the membership of the Church of Christ is more inclusive than the membership of their own church body" (Six Ecumenical Surveys, New York, 1954, p. 13). But since in the preceding point (No. 2) it was stated that "the member Churches of the World Council believe on the basis of the New Testament that the Church of Christ is one," there is either an implicit contradiction or else the profession of a new doctrine — viz., that one can belong to the One Church without believing in her doctrines and without having liturgical unity with her.

The separate statements made in Evanston four years later on behalf of all the Orthodox delegates somewhat improved the situation, because they clearly showed that Orthodox Ecclesiology differs so much in essence from Protestant Ecclesiology that it is impossible to compose a joint statement. Now, however, the Orthodox participants in the World Council of Churches act differently; in an effort to unite truth with error, they have abandoned the principle expressed at Evanston. If all the Orthodox Churches are organic members of the World Council of Churches, then all the decisions of that Council are made in their name as well as in the name of the Protestants. If initially the Orthodox participated in ecumenical meetings only to present the truth, performing, so to speak, a missionary service among confessions foreign to Orthodoxy, then now they have combined with them and anyone can say that what was said at Uppsala was also said by the member Orthodox Churches in the person of their delegates. Alas that it should be said in the name of the whole Orthodox Church!

We regard it as our duty to protest in the strongest possible terms against this state of affairs. We know that in this protest we have with us all the Holy Fathers of the Church. Also with us are not only the hierarchy, clergy, and laymen of the Russian Orthodox Church Outside of Russia, but those members of other Orthodox Churches who agree with us as well. We take the liberty of saying that it seems our Brother Bishops have treated this matter without sufficient attention, without realising how far our Church is being drawn into the sphere of anti-canonical and even of anti-dogmatical agreements with the heterodox. This fact is especially clear if one turns to the initial statements of the representatives of the Orthodox Churches as compared with what is taking place at present.

At the Conference in Lausanne in 1937, the representatives of the Œcumenical Patriarch, Metropolitan Germanos, clearly stated that restoring unity with the Church means for Protestants that they must return to the doctrines of the ancient Church of the Seven Œcumenical Councils. "And what are the elements of the Christian doctrines," he said, "which should be regarded as necessary and essential? According to the understanding of the Orthodox Church there is no need now to make definitions of those necessary elements of faith, because they are already made in the ancient Creeds and the decisions of the Seven Œcumenical Councils. Therefore this teaching of the ancient undividing Church should be the basis of the reunion of the Church." That was the position taken by all the Orthodox delegates at the Lausanne and Oxford Conferences.

As for our Russian Orthodox Church Outside of Russia, her views expressed with particular clarity upon the appointment of a representative to the Committee for Continuation of the Conference on Faith and Order on December 18/31, 1931. That decision was as follows, "maintaining the belief in the One, Holy, Catholic, and Apostolic Church, the Synod of Bishops professes that that Church has never been divided. The question is only who belongs to her and who does not. At the same time the Synod warmly greets the efforts of heterodox confessions to study Christ's teaching on the Church with the hope that by such study, especially with the participation of the representatives of the Holy Orthodox Church, they may at last come to the conviction that the Orthodox Church, being the pillar and the ground of the truth (1 Timothy 3:15), fully and with no faults has maintained the doctrine given by Christ the Saviour to His disciples. With that Faith and with such hope the Synod of Bishops accepts the invitation of the Committee for Continuation of the Conference on Faith and Order."

Here everything is clear and nothing is left unsaid. This statement is essentially in agreement with what also used to be said at that time by official representatives of other Orthodox Churches. What, then, has changed? Have the Protestants abandoned their errors! No. They have not changed, and the Church has not changed; only the persons who are now said to represent her have changed. If the representatives of the Orthodox Churches had only continued firmly maintaining the basic principles of our belief in the Church, they would not have brought the Orthodox Church into the ambiguous position which was created for her by the decision of the Geneva Conference last year.

Since the Assembly of the World Council of Churches in New Delhi, the Orthodox delegates no longer make separate statements, but have merged into one mass with the Protestant confessions. Thus all the decisions of the Uppsala Assembly are made in the name of "the Church," which is always spoken of in the singular. Who is speaking? Who gave these people the right to make ecclesiological statements not merely on their own behalf, but also on behalf of the Orthodox Church? We ask you, Most Reverend Brothers, to check the list of the Churches participating in the Ecumenical Movement and in the World Council of Churches. Take, for instance, at least the first lines of the list on page 444 of The Uppsala 68 Report.

There you will find the following names: Evangelical Church of the River Plata, Methodist Church of Australia, Churches of Christ in Australia, The Church of England of Australia, Congregational Union of Australia, Presbyterian Church of Australia. Is it necessary to continue the list? Is it not clear that beginning with the very first lines, confessions are included which differ greatly from Orthodoxy, which deny sacraments, hierarchy, Church traditions, holy canons, which do not venerate the Mother of God and the Saints, etc.? We should have to enumerate nearly all of our dogmas in order to point out what in our Orthodox doctrines is not accepted by the majority of the members of the World Council of Churches — of which, however, the Orthodox Church is now nevertheless alleged to be an organic member.

Yet in the name of the various representatives of all possible heresies, the Uppsala Assembly constantly states, "the Church professes," "the Church teaches," "the Church does this and that," out of this mixture of errors, which have gone so far astray from Tradition, the published decision on "the Holy Spirit and the Catholicity of the Church" makes the statement "The Holy Spirit has not only preserved the Church in continuity with the past; He is all continuously present in the Church, effecting her inward renewal and re-creation." The question is, where is the "continuity with the past" among those who do not recognise any mysteries? How can one speak of the catholicity of those who do not accept the decisions of the Œcumenical Councils?

If these doctrinal decisions were preceded by words indicating that one part of the Churches observes one doctrine, and the other a different doctrine, and the teaching of the Orthodox Church were stated separately, that would be consistent with reality. But such is not the case, and in the name of various confessions they say, "the Church teaches." This in itself is a proclamation of the Protestant doctrine of the Church as comprising all those who call themselves Christians, even if they have no intercommunion. But without accepting that doctrine, it is impossible to be an organic member of the World Council of Churches, because that doctrine is the basis of the whole ideology on which this organisation rests. True, the resolution "On the Holy Spirit and the Catholicity of the Church" is followed by a note in fine print which says that since this resolution provoked such a great diversity of views, this decision is not final but only a summary of the matters considered in the section. However, there are no such remarks regarding other similar resolutions. The minutes contain no evidence that the Orthodox delegates made any statements to the effect that the assembly might not speak in the name of the Church in the singular and the Assembly does so everywhere, in all its resolutions, which never have such qualifying remarks attached.

On the contrary, His Eminence Archbishop Iakovos, in his reply to the greeting of the Swedish Archbishop, said in the name of the assembly, "As you well know, the Church universal is called by a demanding world to give ample evidence of its faith" (The Uppsala 69 Report, p. 103). Of what "Church universal" did Archbishop Iakovos speak? Of the Orthodox Church? No. He spoke here of the "Church" uniting all confessions, of the Church of the World Council of Churches. A tendency to speak in this fashion is especially conspicuous in the report of the committee on faith and order. In the resolution upon its report, following statements about the success of Ecumenism, it says, "We are in agreement with the decision of the faith and order commission at its Bristol meeting to pursue its study program of the unity of the Church in the wider context of the study of the unity of mankind and of creation. We welcome at the same time the statement of the faith and order commission that its task remains 'to proclaim the oneness of the Church of Jesus Christ' and to keep before the Council and the churches 'the obligation to manifest that unity for the sake of their Lord and for the better accomplishment of His mission in the world'" (ibidem, p. 223).

The implication is clear in all these resolutions that, notwithstanding the outward separation of the Churches, their internal unity still exists. The aim of Ecumenism is in this world to make this inner unity also an outward one through various manifestations of such aspirations. In order to evaluate all this from the point of view of the Orthodox Church, it is sufficient to imagine the reception it would find among the Holy Fathers of the Œcumenical Councils. Can anybody imagine the Orthodox Church of that period declaring itself an organic member of a society uniting Eunomians or Anomoeans, Arians, Semi-Arians, Sabellians and Apollinarians? Certainly not! On the contrary, Canon I of the Second Œcumenical Council does not call for union with such groups, but anathematizes them. Subsequent Œcumenical Councils did the same in regard to other heresies.

The organic membership of Orthodox Christians in one body with modern heretics will not sanctify the latter, but does alienate those Orthodox from the catholic Orthodox unity. That unity is not limited to the modern age. Catholicity embraces all the generations of the Holy Fathers. St. Vincent of Lérins, in his immortal work writes that, "For Christians to declare something which they did not previously accept has never been permitted, is never permitted, and never will be permitted — but to anathematize those who proclaim something outside of that which was accepted once and for ever, has always been a duty, is always a duty and always will be a duty."

Perhaps somebody will say that times have changed, and heresies now are not so malicious and destructive as in the days of the

Œcumenical Councils. But are those Protestants who renounce the veneration of the Theotokos and the Saints, who do not recognise the grace of the hierarchy, — or the Roman Catholics, who have invented new errors — are they nearer to the Orthodox Church than the Arians or Semi-Arians? Let us grant that modern preachers of heresy are not so belligerent towards the Orthodox Church as the ancient ones were. However, that is not because their doctrines are nearer to Orthodox teaching, but because Protestantism and Ecumenism have built up in them the conviction that there is no One and True Church on earth, but only communities of men who are in varying degrees of errors. Such a doctrine kills any zeal in professing what they take to be the truth, and therefore modern heretics appear to be less obdurate than the ancient ones. But such indifference to truth is in many respects worse than the capacity to be zealous in defence of an error mistaken for truth. Pilate, who said "What is truth?" could not be converted; but Saul, the persecutor of Christianity, became the Apostle Paul. That is why we read in the Book of Revelation the menacing words to the Angel of the Church of Laodicea, "I know thy works, that thou art neither cold nor hot I would thou wert cold or hot. So then because thou art lukewarm, and neither cold nor hot, I will spew thee out of my mouth" [Apocalypse 3:15-16].

Ecumenism makes the World Council of Churches a society in which every member, with Laodicean indifference, recognises himself and others as being in error, and is concerned only about finding phrases which will express that error in terms acceptable to all. Is there any room here as an "organic member" for the One, Holy, Catholic, and Apostolic Church which has always professed itself to be holy and without blemish because its Head is Christ Himself [Ephesians 5:27]. The LVII (LXVI in the Athens Syntagma) Canon of Carthage says of the Church that she is "the one spoken of as a dove [Song of Songs 6:9] and sole mother of Christians, in whom all the sanctifying gifts, savingly everlasting and vital, are received — which, however, inflict upon those persisting in heresy the great punishment of damnation."

We also feel it is our duty to declare that it is impossible to recognise the Russian Church as legally and duly represented at the Pan-Orthodox Conferences called by His Holiness Athenagoras. Those Bishops who participate in these Conferences in the name of the Russian Church with Metropolitan Nikodim at their head, do not represent the authentic Russian Church. They represent only those Bishops who by the will of an atheistic Government bear the titles of certain Dioceses of the Church of Russia. We have already had occasion to write about this matter to His Holiness Patriarch Athenagoras. These persons participate in meetings abroad only in so far as such participation is profitable to their civil authorities, the most cruel in the history of the world. Nero's ferocity and Julian the Apostate's hatred of Christianity are pallid in comparison.

Is it not to the influence of that government that we must largely ascribe the political resolutions of the Uppsala Assembly, which repeat many slogans widely observable in Communist propaganda in the West? In the concluding speech of the Chairman, Dr. Payne, it was said that "the Church of Jesus Christ must show actively the compassion of Christ in a needy world." But neither he nor anybody else said a word about the millions of Christians martyred in the U.S.S.R.; nobody spoke a word of compassion about their plight. It is good to express compassion for the hungry in Biafra, for those who constantly suffer from fighting in the Middle East or in Vietnam, but does that cover all the human afflictions of the present time? Can it be that the members of the World Council of Churches know nothing about the persecutions of religion in the U.S.S.R.?

Do they not know what iniquity is reigning there? Do they not know that martyrs for the Faith there are counted in the millions, that the Holy Scriptures are not published there and that people are sentenced to banishment with hard labour for distributing them? Do they not know that children there are prevented from lessons in the basic principles of religion, and even from attending religious services? Do they not know of the thousands who have been banished for their faith, about the children wrested from their parents to prevent them from receiving religious upbringing? All this is certainly well known to anybody who reads the newspapers, but it is never mentioned in any resolution of the World Council of Churches. The ecumenical priests and Levites are passing by in silence and without interest, without so much as a glance in the direction of the Christians persecuted in the U.S.S.R. They are silent because the official representatives of the Church of Russia, in spite of all evidence to the contrary, deny the existence of these persecutions in order to please their civil authorities.

These people are not free. Whether they wish to or not, they are forced to speak in obedience to orders from Communist Moscow. The burden of persecution makes them more deserving of compassion than of blame. But being moral prisoners of the godless, they cannot be true spokesmen for the Russian Orthodox Church, suffering, deprived of any rights, forced to be silent driven into catacombs and prisons. The late Patriarch Sergius and the present Patriarch Alexis were elected in violation of the rules which were instituted by the All-Russian Church Council of 1917 at the restoration of Stalin, the fiercest persecutor of the Church in history. Can you imagine a Bishop of Rome chosen according to the instructions of Nero? But Stalin was many times worse.

The hierarchs selected by Stalin had to promise their obedience to an atheistic Government whose aim, according to the Communist program, is the annihilation of religion. The present Patriarch Alexis wrote to Stalin immediately after the death of his predecessor that he would observe fidelity to his Government, "acting fully in concert with the Council for the Affairs of the Russian Orthodox Church and also with the Holy Synod instituted by the late Patriarch, I will be secure from mistakes and wrong actions." Everybody knows that "mistakes and wrong actions" in the language of the Moscow masters means any violation of the instructions given by the Communist authorities. We can pity an unfortunate old man, but we cannot recognise him as the Head of the Russian Church, of which we regard ourselves an inseparable part. Both to Patriarch Alexis and his collaborators the sanctions of the 30th Apostolic Canon and [the] 3rd Canon of the Seventh Œcumenical Council can be doubly applied, "if any Bishop, making use of the secular powers, shall by their means obtain jurisdiction over any church, he shall be deposed, and also excommunicated, together with all who remain in communion with him."

Bishop Nikodim of Dalmatia in his commentary on the 30th Apostolic Canon says, "if the Church condemned the unlawful influence of civil authorities on the appointment of a Bishop at a time when the rulers were Christians, how much the more so, consequently, she had to condemn it when they were heathens." What is there to say therefore, when a Patriarch and Bishops are installed by the open and militant enemies of their religion? When one part of the Russian Episcopate, together with the late Patriarch (at that time Metropolitan) Sergius, took the course of agreeing with the enemies of the Church in 1927, a large (and the most respected) part of that Episcopate, with Metropolitan Joseph of Leningrad and the first candidate of Patriarch Tikhon for the office of locum tenens, Metropolitan Cyril of Kazan, did not agree to go along with him, preferring banishment and martyrdom. Metropolitan Joseph by that time had already come to the conclusion that, in the face of a government which openly had as its goal the destruction of religion by the use of any available means, the legal existence of a Church administration becomes practically impossible without entailing compromises which are too great and too sinful. He therefore started secret ordinations of Bishops and Priests, in that way organising the Catacomb Church which still exists in hiding.

The atheists seldom mention the Catacomb Church, being afraid of giving her too much publicity. Only very rarely in the Soviet Press is the news of some trial of her members mentioned. Information about her, however, is given in manuals for anti-religious workers in the U.S.S.R. For instance, the basic information about this Church, under the name of "The Truly Orthodox Church," is given in a manual with the title of Slovar Ateista ("The Atheist's Dictionary"), published in Moscow in 1964. With no open churches, in secret meetings similar to the catacomb meetings of the early Christians, these confessors of the faith perform their services unseen by the outer world. They are the true representatives of the

Russian Orthodox Church, whose greatness will become known to the world only after the downfall of the Communist power.

For these reasons, although representatives of the Moscow Patriarchate participated in the decisions of the Pan-Orthodox Conference in Geneva last year, and particularly in regard to making the Orthodox Church an organic member of the World Council of Churches — we look upon that decision as having been accepted without the participation of the Russian Orthodox Church. That Church is forced to stay silent, and we, as her free representatives, are grieved by the fact that such a decision was accepted. We categorically protest that decision as being contrary to the very nature itself of the One, Holy, Catholic, and Apostolic Church.

The poison of heresy is not too dangerous when it is preached only from outside the Church. Many times more perilous is that poison which is gradually introduced into the organism in larger and larger doses by those who, in virtue of their position, should not be poisoners but — spiritual physicians. Can it be that the Orthodox Episcopate will remain indifferent to that danger? Will it not be too late to protect our spiritual flock when the wolves are devouring the sheep before their pastors' eyes, inside the very sheepfold itself? Do we not see the divine sword already raised [Matthew 10:34], separating those who are true to the traditional faith of the Holy Church from those who, in the words of His Holiness Patriarch Athenagoras in his greeting to the Uppsala Assembly, are working to shape the "new drive in the ecumenical movement" for the "fulfillment of the general Christian renewal" on the paths of reformation and indifference to the truth?

It seems that we have shown clearly enough that this apparent unity is not unity in the truth of Orthodoxy, but a unity that mixes white with black, good with evil, and truth with error. We have already protested against the un-Orthodox ecumenical actions of His Holiness Patriarch Athenagoras and Archbishop Iakovos in letters which were widely distributed to Bishops of the Orthodox Church in various countries. We have received from different parts of the world expressions of agreement with us. But now the time has come to make our protest heard more loudly still and then even yet more loudly, so as to stop the action of this poison before it has become as potent as the ancient heresies of Arianism, Nestorianism, or Eutychianism, which in their time so shook the whole body of the Church as to make it seem that heresy was apt to overcome Orthodoxy. We direct our appeal to all the Bishops of the Orthodox Church, imploring them to study the subject of this letter and to rise up in defence of the purity of the Orthodox Faith. We also ask them very much to pray for the Russian Orthodox Church so greatly suffering from the atheists, that the Lord might shorten the days of her trial and send her freedom and peace.

> \+ Metropolitan Philaret
> In New York,
> Sunday of the Sixth Œcumenical Council,
> 4/27 July 1969

The Second Sorrowful Epistle
(First Sunday in Lent, 1972)

Preface[34]

TWO YEARS AGO, in his first "Sorrowful Epistle," Metropolitan Philaret, Chief Hierarch of the Russian Orthodox Church Outside of Russia, clearly pointed out to the Orthodox Bishops of the world how contrary to the very foundation of Orthodoxy is the "organic membership" of the Orthodox Churches in the World Council of Churches. Since then there has been very little healthy reaction on the part of Orthodox hierarchs against the ecumenical movement, and no Orthodox Church has withdrawn its membership from the WCC. Accordingly, Metropolitan Philaret, authorized by the entire Council of Bishops of the Russian Church Abroad, has written a second Sorrowful Epistle, addressed again to all Orthodox Bishops, and stating even more clearly that ecumenism is a dangerous heresy which is now leading its Orthodox participants to the utter annihilation of their churches.

---

34 St. Herman of Alaska Brotherhood, "Second Sorrowful Epistle of Metropolitan Philaret," *Orthodox Word* 8, no. 2 (March-April 1972): 42.

This Epistle, which comprises four pages of fine print, is well documented with references to the radical departures from Orthodoxy of the Orthodox renovationists from the time of the "Living Church" and the calendar reform of the 1920's to the recent statements of Patriarch Athenagoras of Constantinople which clearly indicate his abandonment of the Orthodox Church and his desire to form a new church together with the heterodox. With this new Epistle there can be no doubt that Metropolitan Philaret, with the full support of the Hierarchs of the Russian Church Abroad, has become the leader and champion of true Orthodoxy throughout the world. It remains to be seen whether the voice of conscience is still alive in the Orthodox episcopate to which this new Sorrowful Epistle is addressed. If it is, we should expect to hear at least a few voices, even at great personal risk, raised in solidarity with Metropolitan Philaret, who, in an age of apostasy and madness, has had the courage to remind the Orthodox Bishops that what the Church of Christ has always and unchangingly believed, is still true.

The Second Sorrowful Epistle of Metropolitan Philaret[35]
PRESIDENT OF THE SYNOD OF BISHOPS OF THE
RUSSIAN ORTHODOX CHURCH OUTSIDE OF RUSSIA
75 EAST 93rd STREET, NEW YORK, N.Y. 10028
Telephone: LEhigh 4-1601

A SECOND SORROWFUL EPISTLE

TO THEIR HOLINESSES AND THEIR BEATITUDES,
THE PRIMATES OF THE HOLY ORTHODOX CHURCHES,
THE MOST REVEREND METROPOLITANS, ARCH-
BISHOPS AND BISHOPS

The People of the Lord residing in his Diocese are entrusted to the Bishop, and he will be required to give account of their souls according to the 39th Apostolic Canon. The 34th Apostolic Canon

---

35 "The Second Sorrowful Epistle of Metropolitan Philaret," Orthodox Christian Information Center, accessed July 9, 2022, http://orthodoxinfo.com/ecumenism/sorrow2.aspx

orders that a Bishop may do "those things only which concern his own Diocese and the territories belonging to it." There are, however, occasions when events are of such a nature that their influence extends beyond the limits of one Diocese, or indeed those of one or more of the local Churches. Events of such a general, global nature cannot be ignored by any Orthodox Bishop, who, as a successor of the Apostles, is charged with the protection of his flock from various temptations. The lightening like speed with which ideas may be spread in our times make such care all the more imperative now.

In particular, our flock, belonging to the free part of the Church of Russia, is spread out all over the world. What has just been stated, therefore, is most pertinent to it. As a result of this, our Bishops, when meeting in their Councils, cannot confine their discussions to the narrow limits of pastoral and administrative problems arising in their respective Dioceses, but must in addition turn their attention to matters of a general importance to the whole Orthodox World, since the affliction of one Church is as "an affliction unto them all, eliciting the compassion of them all" (Philippians 4:14-16; Hebrews 10:30). And if the Apostle St. Paul was weak with those who were weak and burning with those who were offended, how then can we Bishops of God remain indifferent to the growth of errors which threaten the salvation of the souls of many of our brothers in Christ?

It is in the spirit of such a feeling that we have already once addressed all the Bishops of the Holy Orthodox Church with a Sorrowful Epistle. We rejoiced to learn that, in harmony with our appeal, several Metropolitans of the Church of Greece have recently made reports to their Synod calling to its attention the necessity of considering ecumenism a heresy and the advisability of reconsidering the matter of participation in the World Council of Churches. Such healthy reactions against the spreading of ecumenism allow us to hope that the Church of Christ will be spared this new storm which threatens her.

Yet, two years have passed since our Sorrowful Epistle was issued and alas! Although in the Church of Greece we have seen the new statements regarding ecumenism as un-Orthodox, no Orthodox

Church has announced its withdrawal from the World Council of Churches. In the Sorrowful Epistle, we depicted in vivid colors to what extent the organic membership of the Orthodox Church in that Council, based as it is upon purely Protestant principles, is contrary to the very basis of Orthodoxy. In this Epistle, having been authorized by our Council of Bishops, we would further develop and extend our warning, showing that the participants in the ecumenical movement are involved in a profound heresy against the very foundation of the Church.

The essence of that movement has been given a clear definition by the statement of the Roman Catholic theologian Yves M. J. Congar. He writes that "this is a movement which prompts the Christian Churches to wish the restoration of the lost unity, and to that end to have a deep understanding of itself and understanding of each other." He continues, "it is composed of all the feelings, ideas, actions or institutions, meetings or conferences, ceremonies, manifestations and publications which are directed to prepare the reunion in new unity not only of (separate) Christians, but also of the actually existing Churches." Actually, he continues, "the word ecumenism, which is of Protestant origin, means now a concrete reality; the totality of all the aforementioned upon the basis of a certain attitude and a certain amount of very definite conviction (although not always very clear and certain).

It is not a desire or an attempt to unite those who are regarded as separated into one Church which would be regarded as the only true one. It begins at just that point where it is recognized that, at the present state, none of the Christian confessions possesses the fullness of Christianity, but even if one of them is authentic, still, as a confession, it does not contain the whole truth. There are Christian values outside of it belonging not only to Christians who are separated from it in creed, but also to other Churches and other confessions as such" (*Chretiens Desunis*, Ed. Unam Sanctam, Paris, 1937, pp. XI-XII). This definition of the ecumenical movement made by a Roman Catholic theologian 35 years ago continues to be quite as exact even now, with the difference that during the intervening years this movement has continued to develop further with a newer and more dangerous scope.

In our first Sorrowful Epistle, we wrote in detail on how incompatible with our Ecclesiology was the participation of Orthodox in the World Council of Churches, and presented precisely the nature of the violation against Orthodoxy committed in the participation of our Churches in that council. We demonstrated that the basic principles of that council are incompatible with the Orthodox doctrine of the Church. We, therefore, protested against the acceptance of that resolution at the Geneva Pan-Orthodox Conference whereby the Orthodox Church was proclaimed an organic member of the World Council of Churches. Alas! These last few years are richly laden with evidence that, in their dialogues with the heterodox, some Orthodox representatives have adopted a purely Protestant ecclesiology which brings in its wake a Protestant approach to questions of the life of the Church, and from which springs forth the now popular modernism.

Modernism consists in that bringing down, that re-aligning of the life of the Church according to the principles of current life and human weaknesses. We saw it in the Renovation Movement and in the Living Church in Russia in the twenties. At the first meeting of the founders of the Living Church on May 29, 1922, its aims were determined as a "revision and change of all facets of Church life which are required by the demands of current life" (The New Church, Prof. B. V. Titlinov, Petrograd-Moscow, 1923, p. 11). The Living Church was an attempt at a reformation adjusted to the requirements of the conditions of a communist state. Modernism places that compliance with the weaknesses of human nature above the moral and even doctrinal requirements of the Church. In that measure that the world is abandoning Christian principles, modernism debases the level of religious life more and more. Within the Western confessions we see that there has come about an abolition of fasting, a radical shortening and vulgarization of religious services and finally, full spiritual devastation, even to the point of exhibiting an indulgent and permissive attitude toward unnatural vices of which St. Paul said it was shameful even to speak.

It was just modernism which was the basis of the Pan-Orthodox Conference of sad memory in Constantinople in 1923, evidently not without some influence of the renovation experiment in Russia. Subsequent to that conference, some Churches, while not adopting all the reforms which were there introduced, adopted the Western calendar, and even, in some cases, the Western Paschalia. This, then, was the first step onto the path of modernism of the Orthodox Church, whereby Her way of life was changed in order to bring it closer to the way of life of heretical communities. In this respect, therefore, the adoption of the Western Calendar was a violation of a principle consistent in the Holy Canons, whereby there is a tendency to spiritually isolate the faithful from those who teach contrary to the Orthodox Church and not to encourage closeness with such in our prayer life (Titus 3:10; 10th, 45th, and 65th Apostolic Canons; 32nd, 33rd, and 37th Canons of Laodicea, etc.). The unhappy fruit of that reform was the violation of the unity of the life in prayer of Orthodox Christians in various countries. While some of them were celebrating Christmas together with heretics, others still fasted. Sometimes such a division occurred in the same local Church, and sometimes Easter [Pascha] was celebrated according to the Western Paschal reckoning. For the sake, therefore, of being nearer to the heretics, that principle, set forth by the First Ecumenical Council that all Orthodox Christians should simultaneously, with one mouth and one heart, rejoice and glorify the Resurrection of Christ all over the world is violated.

This tendency to introduce reforms, regardless of previous general decisions and practice of the whole Church in violation of the Second Canon of the VI Ecumenical Council, creates only confusion. His Holiness, the Patriarch of Serbia, Gabriel, of blessed memory, expressed this feeling eloquently at the Church Conference held in Moscow in 1948. "In the last decades," he said, "various tendencies have appeared in the Orthodox Church which evoke reasonable apprehension for the purity of Her doctrines and for Her dogmatical and canonical Unity. "The convening by the Ecumenical Patriarch of the Pan-Orthodox Conference and the Conference at Vatopedi, which had as their principal aim the preparing of the pro-synod, violated the unity and cooperation of the Orthodox Churches. On the one hand, the absence of the Church of Russia at these meetings and on the other, the hasty and unilateral actions of some of the local Churches and the hasty actions of their representatives have introduced chaos and anomalies into the life of the Eastern Orthodox Church.

"The unilateral introduction of the Gregorian Calendar by some of the local Churches while the Old Calendar was kept yet by others, shook the unity of the Church and incited serious dissension within those of them who so lightly introduced the New Calendar" (Acts of the Conferences of the Heads and Representatives of the Autocephalic Orthodox Churches, Moscow, 1949, Vol. II, pp. 447-448). Recently, Prof. Theodorou, one of the representatives of the Church of Greece at the Conference in Chambesy in 1968, noted that the calendar reform in Greece was hasty and noted further that the Church there suffers even now from the schism it caused (Journal of the Moscow Patriarchate, 1969, No. 1, p. 51).

It could not escape the sensitive consciences of many sons of the Church that within the calendar reform, the foundation is already laid for a revision of the entire order of Orthodox Church life which has been blessed by the Tradition of many centuries and confirmed by the decisions of the Ecumenical Councils. Already at that Pan-Orthodox Conference of 1923 at Constantinople, the questions of the second marriage of clergy as well as other matters were raised. And recently, the Greek Archbishop of North and South America, Iakovos, made a statement in favor of a married episcopate (*The Hellenic Chronicle*, December 23, 1971).

The strength of Orthodoxy has always lain in Her maintaining the principles of Church Tradition. Despite this, there are those who are attempting to include in the agenda of a future Great Council not a discussion of the best ways to safeguard those principles, but, on the contrary, ways to bring about a radical revision of the entire way of life in the Church, beginning with the abolition of fasts, second marriages of the clergy, etc., so that Her way of life would be closer to that of the heretical communities. In our first Sorrowful Epistle we have shown in detail the extent to which the principles of the World Council of Churches are contrary to the doctrines of the Orthodox Church, and we protested against the decision taken in Geneva at the Pan-Orthodox Conference declaring the Orthodox Church to be an organic member of that council. Then we reminded all that, "the poison of heresy is not too dangerous when it is preached outside the Church. Many times more perilous is that poison which is gradually introduced into the organism in larger and larger doses by those who, in virtue of their position, should not be poisoners but spiritual physicians." Alas! Of late we see the symptoms of such a great development of ecumenism with the participation of the Orthodox, that it has become a serious threat, leading to the utter annihilation of the Orthodox Church by dissolving Her in an ocean of heretical communities.

The problem of unity is not discussed now on the level at which it used to be considered by the Holy Fathers. For them unity with the heretics required them to accept the whole of Orthodox doctrine and their return to the fold of the Orthodox Church. Under the prism of the ecumenical movement, however, it is understood that both sides are equally right and wrong; this is applicable to both Roman Catholics and Protestants. Patriarch Athenagoras clearly expressed this in his speech greeting Cardinal Willebrands in Constantinople on November 30th, 1969. The Patriarch expressed the wish that the Cardinal's activities would "mark a new epoch of progress not only in regard to the two of our Churches, but also of all Christians." The Patriarch gave the definition of the new approach to the problem of unity by saying that, "none of us is calling the other to himself, but, like Peter and Andrew, we both direct ourselves to Jesus, the only and mutual Lord, Who unites us into oneness" (Tomos Agapis, Rome-Istanbul, Document No. 274, pp. 588-589).

The recent exchange of letters between Paul VI, the Pope of Rome, and the Patriarch Athenagoras further elaborates and develops this un-Orthodox idea to our great vexation. Encouraged by various statements of the Primate of the Church of Constantinople, the Pope wrote to him on February 8th, 1971, "we remind the believers assembled in the Basilica of St. Peter on the Week of Unity that between our church and the venerable Orthodox Churches there is an already existing, nearly complete communion, though not fully complete, resulting from our common participation in the mystery of Christ and His Church" (Tomos Agapis, pp.614-615).

A doctrine, new for Roman Catholicism but of long-standing acceptance for Protestantism, is contained in these words. According to it, the separations existing between Christians on earth is actually illusory — they do not reach the heavens. So it is that the words of our Savior regarding the chastisement of those who disobey the Church (Matthew 18:18) are set at naught and regarded as without validity. Such a doctrine is novel not only for us Orthodox, but for the Roman Catholics as well, whose thought on this matter, so different from that of the present, was expressed in 1928 in Pope Pius IX's Encyclical Mortaliun Animos. Though the Roman Catholics are of those "without" (1 Corinthians 5:13), and we are not directly concerned with changing trends in their views, their advance nearer to Protestant ecclesiology interests us only insofar as it coincides with the simultaneous acceptance of similar attitudes by Constantinople. Ecumenists of Orthodox background and ecumenists of Protestant-Roman Catholic background arrive at a unanimity of opinion in the same heresy.

Patriarch Athenagoras answered the above quoted letter of the Pope on March 21st, 1971, in a similar spirit. When quoting his words, we will italicize the most important phrases. While the Pope, who is not interested in dogmatical harmony, invites the Patriarch "to do all that is possible to speed that much desired day when, at the conclusion of a common concelebration, we will be made worthy to communicate together of the same Cup of the Lord" (ibid.); the Patriarch answered in the same spirit addressing the Pope as "elder brother" and saying that, "following the holy desire of the *Lord Who would that His Church be One, visible to the entire world, so that the entire world would fit in Her,* we constantly and unremittingly surrender ourselves to the guidance of the Holy Spirit unto the firm continuation and completion of the now begun and developing *holy work begun with You in our common Holy desire, to make visible and manifest unto the world the one, holy, catholic and apostolic Church of Christ*" (ibid., pp. 618-619).

Further on the Patriarch writes, "truly, even though the Church of both east and west have been estranged from each other for offenses known but to the Lord, they are not virtually separated from the communion in the mystery of the God-Man Jesus and His Divine-Human Church" (ibid., pp. 620). The Patriarch bitterly mentions that, "we were estranged from reciprocal love and the blessed gift of confession in oneness of mind of the faith of Christ was taken from us." He says that, "we were deprived of the blessing of going up together to the one altar and of the full and together communion of the same eucharistic honorable Body and Blood, *even though we did not cease to recognize each in the other the validity of apostolic priesthood and the validity of the mystery of the Divine Eucharist*" (ibid.). It is at this point in time, however, that the Patriarch notes that, "we are called positively to proceed to the final union in concelebration and communion of the honorable Blood of Christ from the same holy cup" (ibid., pp. 620-623).

In this letter many un-Orthodox ideas are expressed, which, if taken to their logical end, lead us to the most disastrous conclusions. It follows from the quoted words that the ecumenists led by Patriarch Athenagoras do not believe in the Church as She was founded by the Savior. Contrary to His word (Matthew 16:18), that Church no longer exists for them, and the Pope and Patriarch together would "make visible and manifest" a new church which would encompass the whole of mankind. Is it not dreadful to hear these words "make visible and manifest" from the mouth of an Orthodox Patriarch? Is it not a renunciation of the existing Church of Christ? Is it possible to render a new church visible without first renouncing that very Church which was created by the Lord? But for those who belong to Her and who believe in Her, there is no need to make visible and manifest any new Church. Yet even the "old" Church of the Holy Apostles and Fathers is presented by the Pope and the Patriarch in a distorted manner so as to create the illusion in the mind of the reader that She is somehow connected with the new church that they wish to create. To that end they attempt to present the separation between Orthodoxy and Roman Catholicism as if it never existed.

In their common prayer in the Basilica of St. Peter, Patriarch Athenagoras and Pope Paul VI stated that they find themselves already united "in the proclamation of the same Gospel, in the same baptism, in the same sacraments and the charismas" (ibid., p.660). But even if the Pope and Patriarch have declared to be null and void the Anathemas which have existed for nine centuries, does this mean that the reasons for pronouncing them, which are known to all, have ceased to exist? Does this mean that the errors of the Latins which one was required to renounce upon entering the Church no longer exist? The Roman Catholic Church with which Patriarch Athenagoras would establish liturgical communion, and with which, through the actions of Metropolitan Nikodim of Leningrad and others, the Moscow Patriarchate has already entered into communion, is not even that same Church with which the Orthodox Church led by St. Mark of Ephesus refused to enter into a union. That church is even further away from Orthodoxy now, having introduced even more new doctrines and having accepted more and more the principles of reformation, ecumenism and modernism.

In a number of decisions of the Orthodox Church the Roman Catholics were regarded as heretics. Though from time to time they were accepted into the Church in a manner such as that applied to Arians, it is to be noted that for many centuries and even in our time the Greek Churches accepted them by Baptism. If after the centuries following 1054 the Latins were accepted into the Greek and Russian Churches by two rites, that of Baptism or of Chrismation, it was because although everyone recognized them to be heretics, a general rule for the entire Church was not yet established in regard to the means of their acceptance.

For instance, when in the beginning of the XII century the Serbian Prince and father of Stephan Nemania was forced into having his son baptized by the Latins upon his subsequent return later to Rasa he baptized him in the Orthodox Church (*Short Outline of the Orthodox Churches, Bulgarian, Serbian and Rumanian*, E. E. Golubinsky, Moscow, 1871, p. 551). In another monumental work, *The History of the Russian Church* (Vols. I/II, Moscow, 1904, pp. 806-807), Professor Golubinsky, in describing the stand taken by the Russian Church in regard to the Latins, advances many facts indicating that in applying various ways in receiving the Latins into the fold of the Orthodox Church, at sometimes baptizing them and at others chrismating them, both the Greeks and Russian Churches assumed that they were heretics.

Therefore, the statement that during those centuries, "we did not cease to recognize in each other the validity of apostolic priesthood and the validity of the mystery of the Divine Eucharist" is absolutely inconsistent with historical fact. The separation between us and Rome existed and exists. Further, it is not illusory but actual. The separation appears illusory to those who give no weight to the words of the Savior spoken to His Holy Apostles and through them, to their successors, "verily I say unto you, whatsoever ye shall bind on earth shall be bound in heaven; and whatsoever ye shall loose on earth shall be loosed in heaven" (Matthew 18:18).

The Savior says, "verily I say unto you," and the Patriarch contradicts Him and declares His words to be untrue. It must be concluded from the Patriarch's words that, although the Latins were regarded as heretics by the whole Orthodox Church, although they could not receive Holy Communion, even though they were accepted into the Church over many centuries by Baptism —and we know of no decision in the East reversing this stand — still, they continued to be members of the Corpus Christi and were not separated from the Sacraments of the Church. In such a statement there is no logic. It evidences a loss of contact with the actual history of the Church. It presents us with an example of application in practice of the Protestant doctrine according to which excommunication from the Church because of dogmatical error does not bar the one excommunicated from membership in Her. In other words, it means that "communion in the mystery of the God-Man Jesus" does not necessarily depend upon membership in the Orthodox Church.

In an attempt to find some justification for their ecumenical theory, they are trying to convince us that membership in the

Church without full dogmatic agreement with Her was permitted in the past. In his official statement at the Phanar, made when his letter to the Pope was published, Patriarch Athenagoras tried to convince us that notwithstanding the facts mentioned earlier, the Eastern Church did not rupture its communion with Rome, even when dogmatical dissent was obvious. One can indeed find some solitary instances of communion. In some places even after 1054, some Eastern hierarchs may not have hastened to brand as heresy various wrong doctrines that appeared in the Church of Rome.

But a long ailment before death is still a disease, and the death it causes remains a death, however long it took for it to come to pass. In the case of Rome that process was already evident at the time of St. Photios, but only later, in 1054, did it become a final separation. The exchange of letters between the Patriarch of Constantinople and the Pope of Rome have made it necessary for us to dwell to no little extent upon the relationship of the Orthodox Church toward the Latins. But Patriarch Athenagoras goes yet beyond equating Papism with Orthodoxy. We speak here of his statement to Roge Schutz, a pastor of the Protestant Reformed Church of Switzerland. "I wish to make you an avowal," he said [Athenagoras]. "You are a priest. I could receive from your hands the Body and Blood of Christ." On the next day he added, "I could make my confession to you" (Le Monde, May 21, 1970).

Ecumenists of Orthodox background are willing to undermine even the authority of the Ecumenical Councils in order to achieve communion with heretics. This happened during the dialogue with the Monophysites. At the meeting with them in Geneva, a clear Orthodox position was held actually only by one or two of the participants, while the rest manifested the typical ecumenistic tendency to accomplish intercommunion at any cost, even without the attainment of a full dogmatic agreement between the Orthodox and Monophysites. Rev. Dr. John Romanides, the representative of the Church of Greece, was fully justified in stating the following of the Orthodox members at the conference, "we have all along been the object of an ecumenical technique which aims at the accomplishment of intercommunion or communion or union without an agreement on Chalcedon and the Fifth, Sixth, and Seventh Ecumenical Councils (Minutes of the Conference in Geneva, *The Greek Orthodox Theological Review*, Vol. XVI, p. 30).

As a result of such tactics, one of the resolutions of this conference is actually an agreement to investigate the possibility of drawing up a formula of concord which would not be a dogmatical statement on the level of a confession of faith, but would rather serve as a basis upon which the Orthodox and the Monophysites could proceed toward union in a common Eucharist (ibid., p. 6).

Despite the categorical statements on the part of the Monophysites that on no account would they accept Chalcedon and the rest of the Ecumenical Councils, the Orthodox delegation signed a resolution recognizing it as unnecessary that the Anathemas be lifted, or that the Orthodox accept Dioscorus and Severus as saints, or that the Monophysites acknowledge Pope Leo to be a saint. The restoration of communion, however, would bear with it the implication that the Anathemas on both sides would cease to be in effect (ibid., p. 6). At yet another conference in Addis Ababa, the un-Orthodox statements of representatives of the Orthodox Churches were buttressed by Metropolitan Nikodim of Leningrad and Rev. V. Borovoy, resulting in a resolution that the mutual Anathemas simply be dropped. "Should there be a formal declaration or ceremony in which the Anathemas are lifted? Many of us felt that it is much simpler to drop these Anathemas in a quiet way as some churches have begun to do" (ibid., p. 211).

Here again we see in practice the Protestant concept of ecclesiology whereby the excommunication of one for dogmatical error does not prevent heretics from belonging to the Church. Rev. Vitaly Borovoy clearly expresses this attitude in his paper, "The Recognition of Saints and the Problem of Anathemas" presented at the conference at Addis Ababa, clearly asserting that both Monophysites and Roman Catholics are full-fledged members of the Body of Christ. He claims that Orthodox, Roman Catholics and Monophysites have "one Holy Writ, one Apostolic Tradition and sacred origin, the same sacraments, and in essence, a single piety and a single way of salvation" (ibid., p. 246). With such attitudes, is it any surprise that compromise reigns supreme in the relationship between the Orthodox promoters of ecumenism and the Roman Catholics, Protestants and Anti-Chalcedonians?

Outdoing even Patriarch Athenagoras, Metropolitan Nikodim, the representative of the Moscow Patriarchate gave communion to Roman Catholic clergymen in the Cathedral of St. Peter on December 14, 1970. He served the Divine Liturgy there, while in violation of Canons, a choir of the students at the Pontifical College sang and Latin clergymen accepted communion from his hands (Diakonia No. 1, 1971). Yet, behind these practical manifestations of the so-called ecumenical movement, other broader aims are discernible which lead to the utter abolition of the Orthodox Church. Both the World Council of Churches and the dialogues between various Christian confessions, and even with other religions (such as, for instance, Islam and Judaism) are links in a chain which in the manner of thinking of ecumenists must grow to include all of mankind. This tendency is already evident at the Assembly of the World Council of Churches at Uppsala in 1967.

According to ecumenists, all this could be accomplished by a special council, which in their eye would be truly "ecumenical" since they do not recognize the historical Ecumenical Councils as being truly so. The formula is given in the Roman Catholic ecumenical Journal Irenicon, and is as follows:

1. The accomplishment of gestures of reconciliation for which the lifting of the Anathemas of 1054 between Rome and Constantinople can serve as an example.
2. Communion in the Eucharist; in other words a positive solution to the problem of intercommunion.
3. Acceptance of a clear understanding that we all belong to a universal (Christian) entity which should give place to diversity.
4. That Council should be a token of the unity of men in Christ (*Irenikon*, No. 3, 1971, pp. 322-323).

The same article states that the Roman Catholic Secretariat for Union is working to achieve the same result as Cardinal Willebrands said at Evian. And the Assembly on Faith and Constitution has chosen as its main theme, "The Unity of the Church and the Unity of Mankind." According to a new definition, everything relates to ecumenism "which is connected with the renewal and reunion of the Church as a ferment of the growth of the Kingdom of God in the world of men who are seeking their unity" (Service d'information, No. 9, February 1970, pp. 10-11). At the conference of the Central Committee in Addis Ababa, Metropolitan George Khodre made a report which actually tends to connect the Church in some way with all religions. He would see the inspiration of the Holy Spirit even in non-Christian religions so that, according to him, when we communicate of the Body of Christ we are united to all whom our Lord embraces in His love toward mankind (*Irenikon*, 1971, No. 2, pp. 191-202).

This is where the Orthodox Church is being drawn. Outwardly this movement is manifested by unending "dialogues." Orthodox representatives are engaged in dialogues with Roman Catholics and Anglicans; they in turn are in dialogue with each other, with Lutherans, other Protestants, and even with Jews, Moslems and Buddhists. Just recently, the Exarch of Patriarch Athenagoras in North and South America, Archbishop Iakovos, took part in a dialogue with Jews. He noted that as far as he knew, at no other time in history has such "a theological dialogue with Jews taken place under the sponsorship of the Greek Church." Besides matters of a national character, "the group also agreed to examine liturgy, with Greek Orthodox scholars undertaking to review their liturgical texts in terms of improving references to Jews and Judaism where they are found to be negative or hostile" (Religious News Service, January 27, 1972, pp. 24-25). So it is that Patriarch Athenagoras and other ecumenists do not limit their plans for unia to Roman Catholics and Protestants; their plans are more ambitious.

We have already quoted the words of Patriarch Athenagoras that the Lord desires that "His Church be one, visible to the entire world so that the entire world would fit within Her." A Greek theologian and former Dean of the Theological Faculty in Athens writes in much the same vein. In evolving the ecumenical idea of the Church, his thought arrives at the same far-reaching conclusions. He asserts that the enemies of ecumenism are thwarting the will of God. According to him, God embraces all men in our planet as members of His one Church yesterday, today and tomorrow as the fullness of that Church (*Bulletin Typos Bonne Presse*, Athens, March-April 1971).

Although it is obvious to anyone with an elementary grasp of Orthodox Church doctrine that such a conception of the Church differs greatly from that of the Holy Fathers, we find it necessary to underscore the depth of the contradiction. When and where did the Lord promise that the whole world could be united in the Church? Such an expectation is nothing more than a chiliastic hope with no foundation in the Holy Gospels. All men are called unto salvation; but by no means do all of them respond. Christ spoke of Christians as those given Him from the world (John 17:6). He did not pray for the whole world but for those men given Him from the World. And the apostle St. John teaches that the Church and the world are in opposition to each other, and he exhorts the Christians, saying, "Love not the world, neither the things that are in the world. If any man love the world, the love of the Father is not in him" (1 John 1:16).

Concerning the sons of the Church, the Savior said, "They are not of the world, even as I am not of the world" (John 17:16). In the persons of the Apostles the Savior warned the Church that in the world She would have tribulation (John 16:33), explaining to His Disciples, "If you were from the world, the world would love its own; but because you are not of the world, but I have chosen you out of the world, therefore the world hateth you" (John 15:19). In Holy Scriptures, therefore, we see that a clear distinction is made between the sons of the Church and the rest of mankind. Addressing himself to the faithful in Christ and distinguishing them from unbelievers, St. Peter writes, "But ye are a chosen generation, a royal priesthood, a peculiar people" (1 Peter 2:9).

We are in no manner assured in Scripture of the triumph of truth on earth before the end of the world. There is no promise that the world will be transfigured into a church uniting all of mankind as fervent ecumenists believe, but rather there is the warning that religion will be lacking in the last days and Christians will suffer great sorrow and hatred on the part of all nations for the sake of our Savior's Name (Matthew 24:9-12). While all of mankind sinned in the first Adam, in the second Adam — Christ — only that part of humanity is united in Him which is "born again" (John 3:3 and 7). And although in the material world God "maketh His sun to rise on the evil and on the good, and sendeth rain on the just and on the unjust" (Matthew 4:45), He does not accept the unjust into His Kingdom. Rather, He addresses them with these menacing words, "Not everyone who saith unto me Lord, Lord shall enter into the Kingdom of Heaven; but he that doeth the will of My Father which is in Heaven" (Matthew 7:21). Doubtlessly our Savior is addressing the heretics when He says, "Many who say to me in that day, Lord, Lord, have we not prophesied in thy name? And in thy name have cast out devils, and in thy name done many wonderful works? And then I will profess unto them, I never knew you, depart from me, ye that work iniquity" (Matthew 7:22-23).

So it is that our Lord tells the heretics, "I never knew you;" yet Patriarch Athenagoras tries to convince us that "they were not separated from the communion in the mystery of the God-Man Jesus and His Divine-Human Church." It is the belief in the renewal of the whole of mankind within the new and universal church that lends to ecumenism the nature a of chiliastic heresy, which becomes more and more evident in the ecumenistic attempts to unite everyone, disregarding truth and error, and in their tendency to create not only a new church, but a new world. The propagators of this heresy do not wish to believe that the earth and all that is on it shall burn, the heavens shall pass away, and the elements shall melt with fervent heat (2 Peter 3:1-12).

They forget that it is after this that a new Heaven and a new Earth on which truth will abide will come to be through the creative word of God — not the efforts of human organizations. Therefore the efforts of Orthodox Christians should not be directed to the building of organizations, but toward becoming inhabitants of the new Creation after the Final Judgment through living a pious life in the one true Church. In the meantime, activities aimed at building the Kingdom of God on earth through a fraudulent union of various confessions without regard for the Truth, which is kept only within the Tradition of the Holy Orthodox Church, will only lead us away from the Kingdom of God and into the kingdom of the Antichrist. It must be understood that the circumstance which prompted our Savior to wonder if at His Second Coming He would find the Faith yet upon the earth is brought about not only by the direct propagation of atheism, but also by the spread of ecumenism.

The history of the Church witnesses that Christianity was not spread by compromises and dialogues between Christians and unbelievers, but through witnessing the truth and rejecting every lie and every error. It might be noted that generally no religion has ever been spread by those who doubted its full truth. The new, all-encompassing "church" which is being erected by the ecumenists is of the nature of that Church of Laodicea exposed in the Book of Revelation, she is lukewarm, neither hot nor cold toward the Truth, and it is to this new "church" that the words addressed by the Angel to the Laodicean Church of old might now be applied, "So that because thou are lukewarm and neither cold nor hot, I will spew thee out of my mouth" (Apocalypse 3:16). Therefore because they have not received "the love that they might be saved," instead of a religious revival this "church" exhibits that of which the Apostle warned, "And for this cause God shall send them strong delusion, that they should believe a lie that they all might be damned who believe not the truth, but had pleasure in unrighteousness" (2 Thessalonians 2:10-12).

It is, therefore, upon the grounds stated above that the Most Reverend Members of our Council of Bishops unanimously agreed to recognize ecumenism as a dangerous heresy. Having observed its spread, they asked us to share our observation with our Brother Bishops throughout the world. We ask them first of all to pray that the Lord spare His Holy Church the storm which would be caused by this new heresy, opening the spiritual eyes of all unto understanding of truth in the face of error. May our Lord help each of us to preserve the Truth in the purity in which it was entrusted to us undefiled, and to nurture our flocks in its fidelity and piety.

+ Metropolitan PHILARET

The Third Sorrowful Epistle:
On The Thyateira Confession[36]
(December 19, 1975)

AN EPISTLE TO THE PRIMATES
OF THE HOLY CHURCHES OF GOD
AND THE MOST REVEREND ORTHODOX BISHOPS
ON THE THYATEIRA CONFESSION

"BUT THOUGH WE, or an angel from Heaven, preach any other Gospel unto you than that which we have preached unto you, let him be accursed" (Galatians 1:8). With such firmness did St. Paul teach us to maintain the Orthodox Faith which had been delivered unto us. To his disciple Timothy he wrote, "But continue thou in the things which thou hast learned and hast been assured of, knowing of whom thou hast learned them" (2 Timothy 3:14). This is the instruction which should be followed by every Bishop of the Orthodox Church, which indeed he is obliged to keep according to the oath sworn at his consecration. The Apostle describes a Bishop as "holding fast the faithful word as he hath been taught, that he may be able by sound doctrine both to exhort and to convince gainsayers" (Titus 1:9).

In these days of vacillation, confusion of thought and corruption, we confess the true teaching of the Church regardless of the opinions held by those who might hear us and disregarding the skepticism and faithlessness of our environment. If, for the sake of conforming to the errors of the times, we would suppress the truth or yet profess distorted doctrines to please the world, we would in fact be offering stones instead of bread. And the higher the position

---

36 Metropolitan Philaret of New York, "On the Thyateira Confession," *Orthodox Life* 26, no. 2 (March-April 1976): 21-25.

of one who would act in this way, the more profound the temptation and the more serious the consequences. It was for this reason that we felt great sorrow when we read the "Thyateira Confession" which was recently published in Europe with the blessing and authorization of the Patriarch and the Holy Synod of the Church of Constantinople.

We know that the author of this book, the Most Reverend Metropolitan Athenagoras of Thyateira, had in former times acted as a guardian of the Orthodox Faith. Therefore least of all did we expect from him a Confession of Faith which would be so far from Orthodoxy! Yet if it were only his own personal statement, we would write nothing about it. We are, however, forced to comment because this work bears the seal of approval of the Church of Constantinople in the persons of Patriarch Demetrios and the Synod of that Church. In a special letter addressed to Metropolitan Athenagoras by Patriarch Demetrios, it is stated that this work has been examined by a special Synodical Committee. After approval by that Committee, the Patriarch, in accordance with the decision of the Synod, extended his blessing for the publication of this, as he describes it, "excellent work." Therefore the responsibility for this work is transferred from Metropolitan Athenagoras alone to the entire hierarchy of the Church of Constantinople.

In our former "Sorrowful Epistles" we have already expressed the grief that we feel when from the See of St. John Chrysostom, Saints Proclos, Tarasios and Photios, the See of Fathers and Confessors of our Faith, we hear expressed doctrines which without doubt they would have anathematized. We are heart-struck as we write these words. How much would we rather hear the true doctrine of the Church expressed in the spirit of the blessed and great Hierarchs of the See of the Church of Constantinople which gave birth to our Russian Church! With what joy would we accept such a declaration and transmit it for the instruction of our pious flock! And conversely, how grieved we are when we are obliged to warn our people that from this former fountain of pure Orthodox confession, there now flow the putrid streams of error.

When we turn to the Thyateira Confession itself, alas, in it we find so many un-Orthodox thoughts and contradictions that to deal with all of them would require us to write volumes. But this is not necessary, for it is sufficient to point out the basis upon which all the un-Orthodoxy of the Confession is founded. On page 60, Metropolitan Athenagoras justly says that the Orthodox people believe that their Church is the One, Holy, Catholic and Apostolic Church, and that She teaches the true fullness of the Catholic Faith. He also recognizes that the other bodies have failed to maintain this fullness. But further on, he forgets that if a doctrine in some way deviates from the truth, it becomes in this regard false. By belonging to a religious association which professes this doctrine, one is already separated from the true Church. Metropolitan Athenagoras is prepared to accept this position in regard to some ancient heretics such as the Arians, but when he addresses contemporary heresies, he is not so inclined. In regard to them, he wishes to be guided not by the ancient Tradition, not by Sacred Canons, but by a "new understanding which prevails today among Christians" (p. 12), and by "the signs of our time" (p. 11).

But is this in agreement with the teachings of the Holy Fathers? Let us recall the first canon of the Seventh Ecumenical Council which gives us a very different criterion for the direction of our thoughts and for the regulation of the life of the Church. "For those who have been allotted the sacerdotal dignity, the representations of canonical ordinances amount to testimonies and directions." And further, "we welcome and embrace the divine canons, and we corroborate the entire and rigid fiat of them that have been set forth by renowned Apostles, who are the trumpets of the Holy Spirit, and those of the six holy Ecumenical Councils and of those of our Holy Fathers. For all those men, having been guided by the light dawning out of the same Spirit, prescribed rules that are in our best interest." But setting aside this principle, the Thyateira Confession constantly emphasizes the "new understanding." "Christian people," we read there, "now visit churches and pray with other Christians of various traditions with whom they were forbidden in the past to associate, for they were called heretics" (p. 12).

But what was it in the past which forbade such prayers? Was it not Holy Scripture, the Holy Fathers and the Ecumenical Councils? Are we perhaps speaking of those who were only called heretics but were not such in reality? Yet the first canon of St. Basil the Great gives a clear definition of those who are heretics, "Heresies is the name applied (by the Holy Fathers) to those who have broken entirely and have become alienated from the Faith itself." Does this not apply to those Western confessions which have fallen away from the Orthodox Church?

St. Paul teaches us, "A man that is a heretic, after the first and second admonition, reject" (Titus 3:10). But the Thyateira Confession would have us draw together with them and enter into communion of prayer. The 45th Canon of the Holy Apostles orders us, "Let any Bishop or Presbyter or Deacon that merely joins in prayer with heretics be suspended." We find the same injunction in the 65th Apostolic Canon and in the 33rd Canon of the Council of Laodicea. The 52nd Canon of the latter forbids us to accept even the blessing of a heretic. The Thyateira Confession, on the contrary, urges us to common prayer with them and goes so far as to permit the Orthodox to receive communion from them and to offer it to them!

Metropolitan Athenagoras himself informs us that among the Anglicans, many of their Bishops and laity accept neither the special grace of the priesthood, nor the infallibility of the decisions of the Ecumenical Councils, nor the Eucharistic Reality of the Holy Gifts in the Divine Liturgy, nor most of the other Mysteries, nor the veneration of the holy relics of saints. The author mentions the actual articles of their faith in which these views are expressed; yet putting all this aside, he finds it permissible for the Orthodox to receive communion from Anglicans and Roman Catholics and he finds it possible to administer communion to them in an Orthodox Church. And what is the foundation of such a practice? The teachings of the Holy Fathers? The canons? No. The grounds for such actions is the fact that such lawlessness has already occurred previously. And there exists "friendship" between Orthodox and Anglicans.

Yet, whatever might be the office of a person who commits a forbidden act, and whatever "friendship" might have served as the incentive, neither can serve as a justification for a practice which violates the Canons. What answer will justify a Bishop before the dread Throne of the Heavenly Judge when he must explain why he advised his spiritual children to accept, instead of True Communion, something which even those who give it do not believe that it is the very Flesh and Blood of Christ?

Such lawless actions ensue from the absolutely heretical, protestant or, in modern terminology, ecumenical doctrine of the Thyateira Confession in regard to the Holy Church. The Church is seen as without limits. "The Holy Spirit," we read there, "is active both within the Church and outside the Church. For this reason its limits are ever extended and its bounds are nowhere. The Church has a door but no walls" (p. 77). But if the Holy Spirit acts equally within the Church and outside Her, why, may we ask, was it necessary for our Savior to come to earth and establish Her? If we accept this doctrine of the Church, the legacy left us by our Lord, the Apostles and the Holy Fathers enjoining us to keep and confess true doctrine become unnecessary. Although the Confession says on page 60 "that the Orthodox Church can rightly claim at this moment of history to be the one true Church that Christ the Son of God founded upon earth," it does not see any need to keep the Faith of this Church unaltered thereby permitting the coexistence of truth and error.

In direct contradiction to the words of the Apostle that Christ presented Her to Himself "a glorious Church, not having spot, or wrinkle, or any such thing" (Ephesians 5:27); the Thyateira Confession presents the Church as combining the truth with what this confession recognizes as a deviation from it, in other words a heresy, though it refrains from using that description in this instance. The refutation of such a teaching is clearly expressed in the well-known Epistle of the Eastern Patriarchs (1848) concerning the Orthodox Faith, "We confess with no doubts, as a firm truth, that the Catholic Church cannot make mistakes or fall into error and express lies instead of truth; because the Holy Spirit, always acting through truly serving Fathers and Doctors of the Church, preserves Her from any error" (Article 12).

In submitting to the novel dogma of conforming and compromising with modern trends, the author of the Thyateira Confession seems to forget the Lord's command that if thy brother "neglect to hear the Church, let him be unto thee as a heathen man and a publican" (Matthew 8:17), and a similar instruction of the Apostle, "A man that is a heretic, after the first and second admonition, reject" (Titus 3:10). It is therefore with much grief that we must declare that in this Thyateira Confession, which comes to us from the Church of Constantinople, we hear not the voice of Orthodox Truth, but the voice of the ever-spreading heresy of Ecumenism. But what will follow on the part of those "whom the Holy Spirit hath made overseers, to feed the Church of God, which he hath purchased with His own Blood" (Acts 20:28)? Will this false doctrine, proclaimed officially in the name of the entire Church of Constantinople, be left with no protests on the part of the Bishops of the Churches of God? Will the Truth be betrayed by this very silence, in the words of St. Gregory the Theologian, by all?

Being the least of the Primates of the Churches, we would have rejoiced to have heard the voices of our Elders before we ourselves spoke out. But, alas, we have heard nothing. If it should be that they have not yet familiarized themselves with the content of this Confession, we ask that they do so without delay, so that it will not escape their condemnation. It is terrible to think that the words of the Lord addressed to the Angel of the Church of the Laodiceans might be applied to us, "I know thy works, that thou art neither cold or hot I would thou wert cold or hot. So then because thou art lukewarm, and neither cold nor hot, I will spew thee out of my mouth" (Apocalypse 3:15-16).

We now warn our flock and we appeal to our brothers, to their belief in the Church and to their understanding of our mutual responsibility for our flock to the Heavenly Archpastor. We beg them not to disregard the information that we herewith furnish them, thereby allowing the deliberate falsification of Orthodox Doctrine to remain covered and unconvicted, for the widespread propagation of this untruth has prompted us to make our sorrow known to the whole Church; we pray that our lament will be heard.

+ Metropolitan Philaret
Feast of St. Nicholas

The Triumph of Orthodoxy[37]

When our Lord Jesus Christ at the Mystical Supper conversed with His disciples, having warned them at the end of His talk with the words, in the world ye shall have tribulation, He then concluded with the words, But stand firm I have overcome the world. The Apostle and Evangelist John the Theologian in one of his epistles in a certain way continued the words expressed by his Divine Teacher by writing, This is the victory that overcometh the world — our faith. Therefore the Orthodox Church on the first Sunday of Great Lent celebrates the Triumph of Orthodoxy, the Church celebrates her victory, the victory of the Orthodox Faith over all false teachings, over persecutions and oppression, that great multitude of which she experienced in her bright but sorrowful path.

In the very beginning the Jews fiercely and wickedly fell upon the young Church, and although they had no independent government, they still caused the Church no few problems and sorrows. After them the powerful Roman Empire attacked the Church, persecuting her. The last persecutors expended all their strength in order to completely destroy Christianity. They were totally unsuccessful, for in the end, after those persecutions, the pagan world fell down at the foot of the Christian Cross.

The Apostles, especially St. Paul, still warned the Christians that among them people would appear who did not reason or teach correctly, and this also came to pass. Immediately after the Apostles, and even during their times, the first heretics appeared with their incorrect reasoning and false teachings. Initially, heresies did not greatly trouble the Church, but when the period of persecution

---

37 Metropolitan Philaret of New York, "The Triumph of Orthodoxy," *Orthodox Life*, 45, no.1 (January-February 1995): 2-4.

ended, the era of heresy began. Heresies were more dangerous than persecution for the Church. Persecution was oppression from outside the Church; the faithful had nothing to fear from persecution. The Church during the period of persecutions was merely embellished by the blood of the martyrs. On the other hand, heresies destroyed the Church from within.

The first of the great and dangerous heresies was the heresy of Arius, which troubled the Church for nearly one hundred years. Arianism disturbed the Church even after Arius died — a death which was like the shameful death of Judas the betrayer. There were other heresies, the last of which troubled the Church for a long period. This was the heresy of iconoclasm. This heresy was especially difficult for the Church because Emperors appeared who were iconoclasts and rose up against the veneration of icons, cruelly persecuting the defenders of icon veneration. All of this passed, and at the last ecumenical council which confirmed the veneration of icons, the triumph of Orthodoxy was proclaimed — the victory of our Faith over all of its enemies, over all false teachings and persecutions.

More than any other day this day reminds us that we all must examine our Orthodoxy. Are you Orthodox in all things? If you call yourself Orthodox and are convinced that you are Orthodox, then the triumph of Orthodoxy is your triumph. You must still strive, however, so that the name Orthodox which has been applied to you corresponds to reality. The basis of our faith is precisely, concisely, and exhaustively contained in our Creed. In the Creed all the essential points of our faith are expounded. It is useful, not only at this time but as often as possible, to check oneself by these points and to remember that if even one point of the Creed is not accepted by us completely and reverently, then our Orthodoxy, as they say, will not stand up to the test. In fact there are many things in our faith which people doubt, although they consider themselves to be Orthodox.

There is an example of a merchant in Moscow who, at his own expense, kept a beautiful perpetually burning lampada before an icon of the Iveron Mother of God. When friends praised him for such piety and zeal he answered, "Yes, yes, of course it just might prove useful, perhaps there really might exist something there [in the next life]." There is Orthodoxy for you! He was completely unconvinced that there, beyond the grave, "was something," but "just in case" he kept that lampada burning. There are people who doubt other aspects of our faith. There are those who not only break the fasts (perhaps because of illness), but simply do not consider themselves obliged to keep the fasts — this is already not Orthodox. St Seraphim of Sarov in his time did not give up the conviction that the person who did not keep the fasts was simply not Christian. That holy father said, "No matter how Orthodox a person considers himself, if he does not keep the fasts, does not obey the Church, then he is not a Christian." Indeed the Lord Himself said that a person who does not listen to the Church, who does not obey her, is like a publican and a pagan. Therefore we must examine our Orthodoxy. If indeed your conscience tells you that you reverently accept all the richness and beauty contained in our faith as something holy, as the teaching about truth brought from Heaven, then you are really Orthodox and the Triumph of Orthodoxy will be your triumph and victory. Amen.

A Conversation of His Eminence Met. Philaret with Students of Holy Trinity Theological Seminary in Jordanville, New York[38]

The following excerpts are from a conversation which the First-Hierarch of the Russian Church Abroad had with students at Holy Trinity Seminary on March 22nd, 1966, the day of the commemoration of the Holy Forty Martyrs. The conversation was published in Russian in the November 1971 issue of *Pravoslavnaya Zhizn* (*Orthodox Life* in Russian) pp. 7-16.

---

38 Metropolitan Philaret of New York, "A Conversation with His Eminence Metropolitan Philaret: With Students of Holy Trinity Theological Seminary in Jordanville, New York," Orthodox Life 49, no. 6 (November-December:1999): 39-48.

Metropolitan Philaret with His Grace the future Bishop LUKE of Syracuse and His Grace the future Bishop GEORGE of Canberra, both as Subdeacons

MAN — THE IMAGE AND LIKENESS OF GOD

You and I know, young friends, that God the Creator made man after His image and likeness and placed the imprint of this image on man's very being, on human nature itself. The Holy Fathers of the Church used to love to point out that this image and likeness of God Almighty Himself shines in man, since man was assigned to rule over all other earthly creatures; this dignity of an earthly king and ruler once shone in man so that all creatures on earth willingly submitted to him. They submitted willingly and naturally, in the normal direct order of things. If the Lord, as the King and Master of all existence, bestowed the royal mastery over the earth on His image, then, as the Creator of all existing things, He placed in His favorite creation — man — creative powers and abilities.

When we see today how varied life has become, how multi-faceted and beautiful it is today, even with all the minuses which unfortunately go along with this flowering of life on earth, nevertheless, this is a manifestation of man's creative power, his ability to create after the image of the Creator who made him. Of course between the creative potential of God and of man there lies an abyss. What is the basic difference between the creative ability of God Omnipotent and of man? God is a Creator in the absolute and unconditional sense of the word. Firstly, He is omnipotent and nothing is impossible for Him and secondly He creates from nothing. This is the absolute power of absolute, unlimited creativity. Man, on the other hand, must use prepared material, he cannot create something from nothing. But, having what his Prototype, God the Creator, has created, man creates out of pre-existing material and he creates in a variety of ways.

Unfortunately, as a result of the fact that man did not preserve his original dignity and purity but fell into sin and blackened himself with sin, his whole being, his whole nature, all his powers and capabilities have become darkened and poisoned. In particular, man's ability to create has become darkened and ruined by sin. At the present time, unfortunately, this ability is in most cases given a wrong direction and, therefore, acquires an incorrect character.

Speaking about the Divine creation, about the creation of man, have you noticed in one prayer, which we are all well acquainted with, in the service for the dead, it starts with the words, "Thou alone art immortal, Who didst create and fashion man..." Why are two words used which mean almost the same thing, "create" and "fashion"? Why could not one just say "created" or just "fashioned?" Why is it said in this manner? Because man also fashions out of material which already existed and man's body consists of the same basic material as the rest of the material world. But the Lord breathed an immortal soul into him, and this is something completely new. You yourselves know, in the history of the creation the Lord always said: Let the earth bring forth grass, Let the earth bring forth the living creature [...] Let the waters bring forth abundantly the moving creature that has life, Remember? He speaks like this each time, but here in the creation of man, it is entirely different. Let us make man in Our image, after Our likeness, says the Lord in the council of the Holy Trinity. After this, it is not the earth that brings forth man, but God Himself creates man. That is why the distinction is precisely made who created and fashioned man. Let everyone remember that the monkey, which now, it seems, can boast that he is considered to be our ancestor, was nevertheless brought forth from the earth; it is an earthly creation. It is one of those things which is spoken of in the Bible, let the earth bring forth, but man was created by God! I have digressed. Subsequently, man in his creative activity, because of his corruption from sin, did not preserve his proper direction and in many instances his creativity became, to use a patristic term, a vain creation.

ALL IS VANITY

Already long ago in antiquity a wise man of the Old Testament, Solomon the Wise, who had experienced and endured much and who, because he was a king, had many possessions, looked about himself and said, vanity of vanities; all is vanity. This was his judgment on the already then luxurious, diverse, elegant and, one would have thought, beautiful life surrounding him. And at the end of his book he says Fear God and keep His commandments: for this is the whole duty of man. Such was the purely practical conclusion which he drew from all he had experienced and observed.

THE EMPTINESS OF MAN FALLEN AWAY FROM GOD

Bishop Theophan the Recluse speaks of the seething activity of fallen man. Concerning such vain, albeit seemingly diverse and even fruitful activity, Bishop Theophan says that man, having fallen away from God, cannot but feel his emptiness. And so it is. Man has torn himself away from God, Who is the fullness of everything. On his own he is empty. He has to fill up the void with something. And so he feverishly labors and works in order somehow to fill up his spiritual hunger and feeling of inner emptiness. He races along, agitates, invents, creates. Virtually the majority of the inventions of our present culture are precisely the product of such feverish activity — activity with which mankind, having departed from God, busies itself. How much there is here that is vain and perhaps, even harmful, even though what is manifested here is man's creative capacity, as I have already said. One feels the root in this — it is from God. But, alas, from its fruits and works one sees how far its goal has departed from God's goal.

I remember how, when I was still living in Harbin, China, in the Far East, the latest product of technology appeared — the so-called sputnik. When the first one was sent up, they asked my opinion. I said that when small children blow soap bubbles, we laugh while looking at them, since we know it is a harmless children's amusement. But when grown men begin to send up "bubbles" and balloons, one only becomes sad, since the time could have been spent doing something else. But then, as you know, it turned out this was no innocent amusement, but alas, had turned into the same Moloch of common destruction, since they seek to use these inventions in order to have the ability to bring down the maximum possible explosive materials upon their neighbors. Thus there occurs what Metropolitan Philaret of Moscow once spoke about "Man," he says, "begins to play with a dangerous toy as if he were playing with an innocent sparrow. Then with horror he sees that he has been playing with a venomous snake and that the snake has bitten him." There is probably something similar here.

THEORETICAL AND PRACTICAL ATHEISM

Thus we have before us the activity of fallen man, who has departed from God and is feverishly attempting to fill up with something a life which is absolutely empty and without content (i.e., without the Lord God). As a result, there flourishes what is called "atheism." But here I would direct your attention to something — namely to the sense, albeit a relative one of course, in which one may say that there exist two kinds of atheism: theoretical or ideological atheism and practical atheism. The former is, as it were, preached by many, but hardly was Fedor Mikhailovich Dostoevsky mistaken when he said through one of his characters (a simple man, Makar Ivanych, in the novel, *The Adolescent*), "'They say concerning atheists that they exist, but I,' says Makar Ivanych, 'have experienced much and almost never met real atheists. Those who call themselves atheists are just engaging in vanity.'" That is what he said, "They are simply vain people." "But real atheists," observes

Dostoevsky through his characters, "that is something terrible, but there are very few of them."

I think you yourselves understand perfectly well without my explanations that so-called atheism — for example Soviet communism — is not at all atheism. They would not fight so furiously with God and with religion if they really knew there was no God. What would you say about me if I, right this minute, brought a spade and shovel and began to destroy a stove which did not exist? It cannot be doubted that they (i.e., the Soviets) themselves feel the presence of God in their darkened, poisoned souls. A dread voice echoes somewhere in their subconscious; a certain sensation of the Divine existence is felt. And it is for this reason that they climb walls. This is the reason for all the fury, all the blasphemy.

But a real atheist — he is something different. He does not even want to think about such foolishness. Why should one think about that which does not exist? Archimandrite Konstantine, when we were acquainted in Harbin, told me about one political activist, who was rather well known. "This is a rare example. I define him in this way only not in the usual sense, but in the exact sense of this Greek word, that in the spiritual sense, he is an idiot, deprived of even the rudiments of religious feelings. For him religion is completely foreign and incomprehensible. He is like a beast, not knowing God or anything religious." There is nothing more terrible than such a blinded man, but, glory to God, there are indeed, as Dostoevsky says, few such men.

THE PRACTICAL ATHEIST

As I have already said, there exists little theoretical, ideological atheism. But there are, alas, many practical atheists. That's something else altogether. He whom I would call a practical atheist does not say that there is no God. He may even go to church and place a candle; at home he may, perhaps, even make the sign of the cross. But God is not in his life. It is as if neither the Divine law, nor anything else exists for him. In life he is de facto an atheist, since all his considerations, all the motives which influence him, the entire, so to speak, external and internal content of his activity excludes the Lord God completely and absolutely. Thus there comes about, as I have said, a life fully without God.

Such a man may even become insulted if you call him an atheist. No, he will say, he believes in God! But, of course, he could not endure any trial, he could not demonstrate his faith by his works, as the Apostle Paul once demanded, since his works are those of a man having, so to speak, nothing in common with God. He will allow that the Lord exists — you know how some persons say, "I believe in something higher." But he does not deem himself under any obligation toward this "something higher." He lives as he takes it into his head, according to his own considerations and desires, not at all checking himself by the Divine commandments, completely without sanctifying either his life or his soul by the light of the Holy Gospel. And it is precisely from this that there appears, like fruit sprung from a root, full indifference to Truth.

You, of course, know Pilate's question, "What is truth?" And you know to whom Pilate put this question. Before him stood the Truth, He Who said, I am the way and the truth and the life. But Pilate was not able to discern truth in the Truth, and he turned away from it with the indifferent question, "What is truth?" Does it exist? And if it does it has nothing to do with me (thought Pilate). Why bother with the question? Pilate turned away from the Truth. He went out and said he found no fault in Him. But from the Truth he turned indifferently away.

It is precisely such indifference to truth which is now very widespread. If the Truth does not interest a man, if it is not dear to him then, in such a case, he has no real Christian revulsion before falsehood. That is why falsehood now overflows everywhere. We live in a kind of kingdom of falsehood. I was speaking about falsehood now, and I remembered something. Perhaps this is not entirely, or directly connected with what I am speaking to you about now, but I would also like to hear your question about what is deception and what is not deception. There is one place in the Bible, the Old Testament, which is very difficult not just for teachers and parents to explain to their curious children, but also for experienced religious instructors.

You probably know the place in the Bible when, in order for her younger son Jacob to receive a blessing of the Patriarch instead of the older son Esau to what measures their mother Rebecca resorted, how she told Jacob she would prepare food that Esau should have prepared, and how she covered his neck and hands with goat skins, so that he would seem to be hairy like his brother Esau. And you know that by this she succeeded in her purpose. The direct reasoning of children here sometimes asks, "Is this not wrong? This deceit, is there not something here that is not good?" Some instructors, in defending Rebecca, do it not so skillfully. They say, "Well, you know, Rebecca knew both of her sons well; she knew that Jacob was good, pious, and obedient, that Esau was not, that he might misuse his birthright and therefore she resorted to deceit." This is not a very successful defense. Do you understand? The notion that Rebecca, as their mother, knew her sons very well, perhaps has a place. But this is sort of a secondary addition to the defense. Yes, perhaps she knew her sons well. But based on what? What happened before this? Remember the pot of lentils, the selling of the birthright — selling it with an oath! Therefore, when what Rebecca did came to pass, the one who received the blessing was the one who was supposed to receive it.

Do you understand? An oath in the Old Testament was a serious matter. As soon as Esau gave up his birthright with an oath — it was finished! The firstborn became Jacob. However, Rebecca realized that this would be difficult to obtain from their father directly. Therefore, she used this well-known deception. Yes! But this was not deceit or falsehood, in the essence of the matter, because Jacob was the firstborn, not Esau. Do you understand? I just wanted to express this idea. Not long ago, I happened to speak about this during courses for choir leaders and singers, when we were reading the Bible. I just remembered and I wanted to share it with you. And so, we live in a kingdom ruled by falsehood, which has been raised to a sort of cult. It not only reigns there, in our unfortunate homeland, Soviet Russia, but it is everywhere and in everything.

THE PRESENT AGE

There has never been such a time as the present in the sense that, on the one hand, evil bares itself openly as never before and, on the other hand, there have never, it seems, been so many clever spiritual shams — such a mass of them — as now. Indeed a sincere, good soul seeking spiritual truth, the truth of the Gospel and the Church, can simply flutter about in all directions, since it is truly difficult for it to make sense out of all the turmoil and chaos about it, and since counterfeit shams are everywhere. It is true, there are also now people with very tractable and flexible consciences, people having no clear inner voice. There are numerous cases, for example, in which an Orthodox man will attend an Eastern rite, Uniate church. And when his Orthodox pastor, having learned of this, begins to speak gently to reproach him of this, saying, "Why did you do it? You are Orthodox," he receives the answer, "Father, they have the same thing there, the same vestments, the same order of services. Everything is the same, except they commemorate their Pope of Rome. But I do not pray for him, and everything else is exactly the same." To this, one Orthodox pastor answered simply and appropriately, "You know what," he said, taking out two half-dollar coins from his pocket, (he luckily just happened to have them on him), "one of these coins is real and the other is fake; they look exactly the same, but one has worth and the other has none." So it is here. In that "same" false (Uniate) church there is everything — except Grace. Everything else is there, including the same services as we have, but the church is not lawful and is without Grace.

To these people who are indiscriminate about where they pray I say, well, all right. One peasant lived next to me. He is educated, he reads Slavonic. If he builds a church with his own hands, sews himself vestments, makes the church vessels and everything he needs, and begins to perform services, will you go to him? Will you say that everything is the same? Is this a lawful priest? Is this the Church? So it is with them [the Uniates], let them be outwardly the same, but obviously there is something internal that one must be able to find. Remember this point. May God grant that if not all of you, most of you will be pastors of the Church. But this concerns not only pastors, but all Orthodox people. Today it is necessary to know the Truth and somehow be able to explain and express It.

CALL TO MISSION

You and I are living in unusual times. Now everyone must, to a certain extent, be a missionary in his circle of acquaintances. This is the duty of every Orthodox Christian since we are completely surrounded by non-Orthodoxy. And in the midst of this non-Orthodox world there are good souls who are striving toward the truth and seeking it out. The Lord, the Highest Pastor of the human soul, Himself sees these souls and Himself draws them toward salvation. Recall the marvelous story from today's Lives of Saints about the soldier, the guard who perhaps even several hours before his martyric death did not think he would do anything like it and was only concerned with carrying out his guard duties. Recall how he became a martyr. The Lord through His ways saw that the soldier's soul was ready to become faithful and drew it to Himself. See how he is able to seek out and find those who are lost! So must act every pastor of the Church. Pastors most of all, of course, but also every convinced believing Orthodox Christian, even one of a young age. Even for the young there are opportunities everywhere to be a missionary and a defender and herald of one's faith. And people are drawn to it from everywhere. This is evident everywhere.

It is in vain to think that now, so to speak, the whole world has completely expired spiritually. Of course the darkness does not disperse but rather thickens as the Saviour foretold because of the increase of lawlessness the love of many is going cold. But there are nevertheless still many faithful souls who seek, men who, if shown the true path, will themselves become faithful. You must never forget this. And remember one thing more. This refers both to a serving pastor and also simply to any Orthodox Christian. A sermon, exhortation, or explanation has an effect only when it does not disagree with the actions in the life of the person speaking. One must always keep this in mind. The Holy Fathers always used to say, "Woe to the preacher who teaches one thing and does another. His word will never have any authority."

I remember how our youth in Harbin — those precisely around your age — how they reacted when the Soviet Red Army arrived. There were no longer any battles, the Red Army occupied Harbin. For the Soviets the population remained what they called "White bandits." The Soviet youth, the soldiers of the Red Army who were resting up in Harbin, came in contact with our students, and of course, arguments immediately began to flare up. It was here that our youth realized intuitively that in order to convince someone words are not enough. So all our fellows immediately put on crosses, began strictly keeping the fasts and as the saying goes, did not set foot outside of Church. And this was not false — do not think so. It was not simply for show. It was a response to a certain inner voice. The youth felt that their word would be convincing only when it was backed up by something, because it first of all acts beneficially on the speaker himself, and not merely on his listener. This then is what I wish for you. One way or another, in the future, you will take on yourselves the cross of the priesthood; one would hope there would be more like this, that all of you might be priests. In any case, whether you become priests or not, remember that the obligation of every believing Orthodox Christian today is to know the Truth, to love the Truth, and to be able to defend it. I must finish now. I will say just a few more words to you.

JURISDICTIONS

Of course you have heard of the so-called "jurisdictional disputes." You have of course heard — jurisdictions, jurisdictions, jurisdictions! This all, unfortunately, sometimes takes on such a tense and unpleasant character. I once heard from someone an amusing anecdote which I liked very much. "A certain Russian (emigre) was drowning in the ocean. He had gone out for a swim, swam too far out and began to drown. His wife raced along the shore pleading for help. She asked a certain Frenchman. The gallant and well brought up Frenchman threw himself into the water to save the victim but, as soon as he reached deep water, he shouted, 'I do not know how to swim! Will it be better if two drown instead of one?' The wife came up to an Englishman. 'Help,' she pleaded, 'He is drowning.' The Englishman brushed aside her plea, saying, 'You cannot save everyone!' and continued to bathe by the shore. Then she came up to a certain Russian (émigré) 'Save that Russian there, your countryman. He is drowning!' The Russian then shouted, 'Which jurisdiction?'"

You see what can be the nature of such so-called jurisdictional disputes, what an ugly character they can bear. Relations are completely strained, tainted, and confused. Here one must firstly, in defending one's truth, always be as gentle as possible toward those travelling an incorrect path. One must not become embittered. Does animosity ever gain anything?

Generally speaking imagine to yourself that three men are travelling along a road, the correct road. They go along and one makes a wrong step and goes off into a swamp; two of the men proceed correctly. Then a second man veers off to the right and begins to proceed incorrectly. Now the third man proceeds alone. Voices ring out, "Why are you separated? You must reconcile." How shall this be done? The one who remained on the correct path on which all three had at first been travelling, ought he to turn off somewhere or not? Who should turn back? The ones who went astray, correct? So it is here. You yourselves know that our Church Abroad never split herself off from anyone, and has never swerved. She travels the same road as when she was founded by His Beatitude Metropolitan Anthony. Those who have deviated — let them return.

Bishop Nektary always says very insistently, "I do not even recognize the subject of three jurisdictions. There is only one jurisdiction — the Church Abroad." The Church in Russia, whatever she may be there — the Moscow Soviet hierarchy and the Catacomb Church — that is another matter. At the present time we have no direct ties with them — but here there is only one jurisdiction, as His Eminence Nektary perfectly correctly says — there is only one Russian Church Abroad and groups that have split off from her. They must think of returning, rather than our Church thinking of going over to them, and having swerved off of the correct path, also allow ourselves to be pulled into the swamp. If people now argue so much about the subject of jurisdictions, it is, again, only for the reason that Truth is not dear enough to them. For the sake of some kind of external peace and reconciliation such persons are prepared to accuse us of not wanting to be reconciled, of harboring bad feelings toward those in error. People do not want to learn the Truth because they are essentially indifferent to it. They want only an external peace, like the peace about which the communists shout so much about peace for the whole world, in order to cast together in one heap principles which are totally irreconcilable and which cannot be reconciled. It is like trying to lump hot coals together with firewood. Will they lie quietly together? It is clear that a fire will flare up. So it is here. This artificial, external peace will never be achieved. The Lord spoke about this very thing through the Prophet. There is no peace, saith my God, to the wicked (Isaiah 57:21) — and there will not be any!

So, I repeat, talk of a reconciliation between the so-called "three jurisdictions" — as people who do not understand the matter explain — is being raised now because people do not hold the Truth dear. He who comes to know the Truth objectively and calmly will always grasp the matter at hand and find the correct path. Take, for example, the wonderful, peaceful, objectively written work, the documentary book about this schism written by our Nikolai Dimitrievich Talberg. Do many know of it? In it, the history of what transpired, is elucidated calmly, intelligently, and objectively. I have given it to people who did not know the history of the schism — once they have read it they say, "Now everything is clear." But people are not interested and they do not want to read. And so, it is my wish that you would be spared this fate, and that the Truth would always be dear to you. And if Truth will be dear to you, then you will always be able to defend it.

Address Before the Memorial Service for Vladyka John[39]

In the name of the Father and of the Son and of the Holy Spirit.

From years long past there has existed among Russian Orthodox people the belief that Bishops of the Orthodox Church die "in threes," meaning within a set space of time. I unwittingly recalled this old belief just now. Just after the last Sobor of Bishops of the Church Abroad, a year and a half ago, a participant in the Sobor, Vladyka Archbishop Stephan, died in advanced old age. Later on, a little more than a year ago, the orphaned Church Abroad prayerfully conducted along the "way of all the earth" her aged primate and spiritual father, the unforgettable elder, Metropolitan Anastassy. And now, at last, there is a third name. Yesterday during the vigil service, an urgent telephone call from Vladyka Nektary in far off California brought sorrowful news to us; one of the most senior hierarchs of our Church, the first vice-chairman of the Synod, archpastor and ascetic, Vladyka Archbishop John died suddenly in Seattle, where he had arrived with the Wonderworking Icon of the Mother of God, accompanied by Vladyka Nektary.

Stunning news. Now, when I think of Vladyka John, I recall that over 30 years ago, already a long time ago, my deceased father, Vladyka Dimitry, knowing of what sorrows and troubles the Primate of the Church Abroad, the Most Blessed Metropolitan Anthony, would have to go through in Yugoslavia, invited him to the Far East, to far off Harbin, where there was a well-established church life. "You take a rest among us," wrote Vladyka Dimitry to the head of the Church abroad. Vladyka Anthony answered thus, "Friend, I am already so old and weak that I cannot think of any other journey than to the cemetery. But in my place, I am sending you, as my soul, my own heart, Vladyka John. In our times of world-wide spiritual

---

39 Metropolitan Philaret of New York, "Address of Metropolitan Philaret before the Memorial Service for Vladika John," *Orthodox Life* 100, no. 4 (July-August:1966): 3-5.

St. John (Maximovich) and Met. Philaret

weakening, this frail little man, well-nigh a child in appearance, comes forth as a miracle of ascetic steadfastness and strictness."

Thus his great Abbah defined Vladyka John, then still very young and just ordained a Bishop. Just as Vladyka John was then such as he remained, and even now, in our own days, before our eyes, he remained just such a "miracle of ascetic steadfastness," a lofty example of spiritual and prayerful mentality. Vladyka John prayed all the time. Vladyka John prayed everywhere. It was not without reason that Hieromonk Methodius, then in Harbin and also of a spiritual mentality, made the subtle remark, "We all start praying, but for Vladyka John there is no need to 'start' praying he is always in a prayerful state of mind." And no matter what changes occurred in the external surroundings and external life and work of Vladyka John, the matter of prayer and service to God was always in the first place. Nothing could tear him away from this.

No one man can contain in himself all the perfections and be the bearer of all gifts. Everybody can make mistakes and does make mistakes; no one is free from this. But those who dealt with Vladyka John, just as a man of prayer, as an archpastor caring for human souls and always ready to come to the help of those experienced in themselves and in those closest to themselves the power of his prayers, these will never forget Vladyka. They will always carry in their hearts a grateful memory of that warmth and radiance which he gave them. Vladyka has died. The unceasing prayer which flamed in our great man of prayer, who constantly prayed "for all the people," has come to an abrupt end. The Church Abroad will not forget him. We hope that Vladyka John will acquire grace and boldness before the Dreadful Throne of the Lord of Glory. There he will pray for his children and for his flock, just as he prayed here on the earth. And our duty, the duty of thankful love, is to answer for his prayer also by prayer. And so, let us pray for his radiant soul, that the Lord may grant him repose with the righteous. Amen.

On Archbishop Saint John of San Francisco[40]

In the Australian "Church Word" a letter of Metropolitan Philaret to Archbishop Sava was featured, in which much interesting information is related. Therefore we are reprinting it here.

"Vladyka died not in San Francisco but in Seattle, where he had arrived with the Wonder-working Icon in the company of Vladyka Nektary. According to the accounts, it happened like this. Having served liturgy, Vladyka in a short time decided to visit the cemetery and with this intention he went to the house where he stayed. Two of his devoted admirers were there, who noticed that Vladyka was abnormally pale and, seeing that he was not completely well, began to ask him not to go to the cemetery. Vladyka answered, 'It's nothing, it's nothing.' And went upstairs to this room on the second floor, after which they heard the noise of a body falling. They rushed upstairs and saw that Vladyka was losing consciousness and his legs beginning to convulse. They hurriedly informed Vladyka Nektary and a doctor. Both quickly arrived, but Vladyka was already passing away, and soon he quietly died."

The body of deceased Vladyka John, who died in Seattle, as a special exception was brought to San Francisco, which is in another state, without an autopsy and embalmment. Here his funeral and burial were performed. "Could there be any doubt at all," Met-

---

40 Metropolitan Philaret of New York, "Metropolitan Philaret on Archbishop John," *Orthodox Life* 101, no. 5 (September-October 1966): 3-4.

Metropolitan Philaret with St. John (Maximovich)

ropolitan Philaret writes further, "that Vladyka manifestly pleased God with his truly ascetic life and great labour of prayer? It is also worth noting that we held the funeral, on the sixth day (for different reasons I was long delayed in my journey, and they waited for me a long time. Instead of on Tuesday, as was planned, the funeral was held on Thursday at six p.m.) The casket was open, and not only were there no signs whatsoever of decay of the body, but Vladyka lay as if asleep. His hands had their normal appearance and color and were soft and warm. Obvious incorruptibility.

"But little of this. One pious lady, who can be completely trusted, told the following, Vladyka John, who knew her for 12 years, often visited her for a spiritual discussion. Now, in May of this year, when Vladyka came to visit her as usual, he stunned her with the words, 'I'm going to die soon, at the end of June.' (His death was indeed on June 20; Vladyka didn't recognize the new calendar), and, what is even more startling, he said, 'I'm going to die not in San Francisco, but in Seattle; I'm going there and there I will die.'"

"Another pious woman told about her dream. Before Vladyka's death, she saw a dream. She sees herself standing in the new cathedral; Vladyka comes up and says, 'Let's go,' and he leads her somewhere deep down below where they came into a dark room beneath the ground. Here Vladyka stopped and said, 'Here is my home.' She remembered this dream, and was staggered when the burial procession went downstairs and took the casket into exactly the same underground room, a burial vault, which Vladyka had showed her in the dream.

"I can say about myself, that the last time that Vladyka was at the meeting of Synod and I served the prayer service for a safe journey for him as he was leaving for San Francisco with the Holy Icon, Vladyka bade me farewell in a completely unusual manner. Instead of taking the sprinkler and sprinkling himself, as a Bishop does, he humbly bowed low and asked me to sprinkle him. After this, instead of the mutual kissing of hands, he firmly took my hand, kissed it, and brusquely pulled away his own. I shook my finger at him, and we both smiled. At the time this was quite touching on his part, but I did not give it any special significance. Now I should think that he truly bade me farewell; we did not see each other again. "All the difficult services, and in particular, of course, the funeral, were triumphant. Five Bishops (in addition to me, Archbishops Leonty and Averky, who arrived from Jordanville, Bishop Sava, and, of course, Bishop Nektary served). The large new cathedral was packed with people. The parting farewell after the funeral lasted two hours. After this the casket was carried around the cathedral three times and was set in a temporary burial vault beneath the new cathedral."

Will the Heterodox Be Saved?[41]

Question: If the Orthodox faith is the only true faith; can Christians of other confessions be saved? May a person who has led a perfectly righteous life on earth be saved on the strength of his ancestry while not being baptized as Christian?

---

41 Archimandrite Philaret (Voznesensky), "Will the Heterodox Be Saved," *Orthodox Life* 34, no. 6 (November-December 1984): 33-35.

Answer: "For He saith to Moses, I will have mercy on whom I will have mercy, and I will have compassion on whom I will have compassion. So then it is not of him that willeth, nor of him that runneth (struggleth), but of God that showeth mercy" (Romans 9:15-16). In the Orthodox Church we have the path of salvation indicated to us and we are given the means by which a person may be morally purified and have a direct promise of salvation. In this sense St. Cyprian of Carthage says that "outside the Church there is no salvation." In the Church is given that of which Apostle Peter writes to Christians (only Christians) "According as His divine power hath given unto us all things that pertain unto life and godliness, through the knowledge of Him that hath called us to glory and virtue; whereby are given unto us exceeding great and precious promises that by these ye might be partakers of the divine nature, having escaped the corruption that is in the world through lust. And beside this, giving all diligence, add to your faith virtue; and to virtue knowledge; and to knowledge temperance; and to temperance patience; and to patience godliness; and to godliness brotherly kindness; and to brotherly kindness charity. For if these things be in you, and abound, they make you that ye shall neither be barren nor unfruitful in the knowledge of our Lord Jesus Christ" (2 Peter 1:3-8). And what should one say of those outside the Church, who do not belong to her? Another Apostle provides us with an idea, "For what have I to do to judge them also that are without? Do not ye judge them that are within? But them that are without God judgeth" (1 Corinthians 5:12-13). God "will have mercy on whom He will have mercy" (Romans 9:18). It is necessary to mention only one thing that to "lead a perfectly righteous life," as the questioner expressed it, means to live according to the commandments of the Beatitudes — which is beyond the power of one outside the Orthodox Church without the help of grace which is concealed within it.

The question: Can the heterodox (i.e. those who do not belong to Orthodoxy — the One, Holy, Catholic, and Apostolic Church) be saved, has become particularly painful and acute in our days. In attempting to answer this question, it is necessary, first of all, to recall that in His Gospel the Lord Jesus Christ Himself mentions but one state of the human soul which unfailingly leads to perdition, i.e. blasphemy against the Holy Spirit (Matthew 12:31-32). The Holy Spirit is, above all, the Spirit of Truth, as the Saviour loved to refer to Him. Accordingly, blasphemy against the Holy Spirit is blasphemy against the Truth, conscious and persistent opposition to it. The same text makes it clear that even blasphemy against the Son of Man — i.e. the Lord Jesus Christ, the incarnate Son of God Himself — may be forgiven men, as it may be uttered in error or in ignorance and, subsequently, may be covered by conversion and repentance (an example of such a converted and repentant blasphemer is the Apostle Paul. See Acts 26:11 and 1 Timothy 1:13). If, however, a man opposes the Truth which he clearly apprehends by his reason and conscience, he becomes blind and commits spiritual suicide, for he thereby likens himself to the devil, who believes in God and dreads Him, yet hates, blasphemes, and opposes Him.

Thus, man's refusal to accept the Divine Truth and his opposition thereto makes him a son of damnation. Accordingly, in sending His disciples to preach, the Lord told them, "He that believeth and is baptized shall be saved; but he that believeth not shall be damned" (Mark 16:16), for the latter heard the Lord's Truth and was called upon to accept it, yet refused, thereby inheriting the damnation of those who "believed not the truth, but had pleasure in unrighteousness" (2 Thessalonians 2:12).

The Holy Orthodox Church is the repository of the divinely revealed Truth in all its fullness and fidelity to Apostolic Tradition. Hence, he who leaves the Church, who intentionally and consciously falls away from it, joins the ranks of its opponents and becomes a renegade as regards Apostolic Tradition. The Church dreadfully anathematizes such renegades, in accordance with the words of the Saviour Himself (Matthew 18:17) and of the Apostle Paul (Galatians 1:8-9), threatening them with eternal damnation and calling them to return to the Orthodox fold. It is self-evident, however, that sincere Christians who are Roman Catholics, or Lutherans, or members of other non-Orthodox confessions, cannot be termed renegades or heretics — i.e. those who knowingly pervert the truth.

They have been born and raised and are living according to the creed which they have inherited, just as do the majority of you who are Orthodox; in their lives there has not been a moment of personal and conscious renunciation of Orthodoxy. The Lord, "Who will have all men to be saved" (1 Timothy 2:4) and "Who enlightens every man born into the world" (John 1:9), undoubtedly is leading them also towards salvation in His own way.

With reference to the above question, it is particularly instructive to recall the answer once given to an " inquirer" by the Blessed Theophan the Recluse. The blessed one replied more or less thus, "You ask, will the heterodox be saved? Why do you worry about them? They have a Saviour, Who desires the salvation of every human being. He will take care of them. You and I should not be burdened with such a concern. Study yourself and your own sins. I will tell you one thing, however, should you, being Orthodox, and possessing the Truth in its fullness, betray Orthodoxy and enter a different faith, you will lose your soul forever." We believe the foregoing answer by the saintly ascetic to be the best that can be given in this matter.

Archimandrite Philaret
(Now Metropolitan Philaret)

Concerning the Old Ritual:
The Decision of the Council of Bishops of the Russian Church Abroad[42]

The Council of Bishops of the Russian Orthodox Church Abroad has considered the question of the attitude of the Russian Church to the customs and rites which She observed in former days, known by the general name of "the old ritual," and contained in the liturgical books printed before the middle of the 17th century and also the interdicts and anathemas which were imposed by the Moscow Councils of 1656 and 1667 and by individual persons in respect of the observation of these customs.

---

42 Metropolitan Philaret of New York, "Concerning the Old Ritual," *Orthodox Life* 33, no. 5 (September-October 1983): 39-41.

Whereas:

1. The Orthodox Church has long ago permitted a diversity of local customs in conditions of unity in the truth of the faith.

2. The old rites do not express any un-Orthodox teaching of which the participants of the above-mentioned councils accused them.

3. The anathemas pronounced by these councils were the cause of many disasters for the Russian Church and led not to peace in the Church which was the aim of their authors, but to the schism and falling away from the Church of many adherents to the old rituals, to a fruitless polemic on the question of ritual, in the midst of which intolerable "slanderous expressions" were employed by both sides, and also to the persecution of those who held differing views, as a result of which many zealots of the old rites suffered.

4. The old rites comprise a part of our common ecclesiastical and historical heritage which should not be eradicated.

5. From the year 1800, the use of old rituals was permitted by the Russian Church, and the interdicts on active members were lifted and revoked.

6. In the last century, the Russian Church, headed by Metropolitan Philaret of Moscow, took steps to revoke the anathemas on the old rituals but this was not achieved due to misunderstandings.

7. The Pre-Council Office of 1906 in which Metropolitan Anthony actively participated, resolved to petition the future local Council "to revoke the anathemas on the two-fingered faithful as they were imposed because of bad feelings" and "to rescind them just as the Council of 1667 rescinded the anathemas of the Hundred Chapter Council on those who did not use two fingers in their devotions."

8. The Council of 1917-1918, although it did not formulate a conciliar act concerning this question (since it had no possibility of peacefully concluding its business), still it resolved, on the testimony of Metropolitan Anthony, to rescind these anathemas, to accept into our Church the Old Ritualist Bishops at the rank they then held and provide Old Ritualist Bishops for the Orthodox Old Ritualists, but Patriarch Tikhon, shortly after his accession to the Patriarchal throne, appointed the first Old Ritualist Bishop (who subsequently

was martyred) as Bishop of Okhten, Simon (Shleev), a defender of the old rites and supporter of the rescinding of the anathemas.

9. Their Beatitudes, Metropolitan Anthony and Anastassy themselves repeatedly served according to the old books in Orthodox Old Ritualist Churches.

10. The Synod of Bishops of the Russian Church Abroad, by a decree dated 26 August/8 September 1964, recognized the old rites as Orthodox and blessed the use of them by those who so desired.

11. The Third Council Abroad, with the participation of the clergy and laity, persistently requested the Council of Bishops to lift these anathemas –

Now the Council of Bishops of the Russian Orthodox Church Abroad Resolves:

1. To consider the ancient liturgical customs and rites contained in the service books of the Russian Church before the middle of the 17th century as Orthodox and salutary.

2. To consider the interdicts and anathemas, imposed in the past on those who adhered to these customs, by the Councils of 1656 and 1667 and also by certain individuals who took part in the councils, because of misunderstandings, as null and void and rescinded.

3. To permit the use of the old rites by those who wish to observe them and who are in communion with the Orthodox Church, provided however that this does not result in any confusion in the Church life of existing parishes of the Russian Orthodox Church Abroad.

4. Not to demand from those Old Ritualists who wish to be accepted into liturgical communion, any renunciation of the old rites and acceptance by them of contemporary rites. Also, to appoint Priests for them and, if necessary, Bishops who will be obliged to observe accurately the ancient ceremonial.

5. To call the Old Ritualists on their part to respect our rites as worthy of equal honor as the old.

6. While grieving over the split that occurred and, in particular, over the persecutions inflicted on the adherents to the old rites, the Council of Bishops, however, does not consider that it has the right

to judge concerning the responsibility of the separate individuals for what took place, since all the participants have long ago appeared before the judgment seat of God to whom they had to give an account for their deeds. The Russian Orthodox Church Abroad has never participated in inimical actions against the Old Ritualists. Therefore, the Council of Bishops appeals to them to forget those previous offences and injustices and instead of remembering this evil, consider rather how to so arrange their Church life in exile in the best way for the salvation of Christian souls.

7. The Council of Bishops calls on all Orthodox Christians not to resume, out of imaginary zeal for Orthodoxy, unnecessary disputes over ritual and in particular, not to repeat the intolerable and censorious expressions, since both rituals have been sanctified. Such expressions, whensoever and by whomsoever they were used in the past, the Council of Bishops rejects and considers rescinded.

+Metropolitan Philaret,
President of the Council of Bishops

12/25 September 1974
New York

Declaration To the Bishops, Clergy and Laity Assembly at St. Tikhon's Monastery (October 20-21, 1970)[43]

A year ago news of negotiations for recognition and autocephaly between the Moscow Patriarchate and the American Metropolia caused a strong emotional reaction. Animated by a spirit of brotherly love, we at that time warned the hierarchy of the Metropolia of the tragic dangers of any such agreement (Letter of Archbishop Nikon to Metropolitan Ireney dated December 9/November 26, 1969). We also further explained the inevitable implications of such

---

43 Metropolitan Philaret of New York, "Declaration To the Bishops, Clergy and Laity Assembly at St. Tikhon's Monastery," *Orthodox Life*, no. 5 (September-October 1970): 3-7.

an agreement in resolutions adopted by our Synod of Bishops on December 31/18, 1969, and in the message of same date, and also in various statements of the public press. The essence of our warnings can be concisely expressed by the following words of St. James' Epistle (3:12): Can a fig tree, my brethren, yield olives, or a grapevine figs? No more can saltwater yield fresh.

It is impossible for the Moscow Patriarchate, under the complete control of the Soviet atheistic regime which has set for itself the goal of destroying all religion, to do anything which could be to the over-all benefit of the Church and it must be remembered that the Moscow Patriarchate cannot engage in foreign affairs without a direct order of the Soviet government. Moreover, the idea of exchanging autocephaly to the American Metropolia (OCA) for recognition of the Moscow Patriarchate originated from nobody else but Metropolitan Nikodim himself, a man whom the entire world knows for his close association with the Soviet government. The testimony of numerous persons who have fled from the U.S.S.R. clearly establishes the strict control exercised by the Soviet government in all matters related in any way to foreign affairs. The Church is not exempt from this control. Despite this background, the leaders of the Metropolia naively accepted the proposal of Metropolitan Nikodim as a great gift, as a glass of fresh and sweet water coming from a bitter salty fount of the enslaved Moscow Patriarchate.

It is not our intention to inflict upon you any hurt, but rather to give you again a brotherly warning of the danger now threatening you and of the fact that, from the proposed agreement, the benefit will accrue only to the Moscow Patriarchate. The Synod of Bishops has not forgotten that until very recently you conceded that we and you were united in one Russian Orthodox Church Abroad. This unity was clearly expressed in the Temporary Statute of the Administration of the Russian Orthodox Church Abroad, which we all accepted. We grieved when this unity was disrupted when, under the influence of temporary political tendencies, the All-American Sobor in Cleveland in 1946 resolved to attempt to terminate all subordination to the Synod of Bishops of the Russian Orthodox Church Abroad.

We never accepted the canonical validity of this unilateral decision which was accepted neither by the whole hierarchy of the Russian Orthodox Church Abroad, nor even by a majority of the Bishops of the North American Metropolitan District. The late Metropolitan Leonty, who was then Archbishop of Chicago, wrote at that time to Metropolitan Anastasius that the decision taken by the Sobor of Cleveland had been provoked by the pro-Moscow sympathies which seized suddenly the majority of its members and you will remember that he himself did not share these sympathies. By its unapproved action, the Sobor in Cleveland introduced once again division into the Orthodox Church in America and left the Metropolia again without any legitimate canonical foundation.

With respect to the proposed agreement with the Moscow Patriarchate, we would like to point out that such agreement could be reached only after the Synod of the Moscow Patriarchate lifted its interdict from the hierarchy of the American Metropolia stating that it had until then been regarded as a schismatic society. The Patriarchate removed its interdict first, on April 3rd, 1970, from the hierarchy of the Japanese Orthodox Church and only after that, on April 9th, 1970, from the rest of the American hierarchy. The leaders of the Metropolia, by recognizing the Moscow Patriarchate as the supreme authority of the Russian Church of which the Metropolia is a part, and by negotiating with said authority for autocephaly after the interdict has been removed, have raised a serious question as to the validity of all the actions of the Metropolia during the period of the interdict, that is from December 12th, 1947, to April 9th, 1970.

It is said that the Metropolia has stated that it did not recognize the validity of the interdict, considering it unjust, but the validity of an interdict depends upon the canonical capacity of the hierarchy by which the interdict was imposed, not upon its acceptance by the hierarchy that has been interdicted. Thus the Metropolia in recognizing the present Moscow Patriarchate as the supreme legal authority of the Russian Orthodox Church, has itself recognized the invalidity of its own hierarchical actions for 23 years. That is the logical consequence of the agreement now before you. It appears that the leaders of the Metropolia have been lured by the Moscow Patriarchate's promises of a prompt canonical recognition of your new "autocephalous" church and by a promised removal of at least its parallel jurisdiction, but we can now clearly see how naive it was to believe that such promises would be fulfilled.

For this is what we now see. Instead of the general recognition of the new autocephalous Church, we have the messages of the Ecumenical Patriarch from January 8th and June 24th, 1970, proclaiming the act of the Moscow Patriarchate unilateral, anti-canonical and invalid. We know the unfavorable opinion of one of the Oriental Patriarchs and the statement of the Serbian Bishops of February 10th, 1970, calls it the "wrong road." As early as February did they warn the Metropolia that it cannot expect a general recognition, calling the hope to obtain it "naive." We also see that the new Church calling itself "autocephalous" does not possess even the principal characteristic of an autocephalous Church — a territory of its own considered as stable and undisputable and subordinated to its jurisdiction. And how can the Metropolia possess such a territory when the jurisdiction that granted the autocephaly did not, in spite of your hopes, even abolish its own organization in America, but on the contrary retained in the same territory a great quantity of parishes headed by their own Bishops and possessing their own property, without obliging these parishes to pray for the hierarchy of the new so-called "autocephalous" church? The "Tomos" granted by Moscow even allows the number of these "patriarchal" parishes in Canada to increase. At the same time there also continue to exist parishes of the more numerous Greek Archdiocese as well as parishes belonging to the many other Orthodox churches.

If members of the Metropolia hope that the granting of autocephaly will protect its inner freedom, they are deeply mistaken, because freedom is more often lost by actual relationships than saved by clauses in a treaty. It is now proposed that you link yourselves with the Patriarchate by the strongest of bonds, for what will you do if the only Church which has recognized your autocephaly and promised to obtain for you such recognition from other Churches, will renounce you? You will inevitably become more and more involved with the Patriarchate and there will be more and more infiltration into your life of the influence of Moscow, the influence not of the true Russian Church but of the powerful atheistic government for which it fronts. Everybody knows that the Moscow Patriarchate, in spite of the warning of the Apostle, has been mismatched with unbelievers (2 Corinthians 6:14). The leaders of the Patriarchate, beginning with the Metropolitan, later Patriarch Sergius, in 1927 ignored this warning and have been trying by their policy to unite Light with Darkness, to serve God submitting themselves at the same time to Belial. Thus they have allowed their own hierarchy to become an instrument of the national and foreign policy of the atheistic communist party in spreading its influence in the religious life of all the world.

Even now your leaders are trying to hide the extent and closeness of their relations with the Moscow Patriarchate, but there is nothing hid, except to be made manifest nor is anything secret except to come to light (Mark 4:22). If they did not wish to make it known that Metropolitan Nikodim did go to Alaska as an honoured guest of the Metropolia, if Metropolitan Ireney's Secretary who accompanied Nikodim to Alaska, has published in the Russian paper *Novoye Russkoye Slovo* an article describing his journey without even mentioning the name of the person whom he accompanied, nevertheless all became known to us. If the papers were not notified that the resident in America of the Moscow Patriarchate, Bishop Makari, had been invited to the meeting of the Russian Orthodox clubs, this became known from a letter published in the *Novoye Russkoye Slovo* by a witness revolted by the sermon pronounced there by the above-named Bishop concerning the "peaceful" policy of the Soviet government.

Moscow well knows how to draw people into the sphere of its influence by means of carefully planned visits, threats and gifts. You will feel its influence now stronger and yet stronger as time goes on. The creeping domination may be largely unseen and many of you will not recognize it. You may merely wonder how you became collaborators of Moscow in its international church policy, and only few of you may ever understand why Metropolitan Nikodim so unexpectedly undertook to organize your canonical position and grant you autocephaly. But by the time these things became apparent, it will be too late to prevent them. In your hearts you must all know that the Moscow Patriarchate in its present form is not the true representative of the Russian Orthodox Church. The voice of the Patriarchate cannot be the voice of the Russian Church once the Patriarchate is bound by its subordination to the godless Soviet authority. The actions of the Patriarchate cannot be binding upon the Russian Church in the future, when God will surely again grant its freedom. As you know, the true Russian Orthodox hierarchy today is not at the Patriarchate, but either in prisons or in the Catacomb Church, and it therefore cannot now make its voice heard, except as we speak for it. Thus, as the only portion of the Russian Church existing in freedom, it is incumbent upon us to protect the rights of the true Russian Church in Russia and throughout the world. It is in this capacity as representatives of the interests of the true Russian Church throughout the world that we recognize and declare that the autocephaly granted to you by Moscow is illegal and invalid; and we call upon you to refuse this proposed agreement which is likewise not recognized as valid by any other responsible representative of Orthodox Christians.

Therefore we are addressing you all, Bishops, Pastors and Laity, for the last time. Let other considerations fall. Think how important it is now to hear a free voice of the representatives of the true Russian Church. Return back to the unity of the free before it is too late! Until now the responsibility for all that has been done with respect to autocephaly rested on the hierarchy of the American Metropolia. Now the day has arrived when the whole clergy and laity in casting their votes will have to take responsibility before God and before men for the establishment of the purported autocephaly and the rejection of the free representatives of the true Russian Church. When we see our neighbor at the edge of a precipice, our duty of love forces us to call him and make an effort to stop him. We are now making our last attempt, praying God that He may enlighten your mind and strengthen your will, in order that you should reject the erroneous path of Moscow and decide to return to the road of Truth and of Good.

+ Metropolitan Philaret
President of the Synod of Bishops
of the Russian Orthodox Church Abroad
October 6/19, 1970

An Epistle to All the Faithful Children of the Russian Orthodox Church Abroad Concerning the Approaching Glorification of the New-Martyrs of Russia[44]

"Thy Church, arrayed with the blood of Thy martyrs throughout all the world, as with purple and fine linen, doth cry out to Thee through them, O Christ God"

Great is the feat of martyrdom!

In the holy Gospel we read the call of our Savior, the Lord Jesus Christ, directed to those who wish to be His followers, "Strive to enter in at the strait gate" (Luke 13:24). "Strive" — walk the path of struggle, carry out the Christian struggle in your life. In other words, the Christian must be a struggler in his life. The ways and aspects of Christian struggle are diverse. Turning to the lives of the saints, we find there examples of holy, God-pleasing life under the most varied conditions of life. Among the saints glorified by the Church we find people of the most disparate ages and widely different states — from mighty sovereigns and exalted hierarchs of the Church to simple hermits and recluses, and those living in the world with families. Yet with all the disparity of the external forms and conditions of their life, the spiritual foundation is one and the same — an all-embracing love for Christ and an unshakeable loyalty to

---

44 Metropolitan Philaret of New York, "An Epistle to All the Faithful Children of the Russian Orthodox Church Abroad Concerning the Approaching Glorification of the New-Martyrs of Russia," *Orthodox Life* 31, no. 4 (July-August 1981): 11-14.

Him throughout all the temptations, tribulations and persecutions which they had to bear.

In particular, this undaunted loyalty to Christ shines forth clearly and triumphantly in the struggle of those whom Christian antiquity called "witnesses" (in Greek, "martyros"). This struggle, the struggle of martyrdom, is the struggle of those who bore witness to their loyalty, commitment and love for Christ by dying for Him, and did not spare even their very lives. And what beautiful, edifying examples of the feat of martyrdom we find in the lives of the saints! Behold, the holy Great martyr George the Victorious stands before us! A handsome, noble youth, wealthy, a favorite of the emperor, he was his faithful servant and could rely upon achieving a great measure of "success" in this life. But when he had to bear witness to his faith and loyalty to Christ, he turned from all the good things of this earth, manfully went forth to the tortures of martyrdom and death, and received a martyr's crown from the hand of Him for whom he had suffered. Behold, the beautiful Christian virgins, the Great martyrs Barbara and Catherine! Noble, richly gifted and comely themselves, they did not spare their youth, beauty of their very life, and in them were fulfilled the words of the Apocalypse, "Be thou faithful unto death, and I will give thee a crown of life" (Apocalypse 2:10).

One must keep in mind that the holy martyrs, men and women both, after courageously enduring the dreadful tortures and torments to which their tormentors subjected them, went forth to their death as to a banquet; they went not as ones defeated, but as victors. The torturers used all the means at their disposal to induce them to renounce Christ. And only when they saw that their efforts were in vain did they send the faithful witnesses of Christ to their death — an act of sheer, impotent malice. Although in the history of the Church of Christ we see examples of martyrdom in every age of her existence, prior to the Russian Revolution the feat of martyrdom took place chiefly in the first centuries of Christianity, when paganism strove to annihilate the Church with iron and blood.

What we see now is something quite different. With the appearance and rise of God-hating communism in Russia, persecutions of the Faith were initiated which have been unprecedented in their cruelty and scope. In the words of one Church writer, Orthodox Russia found itself on Golgotha, the Russian Church on the Cross. Of course, as was the case in antiquity, there have been incidents of apostasy. Yet at the same time, the Church of Russia and the Russian people have produced a multitude of cases of the manful endurance of torture and death for faith in Christ, indeed so great a number as to be incalculable with any precision; for it is beyond doubt that there have been so many cases of martyrdom throughout the long years of communism's existence in Russia, as to surpass any other era in the history of the human race. Here we are not speaking of hundreds or thousands, but of millions who have suffered for the Faith — an unprecedented and incredible phenomenon!

Throughout man's entire history, there has not been such an occurrence as we now behold — there has not been such an outpouring of evil, there has not been such a mindless and open rebellion of creation against the Creator as we now see in our much suffering homeland, which has been enslaved by the communists. Never in history has there risen to Heaven such an abominable, mindless stench of blasphemy against God and all that is holy, as in Soviet Russia. Yet if the enemies of God and the Church, demonic in their malice, have defiled our homeland, the Russian land, with their loathsome blasphemy and hatred for God, it is, at the same time, cleansed of this defilement by the sacred blood of the New-Martyrs of Russia who have suffered for the Faith and for righteousness. With this blood the land of Russia is abundantly bedewed — bedewed, sanctified and purified of the mindlessness of the godless and those who struggle against God Himself.

The Holy Church, glorifying the New-Martyrs, says that by their blood she is adorned, as with purple and fine linen — the richest, most beautiful and costly raiment. With this splendor of the feat of martyrdom, the Russian Church is now adorned — that Church which has not acknowledged the thieves' "authority" of the godless, has refused any dialogue and compromise with it whatsoever, and consequently bears the cross of faith and confession.

The day of the canonization is drawing nigh — the glorification of that innumerable assembly of martyrs and confessors of the Faith whom the Church of Russia and the Russian people have revealed to the world. It will be a day of the greatest triumph of the Orthodox Faith — not only in Russia and in the Russian diaspora, but throughout the whole world, in every place where there are faithful children of the Orthodox Church. And every Russian Orthodox person must prepare himself to take part therein in a fitting manner.

Now, with the approach of the long-awaited day of the glorification of the New-Martyrs, one often hears how the people say that the Church Abroad does not have the right to glorify them, that this can be done only by the whole Church of Russia in its entirety. Of course, this would be so if the Church of Russia were free! But we know well that the portion of the Church of Russia which has not accepted the communists' "authority" as the lawful authority in Russia and has not submitted to it, has gone into the catacombs, and it is not possible to ask its opinion freely; and the hierarchy of the "official" Church has subjected itself to the authority of the godless and acts according to its orders. Therefore, it cannot be considered the real spokesman for the much-suffering, persecuted Church of Russia. Thus, the Church Abroad considers it her own responsibility to do what cannot now be done in Russia. And we know that from beyond the "Iron Curtain" many, many cries have reached us, not only expressing sympathy for the glorification of the New-Martyrs, but begging that the glorification be performed as quickly as possible.

Great, yea, vast is the assembly of the New-Martyrs of Russia. It is headed by the sacred name of His Holiness, Patriarch Tikhon, and the murdered Metropolitans Vladimir and Benjamin; moreover, Metropolitan Vladimir occupies a special place therein as the protomartyr, whose martyrdom constitutes the beginning of this glorious band. At the same time, quite a special place in the company of the New-Martyrs is occupied by the Imperial Family, headed by the Tsar-Martyr, Emperor Nicholas Alexandrovich, who once said, "If a sacrifice is necessary for the salvation of Russia, I will be that sacrifice."

Much is now being said of the glorification of the Imperial Family. Many, many of the faithful children of the Orthodox Church — and not only among the Russians — await the day of glorification with joy and impatience. But there are also audible voices of dissent, which speak against the glorification of the Imperial Family. And in the majority of cases these voices say that the murder of the Imperial Family was a purely political act, that it was not a martyrdom in the sense of dying for the Faith. Is this the case?

Turning to Russian history, we see a great number of examples of how the Church has glorified as saints of God many holy princes who were murdered; moreover, their murders were in no wise dependent upon any demand to renounce their faith in Christ the Savior. For example, from the life of the holy passion-bearers Princes Boris and Gleb, we know with what base and criminal considerations their murders were directed by Svyatopolk, who is rightly called "the accursed." But the question of their renunciation of the Faith did not enter into it in the least. Yet the Church glorified them first of all for their holy and righteous life which ended with the holy brothers' suffering and death.

If Sts. Boris and Gleb were thus glorified (as were many others), then it is all the more natural and correct to view in a positive light the question of the glorification of the Imperial Family. First of all, now, when the memory of the imperial victims has been cleansed of the filth and slander hurled at them in the years immediately following the Revolution, it has become known to the whole world that the family of the late Tsar-Martyr was a model, a most splendid example of a true, Christian family. In particular, this became clear when we learned how the Imperial Family lived in their grievous imprisonment before their repose, and also when letters written by members of that family from prison were published — a priceless treasure, which they have left behind for the edification of the Russian Orthodox people who honor their sacred memory.

But this is not the crux of the matter. One should not forget that the communist malefactors, in slaying the Imperial Family,

did so to annihilate the very memory of how Russia had lived for the many centuries of her existence. They have tried to smash, to put an end to, to destroy within the much-suffering Russian people that radiant spirit by which Holy Orthodox Russia lived — the spirit of the Orthodox state, and to implant in it the abominable spirit of God-hating and fratricidal communism. The criminal murder of the Imperial Family was not merely an act of malice and falsehood, not merely an act of political reprisal directed against enemies, but was precisely an act principally of the spiritual annihilation of Russian Orthodoxy, the aim of which was to instill an unnatural and evil communist spirit in the Russian people. The last Tsar was murdered with his family precisely because he was a crowned ruler, the upholder of the splendid concept of the Orthodox state; he was murdered simply because he was an Orthodox Tsar; he was murdered for his Orthodoxy!

Russian Orthodox people! Children of the Russian Church Abroad! We are preparing ourselves for a great triumph — a triumph not only of the Russian Orthodox Church, but of the whole Church Universal, for the entire Orthodox Church is one in all her parts and lives a single spiritual life. Let this triumph of the Orthodox Faith and the beauty of the feat of martyrdom be not only a Church wide triumph, but a personal triumph for each of us! We call upon all the children of the Church Abroad to ready themselves for it with earnest prayer, preparation, confession, and the communion of the holy Mysteries of Christ, that our whole Church, with one mouth and heart, may glorify Him from whom comes every good gift and every perfect gift — God Who is wondrous in His saints.

+Metropolitan Philaret

An official statement, based on Soviet sources themselves on the existence in the USSR of

The Catacomb Church Epistle to Orthodox Bishops and All Who Hold Dear the Fate of the Russian Church[45]

In recent days the Soviet Government in Moscow and various parts of the world celebrated a new anniversary of the October Revolution of 1917 which brought it to power. We, on the other hand, call to mind in these days the beginning of the way of the cross for the Russian Orthodox Church, upon which from that time, as it were, all the powers of hell have fallen. Meeting resistance on the part of Archpastors, Pastors, and Laymen strong in spirit, the communist power, in its fight with religion, began from the very first days the attempt to weaken the Church not only by killing those of her leaders who were strongest in spirit, but also by means of the artificial creation of schisms.

Thus arose the so-called "Living Church" and the renovation movement, which had the character of a Church tied to a Protestant-Communist reformation. Notwithstanding the support of the Government, this schism was crushed by the inner power of the Church. It was too clear to believers that the "Renovated Church" was uncanonical and altered Orthodoxy. For this reason people did not follow it. The second attempt, after the death of Patriarch Tikhon and the arrest of the locum tenens of the Patriarchal throne, Metropolitan Peter, had greater success. The Soviet power succeeded in 1927 in sundering in part the inner unity of the Church. By confinement in prison, torture, and special methods, it broke the will of the vicar of the Patriarchal locum tenens Metropolitan Sergy, and secured from him the proclamation declaration of the complete loyalty of the Church to the Soviet power, even to the point where the joys and successes of the Soviet Union were declared by the Metropolitan to be the joys and successes of the Church, and its failures to be her failures. What can be more blasphemous than such an idea, which was justly appraised by many at that time as an attempt to unite light with darkness, and Christ

---

45 Metropolitan Philaret of New York, "The Catacomb Church: The Epistle of Metropolitan Philaret," *Orthodox Word* 2, no. 2 (April-June 1966): 63-69.

with Belial! Both Patriarch Tikhon and Metropolitan Peter, as well as others who served as locum tenens of the Patriarchal throne, had earlier refused to sign a similar declaration, for which they were subjected to arrest, imprisonment, and banishment.

Protesting against this declaration — which was proclaimed by Metropolitan Sergy by himself alone, without the agreement of the suppressed majority of the episcopate of the Russian Church, violating thus the 34th Apostolic Rule [Canon] many Bishops who were then in the death camp at Solovki wrote to the Metropolitan, "any government can sometimes make decisions that act foolish, unjust, cruel, to which the Church is forced to submit, but which she cannot rejoice over or approve. One of the aims of the Soviet Government is the extirpation of religion, but the Church cannot acknowledge its successes in this direction as her own successes" (Open Letter from Solovki, Sept 27, 1927). The courageous majority of the sons of the Russian Church did not accept the declaration of Metropolitan Sergy, considering that a union of the Church with the godless Soviet State which had set itself the goal of annihilating Christianity in general, could not exist on principle.

But a schism nonetheless occurred. The minority, accepting the declaration, formed a central administration, the so-called "Moscow Patriarchate," which, while being supposedly officially recognized by the authorities, in actual fact received no legal rights whatever from them; for they continued, now without hindrance, a most cruel persecution of the Church. In the words of Joseph, Metropolitan of Petrograd, Metropolitan Sergy, having proclaimed the declaration, entered upon the path of "monstrous arbitrariness, flattery, and betrayal of the Church to the interests of atheism and the destruction of the Church."

The majority, renouncing the declaration, began an illegal ecclesiastical existence. Almost all the Bishops were tortured and killed in death camps, among them the locum tenens Metropolitan Peter, Metropolitan Cyril of Kazan, who was respected by all, and Metropolitan Joseph of Petrograd, who was shot to death at the end of 1938, as well as many other Bishops and thousands of Priest, Monks, Nuns, and courageous Laymen. Those Bishops and Clergy

who miraculously remained alive began to live illegally and to serve
Divine Services secretly, hiding themselves from the authorities
and originating in this fashion the Catacomb Church in the Soviet
Union.

Little news of this Church has come to the free world. The
Soviet press long kept silent about her wishing to give the impression that all believers in the USSR stood behind the Moscow
Patriarchate. They even attempted to deny entirely the existence of
the Catacomb Church. But then, after the death of Stalin and the
exposure of his activity, and especially after the fall of Khrushchev,
the Soviet press has begun to write more and more often on the
secret Church in the USSR, calling it the "sect" of True-Orthodox
Christians. It was apparently impossible to keep silent about it any
longer, its numbers are too great and it causes the authorities too
much alarm.

Unexpectedly in the "Atheist Dictionary" (State Political Literature Publishers, Moscow 1964), on pp. 123 and 124 the Catacomb
Church is openly discussed. "True-Orthodox Christians." we read
in the Dictionary "an Orthodox sect, originating in the years 1922-
24. It was organized in 1927, when Metropolitan Sergy proclaimed
the principle of loyalty to the Soviet Power." "Monarchist" (we
would say ecclesiastical) "elements, having united around Metropolitan Joseph (Perrovykh) of Leningrad" (Petrograd) Josephites or
as the same dictionary says, Tikhonites "formed in 1928 a guiding
center, the True-Orthodox Church, and united all groups and elements which came out against the Soviet order" (we may add from
ourselves, "atheist" order).

"The True-Orthodox Church directed into the villages a multitude of Monks and Nuns," for the most part of course Priests,
we add again from ourselves, who celebrated Divine Services and
rites secretly and "conducted propaganda against the leadership
of the Orthodox Church," i.e., against the Moscow Patriarchate
which had given in to the Soviet power, appealing to people not to
submit to Soviet laws which are directed, quite apparently, against
the Church of Christ and faith. By the testimony of the "Atheist
Dictionary," the True-Orthodox Christians organized and continue

to organize "house," i.e. secret catacomb churches and monasteries, preserving in full the doctrine and rites of Orthodoxy. They "do not acknowledge the authority of the Orthodox Patriarch," i.e. the successor of Metropolitan Sergy and Patriarch Alexy. "striving to fence off" the True-Orthodox Christians "from the influence of Soviet reality," chiefly of course from atheist propaganda, "their leaders make use of the myth of Antichrist, who has supposedly been ruling the world since 1917." The anti-Christian nature of the Soviet powers is undoubted for any sound-thinking person, and all the more for a Christian.

True-Orthodox Christians "usually refuse to participate in elections," which in the Soviet Union, a country deprived of freedom are simply a comedy, "and other public functions; they do not accept pensions, do not allow their children to go to school beyond the fourth class." Here is an unexpected Soviet testimony of the truth, to which nothing must be added. Honor and praise to the True-Orthodox Christians — heroes of the spirit and confessors, who have bowed before the terrible power which can stand only by terror and force and has become accustomed to abject flattery of its subjects. The Soviet rulers fall into a rage over the fact that there exist people who fear God more than men. They are powerless before the millions of True Orthodox Christians.

However, besides the True Orthodox Church in the Soviet Union and the Moscow Patriarchate, which have communion neither of prayer nor of any other kind with each other, there exists yet a third part of the Russian Church — free from oppression and persecution by the atheists — The Russian Orthodox Church Outside of Russia. She has never broken the spiritual and prayerful bonds with the Catacomb Church in the homeland. After the last war many members of this Church appeared abroad and entered into the Russian Church Outside Russia, and thus the bond between these two Churches was strengthened yet more — a bond which has been sustained illegally up to the present time. As time goes on, it becomes all the stronger and better established.

The part of the Russian Church that is abroad and free is called upon to speak in the free world in the name of the persecuted

Catacomb Church in the Soviet Union, she reveals to all the truly tragic condition of believers in the USSR, which the atheist power so carefully hushes up, with the aid of the Moscow Patriarchate she calls on those who have not lost shame and conscience to help the persecuted. This is why it is our sacred duty to watch over the existence of the Russian Orthodox Church Outside of Russia. The Lord, the searcher of hearts, having permitted His Church to be subjected to oppression, persecution, and deprivation of all rights in the godless Soviet State, has given us, Russian exiles, in the free world the talent of freedom, and He expects from us the increase of this talent and a skillful use of it. And we have not the right to hide it in the earth. Let no one dare to say to us that we should do this, let no one push us to a mortal sin.

For the fate of our Russian Church we, Russian Bishops, are responsible before God, and no one in the world can free us from this sacred obligation. No one can understand better than we what is happening in our homeland, of which no one can have any doubt. Many times foreigners, even Orthodox people and those vested with high ecclesiastical rank, have made gross errors in connection with the Russian Church and false conclusions concerning her present condition May God forgive them this, since they do not know what they are doing. This is why, whether it pleases anyone or not, the Russian Orthodox Church Outside of Russia will continue to exist and will raise her voice in the defense of the faith.

She will not be silent:

1. As long as the Soviet power shall conduct a merciless battle against the Church and believers, about which the whole Soviet press also testifies, except for the Journal of the Moscow Patriarchate.

2. As long as, by the testimony of the same press, there exists in the USSR a secret, Catacomb True Orthodox Church, by its very existence testifying to persecutions against the faith and to complete absence of freedom of religion.

3. As long as the Soviet power shall force the hierarchs of the Moscow Patriarchate manifestly to lie and affirm that there are no persecutions against the Church in the USSR and

that the Church there supposedly enjoys complete freedom in accordance with the Soviet Constitution (Metropolitan Pimen, Nicodem, John of New York, Archbishop Alexy, and others).

4. A long as the Journal of the Moscow Patriarchate at the demand of the authorities, does not mention even a single church that has been closed and destroyed, while at the same time Soviet newspapers speak of hundreds and thousands.

5. As long as Churches in the USSR shall be defiled by atheists, being converted into movie-houses, storehouses, museums, clubs, apartments, etc., of which fact there are living witnesses in the person of tourists who have been to the Soviet Union.

6. Until the thousands of destroyed and defiled Churches shall be restored as Churches of God.

7. Until the representatives of the Moscow Patriarchate in clerical robes shall cease agitating in the free world in the interest of the godless Soviet power, in this way dressing the wolf in sheep's clothing.

8. Until the hierarchs of the Moscow Patriarchate end their evil denial of the terrible and dreadful devastation of the Pochaev Lavra and other monasteries, and stop the almost complete liquidation of monks there and the terrible persecutions of her pilgrims, even to killing and murder (letters from USSR).

9. Until priests accused by Soviet courts shall receive the right to defend themselves through the Soviet press.

10. Until there shall cease calumny and ridicule of faith, the Church, priest monks, and believing Christians, in the Soviet press.

11. Until freedom is given to every believer in the USSR to openly confess his faith and defend it.

12. Until it should be officially permitted children and young people to know the foundations of their faith, and to visit the Churches of God, to participate in Divine Services, and receive communion of the Holy Mysteries.

13. Until it shall be permitted parents who are believers to baptize their children without hindrance and without sad consequences for their careers and personal happiness.

14. Until parents who raise their children religiously shall cease from being accused of crippling them, parents and children both being deprived of freedom for this and shut up in mental institutions or prisons.

15. Until freedom of thought, speech, action, and voting shall be given not only to every believer, but also to every citizen of the Soviet Union, first of all to writers and creative thinkers, against whom the godless power is now waging an especially bitter battle using intolerable means.

16. Until the Church and religious societies in general in the USSR shall receive the most elementary rights, if only the right to be a legal person before Soviet laws, the right to own property, to direct one's own affairs in actual fact, to designate and transfer rectors of parishes and priests, to open and dedicate new churches, to preach Christianity openly not only in churches, but outside them also, especially among young people, etc. In other words until the conditions of all religious societies shall cease from being, one and the same without rights.

Until all this shall come about, we shall not cease to accuse the godless persecutors of faith and those who evilly cooperate with them under the exterior of the supposed representatives of the Church. In this, the Russian Orthodox Church Outside of Russia has always seen one of her important tasks. Knowing this, the Soviet power through its agents wages with her a stubborn battle not hesitating to use any means: lies, bribes, gifts and intimidation. We, however, will not suspend our accusation.

Declaring before the face of the whole world, I appeal to all our brothers in Christ — Orthodox Bishops — and to all people who hold dear the face of the persecuted Russian Church as a part of the Universal Church of Christ, for understanding, support, and their holy prayers. As for our spiritual children, we call upon them to hold firmly to the truth of Orthodoxy, witnessing of her both by one's word and especially by a prayerful, devout Christian life.

First Statement on the American Metropolia (OCA)[46]

On Sunday evening, June 14th (27), in San Francisco Metropolitan Philaret who is now staying at his summer residence in Burlingame, Calif., delivered a brief but important address in which he for the first time publicly discussed the question of the American Metropolia and its relation to the Church Outside of Russia. The address was made at the conclusion of a solemn Akathist celebrated in the new Russian Orthodox Cathedral in San Francisco by visiting hierarchs and the entire clergy of San Francisco area to the visiting Kursk Root Icon of the Mother of God. The Metropolitan began his remarks by emphasizing the necessity of being true to the spiritual testament of the late Metropolitan Anastasy, faithfulness to the Russian Orthodox Church Outside of Russia. There can be no change in the Church of Christ, and every faithful child of the Church must uphold all her canons and traditions; it is impossible either to modify or abrogate any of them.

He had not previously spoken, said the Metropolitan, of a certain matter, but recent unwarranted attacks on our Church and her hierarchs now made it necessary to speak of it. (We may supply here the context which the Metropolitan did not need to supply his audience the hierarchs of the Church Outside of Russia have been accused of a lack of "charity" in refusing to take any official notice of the recent death of Metropolitan Leonty, head of the American Metropolia; in the view of these accusers, the difference between the two Churches is over no essential matter and is maintained only because of petty personal animosities.) The Metropolitan outlined briefly the history of the schism of the American Metropolia. The Church unity that prevailed from 1935 to 1946 was broken in the latter year when the Metropolia left the Mother Church, the

---

46 Metropolitan Philaret of New York, "First Statement of Metropolitan Philaret on the American Metropolia," *Orthodox Word* 1, no. 3 (May-June 1965): 117-118.

Church Outside of Russia, and appealed to and accepted the "Patriarch" of Moscow as her legitimate head. Later it is true, the Metropolia found it impossible to accept the conditions imposed by the "Patriarch" and she left the Patriarchal Church, without, however, returning to the Church Outside of Russia. The subsequently self-proclaimed "autocephality" of the Metropolia is uncanonical, being directly opposed to the universal Orthodox

practice governing the relation of a Mother Church to her daughter Churches. The Russian Church, for example, was for centuries in a state of dependence upon her Mother Church in Constantinople, even when she had become larger than the Mother Church. It is the duty of the Metropolia, if she desires to repair the schism, to petition to return to the Mother Church from which she cut herself off; only then can there be serious talk of reunion. The remarks of the Metropolitan offered a welcome clarity and preciseness to a subject that has been obscured in some circles by wishful thinking and simple ignorance.

LETTERS

An Open Letter to His Eminence Archbishop Iakovos (Koukouzis)[47]

Your Eminence:

Many practices of our Church are based on precedent, and indeed the higher the position of him who sets the precedent, the more important it is. Therefore, the ways that Orthodox Bishops act in their contacts with the representatives of heterodox confessions or religions are of special meaning, and in those cases in which they deviate from the order accepted over the centuries, they cannot leave us indifferent. Our silence might be construed as consent, bringing consequent confusion to our own flock as well as misunderstanding to the heterodox expecting our actions, especially in matters of public worship to be performed by all of us in conformance with our doctrines and canons. Therefore, an incorrect action made by one Bishop may be taken for something permitted by the whole Church, and those who are "without" may form a misconception in regard to Orthodox doctrine. In a time such as this, when so much mutual interest is shown by various confessions, we may be found offering them a stone instead of a loaf of bread.

For this reason, the latest actions of Your Eminence, invested as you are with the added authority of His All-Holiness Patriarch Athenagoras, have greatly perplexed not only us and our flock, but

47 Metropolitan Philaret of New York, "An Open Letter to His Eminence Archbishop Iakovos," *Orthodox Life*, no. 2 (March-April 1969): 21-24.

also many others. We have in mind your recent participation at St. Patrick's Cathedral in the "Week of Prayer for Christian Unity", and the "Ecumenical Doxology" in the Greek Cathedral of the Holy Trinity. The very fact that these services were publicized by the press as novelties with no precedent is indicative of their being introduced into the life of the Church as something extraordinary and not properly pertaining to her nature. Which canon, what tradition gave you the right to introduce such novelties?

Orthodoxy by its implicit nature is marked by its fidelity to the tradition and example of Holy Fathers. It is not without reason that St. Vincent of Lérins in his Commonitorium gave the criteria that what is truly Orthodox is that which is accepted by the Church, "always, by everyone, and everywhere." A novelty which does not conform with that rule bears an implicit stamp of un-Orthodoxy. Your Eminence must be aware of the 45th Apostolic Canon which reads, "Let a Bishop, Presbyter or Deacon who has only prayed with heretics be excommunicated, but if he has permitted them to perform any clerical office, let him be deposed". The renowned canonist Bishop Nikodim of Dalmatia, in his interpretation of this canon remarks that participation in such a prayer with heterodox "means that we not only do nothing for their conversion to Orthodoxy, but are wavering in it ourselves." In this case Your Eminence not only violated an ancient tradition of the Orthodox Church founded on canons (Apostolic 10 and 45, Laodic. 6, 32 and 33) but also in your actions and statements, conforming to those of Patriarch Athenagoras, you have expressed a teaching foreign to the Fathers of our Church.

In your sermon at St. Patrick's Cathedral, you said that Church Unity should be understood as a call "that through such ecumenical practices and experiences as praying and working together we arrive at the full knowledge of the truth that frees the faithful from the sin of false and ungodly apprehensions." The pathos in your sermon is not in proclaiming the truth of the Church, but in seeking something new, even a new definition "of our relationship with the Triune God." The Holy Fathers however always regarded common public prayer as the culmination of the conversion of erring persons to the true Church — the achievement of it; not the means to it. Common Church prayer is a manifestation of an already existing unity of faith and spirit. We cannot have such unity with those who teach otherwise than the Orthodox Church about the Holy Trinity (Filioque), Mother of God (immaculate conception by Catholics, lack of veneration by Protestants), the hierarchy (Papism by the Roman Catholics; denial of the Sacrament of Priesthood by the Protestants), etc. It is of further importance to note that the Roman Catholics and Protestants differ with us regarding the dogma of the Church.

Orthodox ecclesiology has always been based on the understanding that there is only One Holy, Catholic and Apostolic Church, and that schismatics, heretics, and persons of other religions are outside of Her. We, therefore, cannot accept the assertion of His Holiness Patriarch Athenagoras which was made in his Christmas Message of 1968 that, owing to a lack of love among brothers, "The Church which was established by Christ to be glorious, without spot or wrinkle (Ephesians 5:27), perfect and holy, was altered." If our Church was altered and is not the same that was established by our Savior, the One Holy, Catholic, and Apostolic Church against which Jesus Christ said, "the gates of hell shall not prevail" (Matthew 16:18) exists no more and instead there are several Churches, none of which is fully true and holy.

In a speech during his visit to Rome in 1967, His Holiness Patriarch Athenagoras publicly declared in the Basilica of St. Peter that the Church should "return to the solid ground on which the undivided Church was founded" as if since 1054 the Church has lost this foundation and as if before that time there existed no schisms. If, as Your Eminence and His Holiness declare, you are proceeding toward the restoration of this "Undivided Church," then this means that for you the Church is at present non-existent. We are also inescapably brought to the conclusion that Your Eminence and the Patriarch accept the "branch" theory. According to that theory, the Orthodox Church is as guilty of divisiveness as the heretics and schismatics who separated themselves from the Church, and all these separated communities remain "branches" of the Church from which they fell away. But if one can belong to the Church without sharing her doctrines, then doctrines are of only secondary importance. This concept is clearly seen in Patriarch Athenagoras's Christmas Message of 1968 when he speaks with praise of the movement of people to the common chalice "not knowing the difference in their dogmas, nor being concerned about them".

Such words could never have been said by the great predecessors of Patriarch Athenagoras: S.S. Proclos, Gregory the Theologian, John Chrysostom, St. Photios and others. Moreover, even if through the sinfulness of human nature heresy has sometimes been preached from the steps of the Ecumenical Throne under the guise of truth, there has never existed a precedent of a Patriarch who would regard dogmas as unimportant! How sad it is to read of such rejection of the teachings of our Fathers in a message of the Primate of the Church which was the Mother of our Church of Russia!

Honoring that Primate, Your Eminence organized an "Ecumenical Doxology" in your Cathedral, thereby joining him in indifference to the Truth in disregard of the aforementioned canons. Your joining there in prayer with Roman Catholics and Protestants was an actualization of the call of Patriarch Athenagoras to move toward union with no concern for doctrines heedless of the warning of the Apostle Paul against people who "would pervert the Gospel of Christ". Do you not fear the further warning of the Apostle, "But though we or an angel from heaven, preach any other gospel unto you than that ye have received, let him be accursed!" (Galatians 1:7-8). We, therefore, regard it our duty to protest strongly against the distortion of the dogma of the Church so insistently made by His Holiness Patriarch Athenagoras and Your Eminence. We protest against the "Ecumenical Doxology" and against the inclusion into the Diptychs by His All-Holiness Patriarch Athenagoras of the name of the Pope of Rome and of "all the confessions of the East and West", which was announced in His Holiness's Christmas Message. This inclusion into the Diptychs has been testimony that a certain person is recognized as Orthodox.

If the Fifth Ecumenical Council ordered the name of Theodore of Mopsuestia stricken from the Diptychs when his teaching was found un-Orthodox, then how can any Patriarch or Bishop now include in the Diptychs those who do not even nominally belong to the Orthodox Church, and who, on the contrary, continue to proclaim doctrines inconsistent with her dogmas? You are uniting with the heterodox not in truth but in indifference to it. We are not writing these lines simply in order to reproach or offend Your Eminence or His Holiness Patriarch Athenagoras, not in the least, especially as we have no reason for personal animosity toward you or His Holiness. On the contrary, we see our indicating to you and the Patriarch of the perils of Ecumenism which you have chosen as the duty of brotherly love.

Oh! If you would hearken to the calls of the Holy Fathers of the Church who did not build on compromises but on the firm adherence to the traditions and every iota of the divine dogmas instead of to the voices of interconfessional conferences and the press indifferent to religious truth. Their true love toward the heterodox consisted of their zeal to enlighten them with the light of truth and in caring for their genuine reunion with the Holy Church. We are writing this in an open letter since your statements were made public, and so that other Bishops and the faithful might know that not all the Church agrees with your pernicious ecumenical ventures. Let it be clear to everyone that your concelebration with the heterodox is a unique episode which may not serve as a precedent or an example for others, but which causes concern and resolute protest on the part of devoted members of the Church as an action which is clearly un-Orthodox and in violation of the Holy Canons.

I am, Your obedient servant,
+ Metropolitan Philaret
Day of Orthodoxy 1969

In Defense of Orthodoxy:
An Epistle to Met. Ireney[48]

EDITORS' NOTE [from *The Orthodox Word*]: In connection with the Third All-Diaspora Council of the Russian Church Outside of Russia, Epistles were sent to the "Paris" and "American" Russian jurisdictions in the hope of the eventual restoration of unity in a single Russian Orthodox Church Abroad. From "Paris" the response was cool, for, in the words of the reply of Bishop Alexander of this jurisdiction, "our understanding of the very foundations of church order, i.e., the Orthodox teaching of the Church (Ecclesiology) is different from yours." This jurisdiction strives first of all for "recognition" by other jurisdictions, and therefore it has no interest in union with a Church which is now largely "unrecognized" due to its outspoken epistles against the heresy of Ecumenism.

The Epistle to the American Metropolia however, met with greater favor, and Metropolitan Ireney replied with an appeal for the restoration of communion without any discussion of ecclesiological differences. The ecclesiastically illiterate Russian press thereupon filled the air with talk of "peace" and "love" and "joint celebration." Metropolitan Philaret finally placed an end to this talk with the following Epistle. It was received with utter shock and amazement, both by Metropolitan Ireney and much of the Russian press — so foreign has the word of truth become to the lovers of the world. Doubtless it was by the prayers of Blessed Xenia that such an eloquent end — which might seem "foolish" to the "wise" of this world — was put to a "dialogue" that had become pointless.

YOUR EMINENCE!

OUR CORRESPONDENCE in the newspapers has come to a dead end, and there is no point in continuing it. But I consider it necessary to reply to your latest letter. Appealing to my conscience, you quote an excerpt from your previous letter and ask where in it

---

do I see a "pointed polemical approach"? I do not see any — in this excerpt. But you did not quote your whole letter, Your Eminence. In it there are entirely other thoughts and expressions.

Stubbornly avoiding the chief question which divides us, you insistently call for communion in prayer. What can one say? The renewal of such communion would be a great joy. But one can begin with it only when there are disagreements of a personal character. In such a case the matter is clear and simple, let there be peace, and we shall celebrate and pray together. But when there are disagreements on principles, in accordance with the words of the Holy Church — "Let us love one another, that we may confess in oneness of mind" — then the attainment of such oneness of mind is required first. And only when it has been attained is the joy of this attainment crowned by joint prayer. Call to mind the historical conference of hierarchs — Metropolitan Eulogius, Metropolitan Theophilus, Metropolitan Anastassy, and Bishop Demetrius — which was called for the examination of the questions which concerned precisely the Church divisions, just as in the present case. Then the hierarchs who conferred did not begin, but ended, their conference with a joint celebration.

And in general, in the history of the Church there has been no joint celebration without oneness of mind. This latter is a purely ecumenistic attainment of our days. "Love," understood according to ecumenistic thinking, opens wide to everyone and everything its "loving embraces," and these embraces are ready to strangle to death true Orthodoxy, burying it in the bosom of un-Orthodox ways of thinking. It is not for nothing, after all, that the Apostle of love says that a man who incorrectly speaks of the truth should not be received into the house, nor even greeted. For he who greets him participates in his evil deeds.

The chief question separating us is the question of the Soviet hierarchy. The Russian Church Outside of Russia will recognize it as the lawful and actual leadership of the suffering Russian Church only when, with all decisiveness, it renounces the disgraceful and frightful Declaration of Metropolitan Sergius, comes away from its ruinous path, and enters the path of Church righteousness, openly and fearlessly defending it. The disgraceful stain must be washed away. And as long as this does not happen — it remains under the "omophorion" of the God-fighting regime, not daring to take a single step without its "blessing," especially in its activities abroad. This is clear even to a child!

Here I interrupt my letter in order to quote, word for word, what has been said on this question by Archbishop Andrew of Rockland, who for a long time performed his pastoral service in Soviet Russia and knows well all the nightmarishness of Soviet reality. Vladyka said the following, "I am reminded of an incident from the life of Blessed Xenia of Petersburg. She was especially popular among the merchant class. The merchants noticed that every visit by the Blessed one would bring them success in business.

"Once in a certain market place the merchants succeeded in obtaining from a wealthy estate a supply of several sorts of the best honey. There was honey from linden-blossoms, and from buck-wheat, and also from other flowers and plants. Each one had its own special taste and fragrance. And when the merchants mixed all three kinds of honey together in one barrel, such a flavor and such taste reproduced as to be beyond one's wildest dreams. People bought this honey immediately, not sparing any sum of money. And suddenly Blessed Xenia appeared. 'Don't take it, don't take it,' she cried; 'this honey can't be eaten, it stinks of a corpse.' 'You've gone out of your mind, Matushka! Don't bother us! You see what a profit we are making. And how can you prove that this honey shouldn't be eaten?' — 'Here's how I'll prove it!' screamed the Blessed one, leaned with all her might on the barrel and overturned it. While the honey was flowing on the sidewalk, people closely surrounded the barrel; but when all the honey had flowed out, everyone cried out in horror and revulsion; at the bottom of the barrel lay an immense dead rat. Even those who had bought this honey for a dear price and carried it away in jars, threw it out.

"Why did I recall this incident and quote it?" continued Vladyka Andrew. "I will answer willingly. A few days ago an American who is interested in Orthodoxy and has been in almost all the Orthodox Churches, both in the Soviet Union and here in America, asked

me why I and a whole group of Russian Orthodox people were
not participating in the reception of the Patriarchal delegation*[49]
and in general seem to shun everything bound up with Church
life in the Soviet Union, and even here, in America, avoid those
Orthodox groups which somehow or other are bound up with the
Patriarchate. What is the matter? Are not the dogmas the same, or
are the mysteries different, or is there a different Divine Service? I
thought, and replied 'No, that is not what it is. Both the faith and
the Divine Services are the same.

The Orthodox faith is fragrant like good honey. But if you pour
this honey into a barrel at the bottom of which there is a dead
rat, would you want to taste this honey?'— He looked at me in
horror. 'Well, of course not.' 'And so we likewise,' I replied to him,
'avoid everything bound up with Communism. Communism for us
is the same thing as the dead rat at the bottom of the barrel. And
if you would fill this barrel to the very top with the very best, most
aromatic honey… no, we would not want this honey. The honey in
itself is superb, but in it has fallen the poison and stench of a corpse.

"The American nodded his head in silence. He understood, and
you?" Striking and convincing! In concluding my letter I in my turn
ask Your Eminence in your conscience as a Bishop do you really
consider the servants, of the KGB, dressed in cassocks and cowls,
to be the true spiritual leaders and heads of the much suffering
Russian Church? Do you really not see that at the bottom of that
quasi-ecclesiastical Soviet organization, with which you have bound
yourselves,[50] there lies the dead rat of Communism? Or do you
prefer to close your eyes and stop your ears in order not to see and
not to hear and to fend off the unsightly reality? Of course, if this is

---

49 A delegation of clergymen, chiefly from the Moscow Patriarchate, sponsored by the National Council of Churches, which visited the United States in
February and March of this year [1975], making many "Ecumenical" contacts
and being officially received by Bishops of the American Metropolia (OCA).
(*Trans. Note*)

50 That is, the Moscow Patriarchate, to which the Metropolia bound itself
by accepting from it its fictitious "autocephaly," at the cost of proclaiming to the
world the "canonicity" and "Orthodoxy" of this organization. (*Trans. Note*)

so, then all further negotiations concerning union are superfluous, and there can be no talk whatever of joint celebration.

+ Metropolitan Philaret
February 27 / March 12, 1975

The Announcement of the Extraordinary Joint Conference of the Sacred Community of the Holy Mount Athos & An Epistle Response to Mount Athos[51]

The Extraordinary Joint Conference of the Sacred Community on Mount Athos, April 9/22, 1980, noting that the issue of the relations of our Holy Orthodox Church with the heterodox has assumed a serious and resolute character, especially as it relates to the dialogue with Roman Catholics, has resolved publicly to state the opinion of the Athonite Fathers on this subject for general consideration:

1. We believe that our Holy Orthodox Church is the One, Holy, Catholic and Apostolic Church of Christ, which possesses the fulness of grace and truth and, in consequence thereof, unbroken apostolic succession.

On the contrary, the "churches" and "confessions" of the west, having in many ways perverted the Faith of the Gospel, the Apostles and the Fathers, are deprived of sanctifying grace, of real mysteries and apostolic succession. That this is correct, His Eminence, Metropolitan Maximos of Stavropolis stresses, "Orthodoxy is not one of the churches, but the Church herself. She has preserved precisely and authentically the teaching of Christ in its pristine splendor and in all its purity. Over and above a simple, unbroken historical continuity and consistency there exists in her a spiritual

---

51 This section and the following:
Metropolitan Philaret & Bishop Gregory, "The Announcement of the Extraordinary Joint Conference of the Sacred Community of the Holy Mount Athos & An Epistle Response to Mount Athos," *Orthodox Life* 30, no. 3 (May-June 1980): 8-13.

and ontological authenticity. The same Faith, the same Spirit, the same Life. It is this which constitutes the distinguishing feature of Orthodoxy and which justifies her claim that she is and remains the Church" (*Episkepsis*, #227, March 15, 1980.)

2. Dialogue with the heterodox is not reprehensible from the Orthodox point of view if its goal is to inform them of the Orthodox Faith and, thus, make it possible for them thereby to return to Orthodoxy when they receive divine enlightenment and their eyes are opened.

3. Theological dialogue must not in any way be linked with prayer in common, or by joint participation in any liturgical or worship services whatsoever; or in other activities which might create the impression that our Orthodox Church accepts, on the one hand, Roman Catholics as part of the fulness of the Church, or, on the other hand, the Pope as the canonical Bishop of Rome. Activities such as these mislead both the fulness of the Orthodox people and the Roman Catholics themselves, fostering among them a mistaken notion as to what Orthodoxy thinks of their teaching. The Holy Mountain is grievously disturbed by the tendency of certain Orthodox hierarchs who have been invited to participate in Roman Catholic services, celebrations and processions, especially on the occasion of the return of holy relics. Conversely, we congratulate those hierarchs who have publicly expressed their alarm for the fulness of Orthodoxy.

4. We express our complete approval of what His All-Holiness, the Ecumenical Patriarch said during the visit of the Pope to Constantinople, namely that there exist various impediments between Orthodox and Roman Catholics, "first of all, we have serious theological problems which concern fundamental principles of the Christian faith" (*Episkepsis*, #221, Dec. 1, 1979, p. 17). These divergences in the principles of the Christian faith require that we do not advance to participation in common liturgies and worship services before oneness of faith is attained. The mystical character

of the kiss of peace during the divine Eucharist always presupposes harmony of faith, "Let us love one another that
with one mind we may confess." We cannot pray together,
especially during the Divine Liturgy, when we do not believe
in the same faith and are separated by fundamental questions of faith. Only an indifference to the faith could permit
us to do so.

Moreover, the Holy Mountain cannot accept the opinion,
expressed in the joint statement of the Patriarch and the Pope, concerning the "cleansing of the historical memory of our Churches"
and the partial opening, by means of a dialogue of love, of the road
towards "new movements in theological work and a new attitude
to the past which is common to both Churches" (*Episkepsis*, ibid.,
p.19). Actually, the heretics must cleanse their own historical memory of all their own historically acknowledged deviations in faith
and practice from the true, evangelical Orthodox Faith. On the
contrary, the historical memory of the Orthodox, which is based on
the inspiration of the Holy Spirit and on the constant experience
of the apostolic faith of the God-bearing Fathers, must be lived
by all of us in repentance and humility, and must instruct us both
in the present and in the future life if we do not wish to fall from
that faith. As Orthodox we must cleanse ourselves by means of the
historical memory of the Church, but not "cleanse" her with an
egotistical and anthropocentric spirit, setting ourselves up as judges
of the Tradition of the Church.

5. The Holy Mountain is convinced, not without great anxiety,
   that although the Orthodox are making many concessions
   and compromises to the Roman Catholics, the latter an-
   tithetically continue to adhere to their own errors which
   have served as the cause of their schism from the Orthodox
   Church and later led to the Protestant split. Thus, the Pope,
   during his visit to the center of Orthodoxy in the Patriarchal
   Cathedral, did not in the least hesitate to proclaim that he
   was coming to Constantinople as the successor of Peter,
   "who as the ultimate authority has the responsibility of

superintending the unity of all, to guarantee the agreement of the Church of God in fidelity and in the 'faith which was once delivered unto the saints' (Jude 3)" (Episkepsis, ibid., p. 9). In other words, the Pope defended (Papal) Infallibility and Primacy; and there are many other actions and manifestations which Pope has effected on behalf of Uniatism. We remember the establishment of diplomatic relations between the Greek Government and the Vatican which, even though it may justify Papism, is unjust and strikes out at the Mother and Nourisher of our [Greek] nation, the Orthodox Church.

6. The Holy Mountain also expresses its anxiety over the constituency of the commission for the dialogue. Uniates comprise a portion of the Roman Catholic delegation, a fact which is a provocation for the Orthodox. The sensibilities and dignity of the Orthodox delegation demand the immediate substitution of others in place of the Uniates in the membership. No Orthodox whose manner of thinking corresponds to this faith can agree to participate in a commission which includes Uniates. Likewise, the Holy Mountain is disturbed by the great weakness and insufficiency of the Orthodox delegation. The most remarkable Orthodox theologians are not participating. The Holy Mountain is also not represented, despite the fact that it is the sole monastic center which preserves the faith and the theology of the Fathers, and which is far removed from the influence of secularism and scholastic Western theology.

7. From the Orthodox point of view there is no justification for optimism in regard to the dialogue, and for this reason no haste should be exhibited concerning it. The Roman Catholics are pressing the dialogue, hoping to strengthen themselves by annexing Orthodoxy to themselves, for they are confronted by very powerful internal disturbances and crises, as is well known. The number of former Roman Catholics who have converted to Orthodoxy also disturbs them. But Orthodoxy has no reason to hasten towards

dialogue since the Papists remain so obdurate and immovable as regards Infallibility, Uniatism, and the rest of their pernicious teachings.

Hastening the dialogue under such conditions is equivalent to spiritual suicide for the Orthodox. Many facts give the impression that the Roman Catholics are preparing a union on the pattern of a Unia. Can it be that the Orthodox who are hastening to the dialogue are conscious of this?

The Holy Mountain maintains that for it there can be no question of accepting a *fait accompli*, that, by the Grace of God, it will remain faithful, as the Lord's Orthodox people, to the faith of the Holy Apostles and the Holy Fathers, impelled to this also by love for the heterodox, to whom real help is given only when the Orthodox show them the vastness of their spiritual sickness and the means of its cure by maintaining a consistently Orthodox position.

The unsuccessful attempts in the past with regard to union must teach us that steadfast unity in the truth of the Church, in accordance with the will of God, presupposes a different preparation and a path distinct from that taken in the past and from that which, apparently, is now being taken.

> All of the Superiors and Representatives of the
> Twenty Sacred and Pious Monasteries
> of the Holy Mountain of Athos
> at the Extraordinary Joint Conference

An Epistle Response by Metropolitan Philaret and Bishop Gregory to the Holy Mount Athos

To the pious monks of Athos, the Holy Mountain, the Sacred Synod of Bishops of the Russian Orthodox Church Outside of Russia wishes joy. May grace and peace be with all the inhabitants of the Holy Mountain of Athos who are faithful to Holy Orthodoxy. Your epistle on the subject of the dialogue with the Roman Catholics reached us only after a considerable lapse of time. We read it with such attention as befits the importance of that question for each Orthodox person. The Sacred Synod of Bishops has subsequently resolved to inform you of our decision. By the intercession of the All-Holy Theotokos, the fathers of Athos have throughout the ages overcome various misfortunes and temptations, ever standing guard over Holy Orthodoxy. These temptations are growing in the apostate world which surrounds us, in which the might of Antichrist reveals itself ever more manifestly.

They not infrequently lure from the path of truth individual Bishops and the entire hierarchies of certain Churches who forget that their true task is to preserve, protect and preach the faith of the Holy Apostles and Fathers of the Church. The first and second canons of the Seventh Ecumenical Council remind us of this in particular. According to the latter, a hierarch must have the fervor "to read with discernment not cursorily, the Holy Canons, the Holy Gospel, the book of the Divine Apostle and all the Divine Scriptures, to progress in accordance with the commandments of God, and to teach the people entrusted to them." From the writings and decrees of the Holy Hierarchs who were faithful to this command, the Tradition of the Church was formed, which, as the first canon of the Seventh Ecumenical Council expresses it, must serve for all Orthodox as a "testimony and direction." And we, having been driven from our homeland as a result of its enslavement by the enemies of God, see the principal aim of our life to be the preservation of that pure Orthodoxy which we have inherited from our forebears.

At the outset of our exile, we found consolation in the oneness of mind and the love of the other Orthodox Churches, since their leaders had not yet begun to push towards union with the heterodox, setting such a goal above the steadfast preservation of the faith of the Holy Fathers. In recent years, various actions and statements of representatives of the Orthodox Churches, of which you also write, have repeatedly caused us consternation and grief, inasmuch as we have found them to be more attempts to please the heretics than any desire to bear witness to the world of the genuine truth of Holy Orthodoxy. We see particular danger in the modernization and ecumenism foretold in the Apocalypse as the manifestation of indifference to the truth (Rev 3:15-16). The intrusion of modernism began with the acceptance of the new calendar, which was introduced not for the purpose of strengthening Orthodoxy, but in the name of rapprochement with the heretical West.

For this reason our Church has never accepted this calendar and has not participated in the so-called ecumenical movement. We maintain that its fundamental principle, which aims at the unification of all who call themselves Christians without oneness of mind in the dogmas of Orthodoxy, is contrary to the principles established by the Holy Fathers. We know and we understand that the Holy Fathers did not seek to conclude agreements with those in error, but rather called upon them to renounce their heresy, to confess the truth and unite with the Holy Church of Christ. For this reason we declared in the past to His All-Holiness, the Ecumenical Patriarch, that we will not accept any compromising agreements with the heterodox and that we do not recognize the Russian Church which is participating in these negotiations, for, apart from us, it does not have a free, legitimate hierarchy which can speak in its name. There is sufficient evidence that the Patriarch in Moscow and other hierarchs in Russia can neither be elected, nor govern freely, but are appointed and govern in accordance with the directives of the antichristian, atheistic regime. Its seal is set on their right hands, which sign resolutions pleasing to the godless regime.

Under such conditions it has been with great spiritual consolation that we have become acquainted with the statement made on behalf of the monks of the Holy Mountain on the subject of the recent conferences on the island of Rhodes between representatives of the Churches of the East and the Latins. It is in agreement with our faith, is close to our hearts and brings us joy. We give thanks to our Chief Shepherd who has inspired you to make such a statement which is Orthodox in content, and we beseech God, that He instruct you to oppose every manifestation of modernism and the spreading of the heresy of ecumenism, which contradicts the Fathers' dogma that there is but one true Church in the world. Of this, Canon 68 of the Council of Carthage writes that she is "the dove, the sole mother of Christians, wherein all eternal and life-creating mysteries are salvifically received, which, moreover, subject all that remain in heresy to great condemnation and torment."

We hope that all of you God-loving monks of the Holy Mountain will not forsake the struggle for the preservation of true Orthodoxy, just as we do not intend to forsake it, even were we to remain in the world as but half of the minority of which the Savior spoke, saying: "Fear not little flock, for it is your Father's good pleasure to give you the Kingdom" (Luke 12:32). May the All-Holy Mother of God cover us all with her precious omophorion and through her prayers may she strengthen you and us in the fearless confession of the Holy Orthodox Faith.

+ Metropolitan Filaret,
First-Hierarch of the Russian Orthodox Church Outside of Russia

+ Bishop Gregory,
Secretary of the Synod of Bishops

To Patriarch Athenagoras of Constantinople on the Lifting of Anathemas from 1054 against the Latin Papists (1965)
A Statement by the Head of the Free Russian Church on the Orthodox Relation to the Church of Rome[52]

AN APPEAL TO HIS HOLINESS ATHENAGORAS OF CONSTANTINOPLE, NEW ROME, AND ECUMENICAL PATRIARCH

Your Holiness:

From the Holy Fathers we have inherited the testament that in the Church of God all is done according to canonical order, in unity

---

52 Metropolitan Philaret of New York, "An Appeal to His Holiness Athenagoras of Constantinople, New Rome, and Ecumenical Patriarch," *Orthodox Word* 2, no. 1 (January-March 1966): 27-30.

of mind and in agreement with ancient traditions. If, however, any from among the Bishops or even from among the representatives of autocephalous Churches should do anything not in agreement with what the whole Church teaches, each member of the Church may declare his protest. The 15th Rule of the Double Council of Constantinople in 861 acknowledges as worthy of "the honor befitting an Orthodox Christian" those Bishops or clergy who withdraw from communion even with their Patriarch, if he should publicly preach heresy or teach such openly in the Church. Thus we are all guardians of the Church's truth, which has always been defended by concern that nothing possessing significance for the whole Church be done without the agreement of all.

For this reason our relation to various divisions which go beyond the bounds of separate local Churches has also been determined not otherwise than by the agreement of all these Churches. If our division with Rome was originally determined in Constantinople, subsequently it was accepted by the whole Orthodox Church and became an act of the whole Orthodox world. No one local Church separately — and in particular the Church of Constantinople, long respected by all of us, from whom our Russian Church received the treasure of Orthodoxy — can change anything in the matter without the prior agreement of all. Moreover, we the presently ruling Bishops, cannot execute decisions which would be in disagreement with the teaching of the Holy Fathers who have lived before us — in particular, insofar as the matters concerns the West, Sts. Photios of Constantinople and Mark of Ephesus.

In the light of these principals we, though we are the youngest of the representatives of the Church, yet as the head of the autonomous, free portion of the Russian Church, consider it our duty to declare a decisive protest against the act of Your Holiness concerning the solemn declaration, simultaneously with the Pope of Rome, of the removal of the excommunication proclaimed by Patriarch Michael Cerularius in 1054.

We heard many expressions of dismay when Your Holiness, before the whole world, did something novel, unknown to Your predecessors and contrary to the tenth Apostolic rule, by meeting the

Pope of Rome, Paul VI, in Jerusalem. We shall say frankly, without hesitation: the offense was great. We have heard that as a result of this many monasteries on the Holy Mountain of Athos ceased to mention the name of Your Holiness during Divine Services. Now, however, You go yet further when, by decree of Yourself and the Bishops only of Your Synod, You abrogate the decree of Patriarch Michael Cerularius, confirmed and accepted by the entire Orthodox East. Doing this, Your Holiness acts in disagreement with the relation toward Roman Catholicism that has been adopted by our whole Church. It is not a question of one or another valuation of the conduct of Cardinal Humbert; it is not a question of any personal falling out between Pope and Patriarch that could be easily healed by mutual Christian forgiveness; no — the essence of the question lies in those deviations from Orthodoxy which have become rooted in the Roman Church during the course of centuries, first of all the teaching of Papal Infallibility, definitively formulated at the First Vatican Council. The declaration of Your Holiness and the Pope justly acknowledges the act of "mutual pardon" as insufficient for the cessation of former as well as of more recent divergences. But more than that, this act places a sign of equality between error and truth. During the course of centuries the whole Orthodox Church has justly believed that she has departed in nothing from the teaching of the Holy Ecumenical Councils, while at the same time the Roman Church has accepted a series of novelties, discordant with Orthodoxy, in her dogmatic teaching. The more these novelties have been introduced, the deeper has the division become between East and West. The dogmatic deviations of the 11th century Rome did not yet contain such errors as were added later. Therefore the revocation of the mutual interdictions of 1054 might have had a significance in that epoch, but now it serves only as a witness of neglect for the most important and essential, namely, the new teachings, unknown to the ancient Church, that were proclaimed after that, of which several, being indicted by St. Mark of Ephesus as a reason why the Union of Florence was rejected by the Holy Church.

We declare decisively and categorically:

No union of any sort of the Roman Church with us is possible until she renounces her new dogmas, and it is not possible to re-establish communion in prayer with her without the decree of all Churches — which, however, is not regarded by us as possible until the Russian Church, now compelled to live in the catacombs, becomes free. The hierarchy now headed by Patriarch Alexei cannot express the authentic voice of the Russian Church, for it is completely subservient to the atheist authority, executing its will. The representatives of several other Churches in Communist countries are also not free.

Inasmuch as the Vatican is not only a religious center, but also a state, and one's relations to it — as the recent visit of the Pope to the United Nations clearly showed — have also a political significance, one cannot fail to reckon with the possible influence of the atheist powers upon the hierarchy of the captive Churches, on one side or the other, in the question of the Roman Church.

History testifies that negotiations with those of different belief under the condition of pressure from political circumstances, have never brought the Church anything but disturbance and divisions. Therefore we consider it necessary to declare that our Russian Church Abroad, as undoubtedly also the Russian Church now in the "catacombs," will not consent to any "dialogues" whatever with other confessions concerning dogmas, and she rejects beforehand every agreement with them in this connection, acknowledging the possibility of restoration of unity with them only if they accept in full Orthodox doctrine in that form in which it has been preserved until now by the Holy Catholic and Apostolic Church. As long as this condition is unfulfilled, the interdictions of Patriarch Michael Cerularius maintain all their force, and their removal by Your Holiness is an act uncanonical and invalid.

To be sure, we are not opposed to the well-wishing mutual relations with the representatives of other confessions, as long as Orthodox truth is not betrayed thereby. For this reason our Church at one time accepted the kind of invitation to send observers to the Second Vatican Council, just as she had sent observers to the

Protestant Conferences of the World Council of Churches, in order to have information from firsthand concerning the work of these meetings, without any participation in their decisions. We value a good relation to our observers and study with interest their detailed reports, which testify to the beginning of significant changes in the Roman Church. We shall thank God if these changes will serve the cause of her drawing near to Orthodoxy. However, if Rome must change much in order to return to "the confession of the Apostolic faith," the Orthodox Church, which has preserved this faith until now uncorrupted, has nothing to change.

Church tradition and the example of the Holy Fathers teach us that no dialogue is conducted with Churches that have fallen away from Orthodoxy. To them is always directed sooner the monologue of the Church's preaching, in which the Church calls them to return to her bosom through rejection of every teaching not in accord with her. A genuine dialogue supposes an exchange of opinions, admitting the possibility of the persuasion of the participants in it for the attainment of agreement. As is apparent from the encyclical Ecclesiam Suam, Pope Paul VI understands dialogue as a plan for our annexation to Rome, or for the restoration of communion with her with the aid of some kind of formula, which however leaves her doctrine totally unchanged, and in particular her dogmatic teaching on the position of the Pope in the Church. But any agreement with error is foreign to the whole history of the Orthodox Church and to her very being. It could lead, not to unanimous confession of the truth, but to a visionary external union similar to the agreement of the differently minded Protestant societies within the Ecumenical Movement.

May such a betrayal of Orthodoxy not penetrate to our midst! We fervently beg Your Holiness to place a limit to the offense, for the path which You have chosen, if it should further bring You into union with the Roman Catholics, would call forth a division in the Orthodox world; for undoubtedly many of Your own spiritual children also will prefer faithfulness to Orthodoxy above the ecumenical idea of a compromising union with non-Orthodox without their full agreement in the truth.

Begging Your holy prayers I remain Your Holiness' obedient servant,

+ Metropolitan Philaret
Chairman of the Synod of Bishops of the
Russian Orthodox Church Outside of Russia

Paschal Letter to Patriarch Athenagoras of Constantinople (1968)[53]

President of the Synod of Bishops of
the Russian Orthodox Church Outside of Russia
75 East 93rd Street, New York 28, N.Y.

May 21/June 3, 1968

HIS HOLINESS THE ALL HOLY ATHENAGORAS I
ARCHBISHOP OF CONSTANTINOPLE AND
OECUMENICAL PATRIARCH

YOUR HOLINESS:

On the joyous day of Easter, when our Holy Church celebrates the Holiday of Holidays and the Feasts of Feasts, all the Primates of the Holy Churches of God announce to their flocks the joy of the Resurrection of Christ. In accordance with this tradition, Your Holiness has done this also. The joy of the Resurrection, however, as announced by Your Holiness, is dimmed for the zealots of Orthodoxy by the other news which you announced to the Orthodox world as "an additional joy." You proclaimed your decision to proceed with the convening of a "Great Synod" for the purpose of "renewing the Church and establishing the unity of all Christian Churches."

Under certain conditions, this intention of the Oecumenical Throne to convene a Great Synod of the representatives of all the Orthodox Churches could actually be a happy event. But not every

---

53 Ivan N. Ostroumoff, *The History of the Council of Florence* (Boston: Holy Transfiguration Monastery, 1971), 201-207.

calling of a Council brings joy, and not every Great Synod, however well represented all the autocephalic churches are at its session, has been honoured by the recognition of the Church as expressing her authentic voice, true to the traditions of the Apostles and the Holy Fathers. To that end, every new Synod should be in full harmony with the former Occumenical Councils. It would seem that the representation of Churches at the Ephesian Council at which Dioscorus presided was full enough; however, it is known to history as the "Robber Synod."

The Grace of the Holy Spirit illuminates a Synod and makes its voice the voice of the Orthodox Catholic Church only when it is assembled to condemn, in accordance with Holy Tradition, innovative arbitrary doctrines, subservience to the mighty of this world, and the introduction into the Church of a widespread error. In the announcement of Your Holiness, however, it is not a call for the strengthening and propagation of Orthodoxy in the face of rising new errors that is heard, but on the contrary, the introducing of novelties which you call "the renewal of the Church." Your Holiness also very vaguely speaks of "the establishment of the unity of all Christian Churches," as if you are not aware that they all differ very much from the Orthodox Church, and, indeed from each other. Thus, you make the blending of truth with the error that is called "ecumenism" the aim of the future Synod. But the Holy Church teaches us that unity with heterodox is achieved only when they "have thought the true Church to be their own and there believed in Christ and received the mystery of the Trinity. And that all these Mysteries are altogether true and holy and divine is most certain, and in them the whole hope of the soul is placed, although the presumptuous audacity of heretics, taking to itself the name of truth, dares to administer them" (57/68 Canon of Carthage).

In 1965, we were already obliged to raise our voice against certain acts of Your Holiness which support the presently fashionable error of "ecumenism," which has become so widespread that to propagate it has become a craze — and thus a following of the "broad way of this world" against which we were warned by our Saviour (Matthew 7:13-14). In the present Easter message of Your Holiness, as well as in other statements of yours, we hear with distress that same voice, that voice which calls us not to tread the narrow path of salvation by witnessing to the only truth, but which calls us to follow the "broad way" of unity with those who foster various errors and heresies, and of whom the Apostle Peter said that by reason of them "the way of truth shall be evil spoken of" (2 Peter 2:1-2). This is not what has been taught to us by the Holy Church through the example of such Saints as Maximus the Confessor and Mark of Ephesus, who defended Orthodoxy against any compromise in regard to doctrine.

We are all witnessing at present to what tribulations, to what inner weakening, and to what growth of new errors the Roman Catholic Church has been brought by her recent Second Vatican Council, which had approximately the same goals as Your Holiness has for the future Great Synod. Instead of returning to Orthodoxy, the Roman Church sought "renovation" to accommodate itself to modern society, its temptations and ills, and has thus incorporated these diseases into its own life, which now verges more and more on spiritual anarchy. May the Lord preserve us from introducing such stumbling blocks into the life of the Orthodox people!

To us who are members of the Russian Orthodox Church, such confusion is all too well-remembered through the activities of the "Renovation Movement" or "Living Church." This appeared in Russia after the revolution and was sponsored by the atheistic Soviet government, which is hostile to all religions. Its purpose was to weaken the Church from within, adjusting Her to Communism and making Her serve its political and economic goals regardless of Orthodox doctrines and canons. Thank God, the consensus of the Russian faithful has finally rejected this temptation of unholy modernism. We should like to believe that the representatives of the Orthodox Churches, being aware of that unfortunate historical ex-perience of the Russian Church, and witnessing the present events within the Roman Church, will be on guard against following that same dangerous path. Therefore we will not further elaborate on the misgivings caused in that respect by the Easter message of Your

Holiness before we learn of the decisions of the Prosynod Conference called by Your Holiness.

We do, however, feel that it is our duty to warn Your Holiness and those who will be assembled under your presidency, even now, that however broad the constituency of the Great Synod you are calling will be, it cannot have world-wide Orthodox authority, because the authentically representative voice of the largest Church in number of faithful, the Russian Orthodox Church of martyrs, will not be heard there. There will be, of course, at the sessions of the Prosynod Committee and at the Great Synod itself, bishops bearing the titles of Russian dioceses, but they should not be recognised as having any right or authority to do this.

The history of the Christian Church knows no other example of such an inner enslavement of the Church by Her enemies as the one presented to the world by the Moscow Patriarchate. Not only does it resignedly endure the persecution of religion, which is comprehensible, but it has also put itself at the service of the lies of the atheists, praising the persecutors of the Faith as if they granted it freedom, the tormentors of the nation as its benefactors, and the instigators of world conflicts and unrest as peacemakers. Though the communists themselves have disclosed the innumerable crimes of Stalin as a murderer unsurpassed in the history of the world, the Moscow Patriarchate has praised him as an exemplary and virtuous leader elected by God.

While the whole world knows that the Moscow Patriarchate claimed to have 20,000 churches when it was seeking admission to the World Council of Churches, it is no secret to anyone that hardly a third of this number is still open. It is further known that while they were being closed by Soviet authorities, representatives of the Moscow Patriarchate made numerous statements claiming that news about the closing of churches was being invented by the enemies of the Soviets. The truth about the situation of the Church in the U.S.S.R. is now widely known as a result of various petitions received in the west, from the Open Letter of the two Moscow priests, and from other documents. Their authenticity is confirmed by the reaction of the bishops of the Moscow Patriarchate. From all these sources it is clear that the atheistic government, through compliant bishops, has created an artificial hierarchy which now is not only silent in the face of the crimes of the civil authorities, but even actively cooperates with them in their mission.

Recently, the letters of Archbishop Hermogen, formerly of Kaluga, have become known.[54] He openly states to Patriarch Alexis that the real reason for his dismissal from his see was no crime, no weakness in his administration, and no canonical offence, but the request of Kuroyedoff, Chairman of the Committee for Religious Affairs at the Council of Ministers of the U.S.S.R. The Archbishop explains the reason for such a request: "The first cause for complications was my refusal to the Delegate to help him in closing the church in the village of Lunacharsk near Tashkent." He states that after his transfer to another diocese, complications arose with the Delegate of the government because the latter wished to appoint some priests himself and to suspend others, requesting the Archbishop to sign these orders as if they came from him.

The enslavement of the Moscow hierarchy is especially evident in the following case, mentioned in the letter of Archbishop Hermogen to Patriarch Alexis of February 20th, 1968. He quotes the suggestion he received from a permanent member of the Synod, now deceased, Metropolitan Pitirim of Krutitzy: "In order to avoid any complications, act in the following way: When a priest or a member of a parish council visits you on some church matter, listen to him and then send him to the Delegate with the understanding that he will return to you from him. When he comes back and this is reported to you, telephone the Delegate and ask him what he told your visitor. And what the Delegate told him; you tell him also."

Thus the first-ranking bishop after the Patriarch was instructing a diocesan bishop how he must act as a mouthpiece to his clergy and faithful in the administration of the Church, transmitting as his own, the orders of an atheist enemy of the Church, a repre-

---

54 For the text of Archbishop Hermogen's letters see *Religion in Communist Dominated Areas*, Vol. VII, pp. 97-102. Compare also the long letter from the Kirov Diocese to the Attorney-General of the U.S.S.R., protesting the behaviour of the Patriarchal clergy, given in the same, Vol. VII, pp. 123-136.

sentative of the Communist power which has as one of its aims the complete destruction of religion. If Archbishop Hermogen has refused to put himself in the position of a blind executor of the orders of an enemy of the Church and was consequently deprived of his see, the Patriarch of Moscow and his collaborators have, on the contrary, long ago fully surrendered themselves to the orders of the communists, fulfilling their every wish and instruction. Perhaps initially they wished to serve God only. But subsequent persecution has forced them to serve Belial as well, thus acting contrary to the warning of the Holy Apostle Paul (2 Corinthians 6:14). It should, however, soon become evident to them that, according to the words of our Saviour, "no man can serve two masters; for either he will hate the one and love the other; or else he will hold to the one and despise the other" (Matthew 6:24). But the sons of the devil do not tolerate those who give preference to God and therefore the leading bishops of Moscow, for reasons of self-preservation, whether they wish it or not, have become obedient to them and not primarily to God.

For this reason, their voice in a Great Synod would not express the free opinion of the Church, but in many cases would express the thoughts of Her enemies, who are dominating them. Although for those who do not know its real situation, or do not wish to know it, the title of the Church of Russia would seem to stand behind that voice, we, being aware of the actual state of affairs, could not recognise as valid or binding in either a canonical or a moral sense any decision arrived at with the participation of bishops enslaved by atheists. We have the duty to inform Your Holiness of all the foregoing even now, and we remain, Your Holiness' humble servant.

+ Metropolitan Philaret

ROCOR ENCYCLICALS & SYNODAL EPISTLES UNDER METROPOLITAN PHILARET

Epistle of the Sobor of Bishops of the Russian Orthodox Church Abroad to the Faithful (1964)[55]

Christ is Risen!

With these, ever-joyful words do we greet you, our beloved flock. In the holy, after Easter days, when all of God's creation rejoices spiritually; when the Church's children, enlightened by the solemn feast of the Resurrection, embrace and forgive each other, and when in our earthly existence Our Saviour's wish receives fulfillment: as thou, Father art in me and I in thee, that they also may be in us, we, Bishops of the Russian Orthodox Church, free from the yoke of godlessness, obedient to the call of our Primate, the ever honored and beloved by us, Most Eminent Metropolitan Anastassy, gathered in Sobor (General Council) in New York City on May 4/17, 1964.

The main task of our Sobor (in accordance with the expressed desire of the Lord Metropolitan,) was the election of his successor.

---

55 Metropolitan Philaret of New York, "Epistle of the Sobor of Bishops of the Russian Orthodox Church Abroad to the Faithful," *Orthodox Life* 87, no. 3 (May-June 1964): 3-5.

Archbishop Nikon, Metropolitan Philaret, and Archbishop Averky

This election was carried out under his chairmanship with his blessings, and on our part — in full brotherly harmony and love. On Sunday, May 4/17, we Bishops jointly celebrated the Divine Liturgy at the Synod's Cathedral and all received the precious Body and Blood of Christ, so that all of us, as communicants from the One Chalice, be united by Our Lord in the Holy Spirit. By singing a Te Deum before the miracle-working icon of Our Lady of Kursk, we left the act of electing the Metropolitan to the will of Our Most Pure and Most Gracious Queen of heaven and earth. "Most Gra-

Metropolitan Philaret with Bishop Anthony of San Francisco
and Archbishop Sava of Sydney

cious Mother of God, save us and guide us!" — we invoked her with faith and hope. And we believe that we were heard.

Knowing that it is not mortals who decide the fate of Christ's Church but that it is the Almighty who leads her with a firm hand and divine strength; that human life is edified not on human devices but on the blood of martyrs, on selfless deeds and on prayer, we raised as from one mouth and one heart our burning prayers to those of God's great saints, whose memory was celebrated on the days of our sobor conferences.

On May 8/21 we invoked the aid of the great Apostle and Evangelist, St. John the Divine, that Apostle of Love and divine-ly-inspired foreseer of the entire fate of Christ's Church. On May 9/22 we prayed to the great Prelate and Miracle-Worker, St. Nich-olas, knowing how closely he took to his heart the establishment of good order in the Church at the First Ecumenical Council. On May 11/24 we glorified the great organisers of the Slavonic Churches, those co-equals of the Apostles and saintly brothers, Methodius and

Cyril. On May 12/25 we invoked assistance in our sobor labors of Russia's great and holy martyr, His Holiness Hermogen, Patriarch of Moscow and of all [Russia].

Finally, on the day of mid-Pentecost, having been strengthened by the prayers of these saints, we unanimously elected as Metropolitan and head of our Church, Philaret, the Bishop of Brisbane, Australia. At the same time the Sobor unanimously decided to elect His Eminence Metropolitan Anastassy honorary chairman for life of the Sobor and Synod of Bishops, with the title of "His Beatitude". We believe and profess that this is good to the Holy Spirit and to us. We summon you, our beloved flock, to view this election as the obvious will of God, manifested through us sinners. We beseech you to remain in complete obedience to the newly elected Metropolitan, so that in our brotherly unity of mind and love, the grace of the Lord Jesus Christ, and the love of God the Father, and the communion of the Holy Spirit, may remain with us all.

May 14/27, 1964, New York City.
Metropolitan ANASTASSY, Honorary Chairman of the Sobor of Bishops.
Metropolitan PHILARET, Chairman of the Sobor of Bishops.
JOHN, Archbishop of San Francisco and Western America.
ALEXANDER, Archbishop of Berlin and Germany.
ATHANASIUS, Archbishop of Buenos Aires and Argentina.
STEPHEN, Archbishop of Vienna and Austria.
PHILOPHEUS, Archbishop, Comptroller of the North-German Vicariate.
LEONTY, Archbishop of Santiago, Chile and Peru.
SERAPHIM, Archbishop of Chicago and Detroit.
NIKON, Archbishop of Washington and Florida.
VITALY, Archbishop of Montreal and Canada.
ANTHONY, Archbishop of Los Angeles and Texas.
AVERKY, Archbishop of Syracuse and Holy Trinity.
NIKODIM, Bishop of Richmond and England.
SERAPHIM, Bishop of Caracas and Venezuela.
ANTHONY, Bishop of Geneva and Western Europe.
ANTHONY, Bishop of Melbourne.
SAVVA, Bishop of Edmonton.
NEKTARIUS, Bishop of Seattle.

Archpastoral Encyclical of the Synod of Bishops of the Russian Orthodox Church Outside of Russia to the Orthodox Russian People in Diaspora[56]

The Russian People dispersed throughout the whole world by reason of the captivity of our sacred homeland by atheistic communism, were shocked by the announcement of the Russian American Metropolia, published on December 6th, 1969, in New York City, that the Metropolia has entered into spiritual relations with the Moscow Patriarchate and intends to receive autocephaly from it, i.e., existence as a new American Orthodox Church. In so doing, the Russian American Metropolia, which formally receives her independence, is in fact establishing spiritual and practical ties with the Moscow Patriarchate, which is held in slavery by the atheistic communist regime. These ties by the very nature of the case must be strengthened and developed in the future. By this means a fatal blow is dealt to the Russian emigration, the whole meaning of whose existence lies in the fact of its non-reconciliation with the Soviet regime.

We left the borders of our homeland in order to have the possibility, outside the influence and control of the communist regime, to pray freely to God and to rear the younger Russian generation in Orthodox piety. And now, after fifty years of the existence of our emigration, the spiritual meaning of our existence abroad is shaken. Over-ruling its own pastorate and the Russian emigration, the hierarchy of the Metropolia extends a hand to the Soviet Patriarchate of Moscow, which, in the person of its chief hierarchy, is a conscious tool of the God-hating government. The immorality of this act consists in the fact that the boundaries between good and evil, between black and white, are thereby erased.

From 1936, after the first troubles within the Church, and up until 1946, the Russian American Metropolia was a part of the Russian Church Outside of Russia as the North American

---

56 Metropolitan Philaret of New York, "Archpastoral Encyclical of the Synod of Bishops of the Russian Orthodox Church Outside of Russia to the Orthodox Russian People in Diaspora," *Orthodox Life*, no. 1 (January-February1970): 14-18.

Metropolitan District, and fruitfully and peacefully realised her ecclesiastical and missionary activity, not only in the spiritual service
of Russian exiles, but also successfully preaching Holy Orthodoxy
among native Americans. The re-union of all parts of the North
American Metropolia in the Russian Church Outside of Russia
was announced by the local Sobor of Bishops under the presidency
of Metropolitan Theophilus in Pittsburgh in 1936. This Sobor
wrote: "It is with great joy that we announce to you, beloved, that
at the Sobor of Bishops in Pittsburgh the 'Temporary Status of
the Russian Orthodox Church Outside of Russia,' worked out in
November of last year, 1935, by our hierarchs at the Conference
under the presidency of His Holiness Patriarch Varnava of Serbia,
with the retaining of the present autonomy, was accepted by all of
us unanimously."

In 1946, at the Cleveland Sobor, the Russian American
Metropolia recognised the Patriarch of Moscow as its spiritual head
and left the body of the Russian Church Outside of Russia, which
repudiated any such recognition. However, soon after this, in direct
opposition to her own recognition, the Metropolia refused to submit to the Moscow Patriarchate. For this reason she was put under
canonical ban by the latter; but the Metropolia shielded herself in
every way she could from the Moscow Patriarchate, even defending
herself from it in the civil courts. But at the present time, after secret
negotiations (which, as has only now come to light, have been under
way since 1963), the Russian American Metropolia has radically
altered her relationship with the Moscow Patriarchate, recognising
it once again as the Mother Church, and now accepting a blessing
from it for existence as a new autocephalous Orthodox Church.

The Synod of Bishops considers it its duty to make publicly
known the fact that spiritual and practical relations with the Moscow Patriarchate in its present situation are, to the conscience of
any Church endued with grace, out of the question for spiritual as
well as for political reasons. The Moscow Patriarchate's existence
within the communist state has as its basis the agreement published
on July 16/29, 1927, which was concluded in Moscow between
Metropolitan (afterwards Patriarch) Sergius in the name of the Su-

preme Church Authority organised by him, and the Soviet government. This agreement was published in the well-known declaration of Metropolitan Sergius of the same date. In this declaration, the Orthodox faithful are called upon to be loyal to the Soviet regime, to submit to it not only out of fear, but also in good conscience. It was further stated that the joys and successes of the Soviet Union ought to be considered our joys and successes, and its failures, our failures. In return for this declaration the Supreme Church Authority received "legal" existence in the Soviet Union, but in fact it became an obedient tool of the Soviet regime, being the latter's ecclesiastical organ.

The Russian Church Outside of Russia completely disavowed this agreement as being contradictory to Gospel truth, the sacred canons, and the history of the Church. Likewise this declaration was denounced in Russia itself by the better Bishops, a significant number of the clergy, and by many laymen, who paid for this denunciation with brutal persecutions from the Soviet regime, and in many cases with death. After this, Metropolitan Sergius invited all the Russian clergy abroad to give their signature of loyalty to the Soviet Regime — an invitation which was decisively rejected by the Russian Church Outside of Russia, in Europe as well as in America. Patriarch Tikhon had declared this regime itself to be anathema.

Our First-Hierarch at that time, the ever-memorable Metropolitan Anthony, who as Metropolitan of Kiev was also at the same time the senior hierarch of the whole Russian Orthodox Church, not only condemned this agreement but called the author of the declaration, Metropolitan Sergius (before the revolution his student and friend), an apostate from God, and in a personal letter to him summoned him to repentance, pointing out that the Church, to the end of Her days on earth, would not forget his betrayal, and that in the life to come it would lead him to "the bottomless pit of hell." Since the death of Metropolitan Sergius and the Soviet regime's installation of Patriarch Alexis in the Moscow Patriarchate, the activity of the Moscow Patriarchate has, up till now, kept to the same basis of being enslaved to the atheist regime, with the single qualification that at the present time the Moscow Patriarchate, while still denying before the free world the sufferings of the Russian people and the persecution of the Church at the hands of the atheist regime, and refusing honour to the New-Martyrs who have suffered for the same, also shows a zealous concern for the success of the world communist movement.

Thus the Moscow Patriarchate condemned the rebellion against the communist regime in Hungary — vilifies the self-sacrificing effort of America in the defence of Korea, South Vietnam, and of Asia in general from communism, has falsely accused America of the use of bacteriological warfare (infecting the population with fatal diseases) — approves the Soviet oppression of Czechoslovakia, — defends the communists in Greece — condemns the defensive measures of free countries against communism — conducts, according to the plans of the Soviet regime, Church conferences with propaganda filled resolutions in the interests of the communist movement — and thus with the name of Christ and with the robes of the Church covers up the blatant crimes of the communist regime, which is inexorably striving for world mastery and has already caught almost a third of all mankind in its toils.

That is why we, together with a significant part of the flock of the Russian American Metropolia, are deeply concerned by the fact that her hierarchs with their assistants have entered into negotiations and agreements with such agents of the atheist regime. The grace of God cannot rest upon such an agreement. It is understandable that false communist propaganda should deceive the representatives of other local — non-Russian — Orthodox Churches, but for us, the Russian emigration, it is unforgivable to succumb to such deception.

The spiritual nature of the Supreme Church Authority in Moscow after the declaration of Metropolitan Sergius was thus defined by Metropolitan Anthony in his Encyclical of July 22nd, 1928 —

The Synod of Moscow has deprived itself of all authority by entering into agreement with atheists, and by permitting, without struggle, the closing and destruction of holy Churches and the innumerable crimes of the Soviet government, which openly denies all religion and conse-

Eastern American Diocese – Восточно-Американская епархия eadiocese.org

quently wages persecution against it. It must be realised that the institution organised by and entering into union with the enemies of God — which Metropolitan Sergius calls an Orthodox Synod — and recognition of which has been refused by the better Russian Bishops and laymen, is illegal. It must not be recognised in any way by our Orthodox Churches, by our Synod of Bishops with its flock abroad; and the institutors of the Moscow Synod must be held to be the same kind of apostates from the Faith as the ancient "*libellatici*," that is, Christians who, although refusing to blaspheme Christ openly and to offer sacrifices to the idols, still accepted false documents from the priests of the idols stating that they were in full agreement, so to speak, with the followers of the heathen religion.

These documents spared them from the persecutions of the government, but subjected them to total excommunication from the Church, into which those of them who repented were received only after several (15) years. We may add that at present, the Bolsheviks, just like the ancient *libellenses* (registrars), are carrying out the registrations of the clergy of the Church, who are counted as "administrators of the cult." It is all too obvious that the Mother Church — i.e., the Moscow Patriarchate — with the help of the agents of communism which infest it, is striving to bequeath to its daughter Church both its spiritual and its political nature, with the single great difference that the threats of force and coercion do not hang over the Russian American Metropolia.

That is why our second Primate, the ever-memorable Metropolitan Anastassy now reposing in the Lord, as if foreseeing the present events, wisely stated in his last will and testament: "To my dear brethren, co-pastors and co-workers in Christ, I bequeath them to stand steadfast upon the rock of Holy and saving Orthodoxy, to reverently maintain apostolic tradition, abide in brotherly unity, peace, and love among themselves, and to render to the one God chooses after me to lead the ship of the Church Abroad, the same trust and equal obedience of mutual love, which they have always shown my humility. May the 34th Canon of the Apostles serve as the cornerstone for their mutual relations, where the spirit of rule by council in the Church is expressed so deeply and clearly. As regards the Moscow Patriarchate and its hierarchs, then, so long as they continue in close, active, and benevolent co-operation with the Soviet Government, which openly professes its complete godlessness and strives to implant atheism in the entire Russian nation, then the Church Abroad, maintaining Her purity, must not have any canonical, liturgical, or even simply external communion with them whatsoever, leaving each one of them at the same time to the final judgment of the Council (Sobor) of the future free Russian Church."

Although the Russian American Metropolia has now lived in schism from the Russian Church Outside of Russia for more than twenty years, the Synod of Bishops considers it its sacred duty to turn to her archpastors, pastors, and children with the loving brotherly plea decisively to repudiate the temptation coming upon them in the form of relations with the Moscow Patriarchate, and for all Russian people to work together in order that the hope of their eternal salvation might be preserved unimpaired, that the enslavement of the Russian people by the atheist communism might not be strengthened, that the international communist movement might not gain force. Instead, ways must be found for the restoration of the desired ecclesiastical unity and peace in the Russian emigration. Then Holy Orthodoxy will blossom in America, and the time of the liberation of the Russian people and the restoration of Holy Russia will draw near. But if this call of ours goes unheard, the Episcopate of the Russian Church Outside of Russia, in its full membership, will take such further ecclesiastical measures as the development of events shall require. The Grace of our Lord Jesus Christ, and the love of God the Father, and the communion of the Holy Spirit be with you all. Amen.

By the Chairman of the Synod of Bishops,
+ Metropolitan Philaret

Epistle of the Council of Bishops of the Russian Orthodox Church Abroad to the Russian People[57]

RUSSIAN ORTHODOX PEOPLE, our brethren and sisters, akin to us both in spirit and by blood, bound to us with indissoluble natural bonds! In the name of the Council of Bishops of the Russian Orthodox Church Abroad and in the name of all its flock we turn to you with the Apostle's salutation: "Grace and peace be multiplied unto you through the knowledge of God and of Jesus our Lord" (2 Peter 1:2). We kiss your wounds, we bow before your sufferings, before your podvigs of faith and endurance which you bear, submitting to the will of God and to that which He permits. Of the twenty centuries of her earthly existence, the Church of Christ has been subjected to persecution for half of that time, be it by pagans, heretics or evil atheists. Yet, at the most difficult times there arose from the bosom of the Church undaunted confessors of the truth who opposed the persecutors, and the Holy Church placed in their

---

57 Synod of Bishops of the Russian Orthodox Church Outside of Russia, "Epistle of the Council of Bishops of the Russian Orthodox Church Abroad to the Russian People," *Orthodox Life* 28, no. 6 (November-December 1978): 11-14.

mouths all her power, wisdom and grace. Embodying Christianity before the whole world, St. John Chrysostom, St. Philip, Metropolitan of Moscow, and many others censured crowned heads and tyrants, becoming the mouth of the Church and her heralds.

Our Russian Church was subjected to grievous persecution directly after the Revolution, when the first generation of Hierarchs, Priests, Monastics and Laity who remained faithful to the Church was annihilated in horrible underground torture chambers and in concentration camps, so that she fell almost completely silent. But behold, almost two decades after the tomb-like silence of the Church, fearless voices proclaiming the truth of the Church again resound — rarely from the lips of Bishops, but more often from those of Priests and Laymen. With reverence we bow down before this podvig of past and present generations of martyrs and confessors of the Russian Church, paying careful heed to their voices and striving to relate to a cold and indifferent world what they have said.

Alas! This world is foreign both to your suffering and to our own efforts to open its eyes to the true condition of believers in the land of militant atheism. They are controlled, to a significant degree, by the same evil, godless powers. Thus, the so-called Free World more willingly believes the falsehood which the enemies of Christianity in our homeland trumpet about. They wish neither to understand us nor to listen, for they fear that the truth is bitter, painful and unpleasant. For this reason we find no support among the powers of this world, which on the one hand is sad, but on the other hand gives us complete freedom in confessing the truth. Left to ourselves, we value the freedom to which we have been called, as the Apostle has said (Galatians 5:13).

Yet even in our blessed state, which is in no way bound up with anyone or anything, there are peculiar disadvantages. There are persons, or groups of people, who enjoy the support of the powers of this world, who can send you their literature to a much greater extent than we, and thus share their thoughts with you and foist their ideas upon you. And we are disturbed that the ideas and thoughts that you receive from the West are far from being all Orthodox and Churchly. These are frequently those same spiritually harmful, fashionable teachings which hold sway in human minds even amongst us, serving as a stumbling-block for these little ones, and drawing them away from the pure and unsullied truth of the Church of Christ. In the past, the Russian Church survived all these temptations, in the form of "reformism," "renovationism" and the so-called Living Church. Through the podvig of His Holiness Patriarch Tikhon and a multitude of Archpastors, Pastors and Laymen, she overcame the temptations of renovationism, and the stumbling-block of reformism. It would be an unpardonable error and sin to give way to them again.

One must keep in mind that the Church is a theanthropic organism, whose Head is the Lord Jesus Christ and whose life is directed by the Holy Spirit. Thus, the Church is in no need of human reforms, be they in the realm of her dogmatic teaching, in the amending of apostolic traditions, or in the alteration of canon laws and liturgical practices hallowed by centuries of use. Those who wish to reform the Church do not understand that they themselves must turn as quickly as possible to the grace-bearing life of the Church which, as the Apostle says, is the pillar and ground of truth. Those who wish to renovate the Church, alas, do not desire their own personal renovation within her, according to the image of the new man who has put off the old man with his passions and lusts. It is not for us to bring the Church to perfection, but we ourselves who must be perfected within her through the grace of the Holy Spirit.

Why, in various periods of history, have many so insistently striven for ecclesiastical reforms? Were those who strove for them loyal and obedient sons of the Church? We know from history that following the era of terrible persecutions, when all the might of the Roman Empire had not been able to crush the Church, the ancient enemy of God and man attempted to seize the Church internally, by means of the temptations of heresies and schisms. And even now he is working in the same manner, with the sole difference that in the early centuries of Christianity heresies arose around the dogma of the essence of the Holy Trinity and the Person of Christ the Savior, whereas now they distort the Doctrine of the Church.

In the modern world there are many of these wrong, non-eccle-
siastical, often anti-ecclesiastical, spiritually detrimental ideas which
tempt souls and lead them to destruction. One of these is the capit-
ulation of the Church's leaders to the godless, yielding their position
to them, i.e., the readiness to carry out their will. The Church in our
homeland has lost that support of an Orthodox dominion which it
formerly enjoyed; and behold, the false idea has arisen which asserts
that one may seek such support from the godless authorities, despite
the fact that that authority has determined as its goal the annihilation of religion. Another anti-ecclesiastical idea of our times is
the concept of the unprincipled unification of all religious groups,
in spite of differences in belief, and including not only Christian,
but non-Christian groups as well. This idea is born of the fear that
the Church cannot survive in the modern world and that therefore
all religious groups, including the Orthodox Church, should unite,
even though this would mean sacrificing the divine dogmas of our
most Holy Faith and our canons.

To proponents of this idea it seems that all power lies in unity.
Those who think in this manner forget that the power of the Church
lies not in governmental support, nor in the unprincipled unity of
truth with delusion, but in the power of God and in God's guidance
of those that have a pure heart and maintain their faithfulness to
the truth, rich in humility and submission to the will of God. What
is impossible for man is possible for God, our Savior said. And further: "Take heed that no man deceive you. For many shall come in
My name and shall deceive many" (Matthew 24:4,5). And Christ's
Apostle admonishes us to be obedient to "that form of doctrine
which was delivered to [us]" (Romans 6:17).

Nearly one thousand years ago, the Holy Prince Vladimir baptized us and gave us the joy of being Orthodox. The Church has
bestowed upon us a great heritage, giving us a lofty ideal of sanctity,
a beacon of culture, a national consciousness and a Christian life.
And let us in our desire to remain loyal to the Church and her truth
until the end, tearfully repeat from the depths of our hearts the
prayer of repentance of the three youths who were cast to certain
death in the Babylonian furnace. We believe that this prayer, which

Archbishop Antony of Geneva (Bartoshevich) with Metropolitan Philaret

corresponds so closely to our present situation will also save us, who are in the blazing furnace of temptations and persecutions, as it saved the young men. Here are the words of that marvelous prayer:

"Blessed art Thou, O Lord, the God of our fathers, and praised and glorified is Thy name unto the ages for in truth and judgment hast Thou brought all these things upon us for our sins. For we have sinned and transgressed in departing from Thee and Thy commandments have we not heard, nor have we given heed, nor done as Thou hast enjoined us, that it might go well with us. For, O Sovereign Master, we are become the least of all the nations, and are humbled this day in all the earth because of our sins. And there is not at this time any prince, nor prophet, nor leader, nor whole-burnt offering, nor sacrifice, nor oblation, nor incense, nor place to bring first-fruits before Thee and to find mercy. But in a contrite soul and in a spirit of humility may we be accepted."

And now we have the same Lord and His same inexhaustible, almighty power awaiting our conversion, repentance and prayer. In view of the approaching millennial jubilee of the anniversary of the

Baptism of Russia, our Council of Bishops has decided to glorify the vast multitude of Russian New-Martyrs, numbering them in the choir of God's favored ones. This glorification is to take place at the next session of the Council, in approximately three years' time.

May God assist us! All saints of the Russian land and ye holy Russian New-Martyrs, pray to God for us!

SIGNATURES:

Metropolitan PHILARET, Presiding Bishop of the Council
Archbishop SERAPHIM of Chicago and Detroit
Archbishop ATHANASIOS of Buenos Aires and Argentina-Paraguay
Archbishop PHILOTHEOS of Berlin and Germany
Archbishop VITALY of Montreal and Canada
Archbishop ANTHONY of Los Angeles and Southern California
Archbishop ANTHONY of Geneva and Western Europe
Archbishop ANTHONY of San Francisco and Western America
Archbishop SERAPHIM of Caracas and Venezuela
Archbishop THEODOSY of Sydney and Australia-New Zealand
Bishop NATHANAEL of Vienna and Austria
Bishop LAURUS of Syracuse and Holy Trinity
Bishop NIKANDR of Sao Paolo and Brazil
Bishop NEKTARY of Seattle
Bishop PAUL of Stuttgart and Southern Germany
Bishop ALYPY of Cleveland
Bishop CONSTANTINE of Boston
New York, Sept. 1978

Epistle to the Flock of the Russian Church Abroad, Beloved of God[58]

REJOICE IN THE LORD ALWAYS (Philippians 4:4). With these words of the Holy Apostle Paul we turn to you and greet you, our flock in diaspora, entrusted to our care by the Chief Shepherd,

---

58 Synod of Bishops of the Russian Orthodox Church Outside of Russia, "Epistle to the Flock of the Russian Church Abroad, Beloved of God," *Orthodox Life* 28, no. 6 (November-December 1978): 19-22.

the Lord Jesus Christ Himself. Rejoice, for the Lord has chosen you to be children of the Holy Orthodox Church, has made you partakers of the grace of the Holy Spirit, has illumined you with the light of truth. To live and walk in His light is a great honor and a great joy. Therein lies the fulfilment of the promises made by God to His people. You are the people of God, and joy must be your heritage for the "love of God is shed abroad in our hearts" (Romans 5:5).

We know that to be Orthodox in our times, so full of trials and hitherto unprecedented temptations, to belong to the Russian Orthodox Church Abroad, is a great podvig, and requires the utmost exertion of the powers of the soul. Our Church follows the path of faithfulness to God, which is so contrary to the modern world; and on this account the world subjects her to various oppressions and assaults. Our membership in the free Church Abroad is not only a gift of God, but is also a great responsibility which places us under moral obligation. All who belong to the persecuted "True Orthodox" or "Catacomb" Church look to our Church as the repository and receptacle of true piety and the pure Orthodox Faith. For the sake of our own salvation and of our persecuted, suffering brethren, we must not betray their trust, but vindicate it. Let us pray at home, assiduously attending the Divine Services; and having frequent recourse to the Mysteries of Confession and Communion, let us be diligent in keeping the Church's fasts and in reading books spiritual in content which are now so easily obtained. All of this is a living source for the acquisition of spiritual strength, without which it is impossible to bear the exalted appellation of Orthodox Christian.

As of old God notified Nineveh of its impending destruction through the Prophet Jonas, so now He warns us through "rumors of wars, famines, and pestilences, and earthquakes" of the tremendous shocks which will threaten the whole world if we do not set ourselves aright. But the Lord promises to cut short the days of suffering "for the elects' sake." And as God's command concerning Nineveh was withdrawn because of the repentance of the inhabitants of that land, so even now, in our own hands lies the future of today's life of vacillating peace. The Lord began His preaching with a call to repentance, continued it with a sermon on repentance, "I came not

Fr. Rostislav Gan, Metropolitan Philaret, Bishop Anthony (Medvedev) of
Melbourne and San Francisco in Sydney Australia.

to call the righteous, but sinners to repentance," and finally warned
that "Except ye repent, ye shall all likewise perish" (Luke 13:3).

Our Savior has called us to be children of the True Church;
He calls us to be participants in His Kingdom, and awaits our
good deeds, that we may become heirs of eternal life. Yet, at the
same time, we see how representatives of certain local Orthodox
Churches are turning aside from this path of salvation and are seeking out paths new and foreign to our Church. We stand apart from
their activity. And our Church has been ostracized by them, either
because our faithfulness to Christ denounces them, or to please the
Soviet authorities.

In our difficult times, we believe that the Lord, in the ways of
His Providence, has found a special Church Body — our Russian
Church Abroad — to be a necessity, i.e. a Church not connected
with the territory of the Soviet Union and its rulers, the militant
atheists. In other words, only the Church Abroad can be free in our
evil times. Our Church exists in a fully canonical manner in the
Orthodox diaspora, is guided by a canonical hierarchy, and has no
other Master, save the Head of the Church, our Lord Jesus Christ.

Here we have two tasks, preserving True Orthodoxy and bearing witness before the whole world concerning the truly bestial face of atheistic communism and perhaps, to warn all the nations for one last time to avoid being deceived by this terrible evil.

Our situation in the diaspora has drawn to the Church many heterodox who have sought the truth of Orthodoxy and have become faithful children of the Church. And now they are going forth to preach Orthodoxy, principally in the name of our Church, together with the sons and grandsons of former Russian, Serbian, Romanian and other political refugees. This generation of Orthodox citizens of many countries bears witness to True Orthodoxy before the world. Thus, by God's mercy, the Russian Orthodox Church Abroad has outgrown its name and has come to occupy a special, unusual place in the conscience of all Orthodox Christians. Despite our weakness, we have been vouchsafed so great an honor; on this account they may but love us or despise us. Without separating ourselves from the Mother Russian Church, our Church is truly the free, multinational, multilingual Church of the diaspora.

Our Church fully confesses her unity with the tormented and persecuted Church in our homeland, with her martyrs and confessors. Indeed, each martyr represents the victory of the whole Church over the powers of evil; each courageous confessor of the Faith is the joy of the whole Church. In her entirety, she lives by its victory which has conquered the world — our Faith. Our persecuted brethren in our much suffering homeland tell us: You are on the right path; stand firm and steadfast thereon. Yes, all true children of the Church know us and trust that with God's help we will preserve Holy Orthodoxy in all its purity.

While our fatherland has been deprived of the most basic of freedoms, we here abroad can openly confess our Faith and witness to the truth. But even here we have an enemy. It is not militant atheism or any organized evil, but overabundance and prosperity in freedom. How many of us, imperceptively, but in actuality, has this insidious enemy torn away and continues to tear away from God! Let us not forget the words told us from "over there", that true freedom is only in God; that there is no freedom in man if he has slain the knowledge of God and buried the very memory of Him. The possession of freedom and prosperity places a great responsibility on man. One must know how to use them correctly. And this is possible only when we use them for the implementation of the teaching of the Gospel.

Thus, we call you to faithfulness and steadfastness in Holy Orthodoxy. Be not troubled that more and more often we see ourselves as though abandoned by all. Our path is the path of faithfulness to Christ. Therefore, we prefer to be with the Church which is persecuted and torn apart, not only by enemies from without, but by enemies within as well. It is our desire to glorify the new, undaunted martyrs, to confess our own spiritual unity with them, and to kiss their bloody wounds with love. We pray for the courageous confessors, striving to stretch forth a helping hand to them. Is this not why we are persecuted and not recognized by individual official representatives of the Churches? If so, we are happy to share even one hundred thousandth of the struggles of the persecuted.

We want to be with the new confessors, with the hundreds of thousands incarcerated in camps and prisons, with those lamps hid beneath the bushel, of which the world is not worthy. "Ye are the light of the world," Christ says to them. By the reflection of this light do we also wish to live, despite our being completely unworthy, which we sorrowfully acknowledge. O Holy New-Martyrs and all Saints of the Russian Church, pray to God for us!

Metropolitan **PHILARET**, Presiding Bishop of the Council
Archbishop **SERAPHIM** of Chicago and Detroit
Archbishop **ATHANASIOS** of Buenos Aires and Argentina-Paraguay
Archbishop **PHILOTHEOS** of Berlin and Germany
Archbishop **VITALY** of Montreal and Canada
Archbishop **ANTHONY** of Los Angeles and Southern California
Archbishop **ANTHONY** of Geneva and Western Europe
Archbishop **ANTHONY** of San Francisco and Western America
Archbishop **SERAPHIM** of Caracas and Venezuela
Archbishop **THEODOSY** of Sydney and Australia-New Zealand
Bishop **NATHANAEL** of Vienna and Austria

Bishop LAURUS of Syracuse and Holy Trinity
Bishop NIKANDR of Sao Paolo and Brazil
Bishop NEKTARY of Seattle
Bishop PAUL of Stuttgart and Southern Germany
Bishop ALYPY of Cleveland
Bishop CONSTANTINE of Boston

New York, September 1978

Encyclical Letter of the Council of Bishops of the Russian Orthodox Church Outside Russia (1983)[59]

May God's grace and peace be with and increase among all the clergy and faithful of our Russian Orthodox Church Outside Russia. In the name of the Council of Bishops we address all our pious flock scattered all over the world. We greet our beloved children and bless them for their further labors in Christian Orthodox living in a world departing ever more and more from all the principles which our Lord Jesus Christ, His Apostles, and the Holy Fathers commanded us to observe. In our unfortunate homeland, formerly called Holy Russia, there has been established a worldwide center of all-encompassing evil which hopes at the present time to eradicate all traces of former sanctity and piety. For all these decades we have observed the sufferings of our brothers with sorrow, and we have noetically kissed their wounds and glorified as Holy Martyrs all those millions of faithful who, led by Patriarch Tikhon and the Tsar-Martyr Nicholas II, have testified to their faithfulness to God even unto death.

The Seer prophetically saw them standing "before the Throne and before the Lamb in white robes" (Apocalypse 7:9). He was told about them, "These are they who came out of great tribulation, and have washed their robes, and made them white in the Blood of the Lamb. Therefore are they before the throne of God, and serve Him

---

59 Synod of the Russian Orthodox Church Outside of Russia, "Encyclical Letter of the Council of Bishops of the Russian Orthodox Church Outside Russia," *Orthodox Life* 33, no. 6 (November-December 1983): 11-19.

day and night in His temple: and He Who sits on the throne shall dwell among them" (Apocalypse 7:14). Having assembled together in this Council to consider questions of our Church life, we have felt our spiritual unity with them and with those of our brethren who are following their path, being still "in great tribulation."

Dwelling in freedom, we only spiritually experience with them this "great tribulation," but we have our own tribulation which is united with theirs and is called forth by the unbelief and apostasy from the true faith even of many who bear the name of Orthodox Christians, and which is spreading more and more in the world. In the world which surrounds us we often feel that the words of the Saviour, "in the world you shall have tribulation" (John 16:33), are coming true for us. If the Apostle Paul saw that while living in this world it was impossible not to have contact "with the fornicators of this world, or with the covetous, or extortioners, or with idolators" (1 Corinthians 5:10), then what can we say about our times? Now we are not only obliged to have contact with them, but, more than that, the way of life surrounding us is built on recognition not just of the permissibility, but of the legality of the lowest and crudest forms of sin.

We are especially concerned for our children, our youth, who are growing up in this environment. It is very difficult for them to grow up as "sons of God," when they are surrounded by a way of life founded on unbelief and a denial of all the basic principles of the Christian faith and of the family. We have therefore indicated to our pastors that they should devote special attention to instructing their flocks in family living. For children to be able to grow up as sons of God's Kingdom, the parents' educational efforts must begin from the time their children are still in the mother's womb. Even unbelieving doctors now recognize that this period is very significant for the child's future development.

Parents should nourish their children from their earliest years with good and holy impressions, themselves providing an example of prayer and virtue, so that sin and immorality will be something foreign to them and will not attract them, but, on the contrary, will repel them. They should remember that their children, when they reach adulthood, will bring them joy and comfort only to the measure of that good which was instilled in their hearts by their family. For this reason pastors should constantly instruct both parents and children, and in conjunction with that be concerned with the establishment of church schools and the attraction of young parishioners from childhood on to active participation in church life.

It is good to attract to oneself young souls, if they are not poisoned by evil exemplified as something permissible and even positive. Let pastors and parents see to it that their children see and know examples of good in the saints and in the efforts of great men. It is especially necessary persistently to teach them to love truth and to turn away from all kinds of falsehood. Falsehood has now acquired special strength, having deeply penetrated into people's consciousness. Alas, those who disseminate it are not just political activists, who consider everything permissible to obtain power, but also representatives of various religions. A clear manifestation of this was the Sixth Assembly of the World Council of Churches, which met in Vancouver at almost the same time as the sessions of our Council.

In its decision of 28 July/10 August our Council explained that the Russian Orthodox Church Outside Russia does not participate in the World Council of Churches since the latter attempts to represent those assembled in it, representatives of confessions differing in their opinions, as though they had some sort of unity in their faith. In reality, though, this position is a lie, inasmuch as they, members of various confessions and sects, have not given up their points of disagreement with each other, much less with the Orthodox Church, in dogmas and in fundamental attitudes. In the name of unifying formulas these differences of opinion are not removed, but are just set aside. Instead of the unshakable truths of the faith, they try to see only opinions, not obligatory for anyone. In reply to the confession of the one Orthodox Faith they say together with Pilate: "What is truth?" And the nominally Orthodox members of the Ecumenical Movement more and more deserve the reproach to the Angel of the Church of Laodicea, "I know your works...you are neither hot nor cold. O if only you were hot or cold! (Apocalypse 3:15).

A clear manifestation of such false union was the serving of the so-called Lima liturgy, i.e. a supposed eucharistic service, performed by the Archbishop of Canterbury and various Protestant pastors. This liturgy, composed at a conference in Lima, is supposed to return its participants to the beginnings of the ancient Orthodox liturgy, but without the chief thing, unconditional faith in the transformation of the bread and wine into the Body and Blood of our Lord Jesus Christ and the necessity of its being performed only by a celebrant having the apostolic succession.

In describing this liturgy, the magazine Newsweek for August 22nd, 1983, wrote: "Facing the altar was a multi-racial congregation of 3,500 Christians from every corner of the earth, including Roman Catholic Priests and bearded Orthodox Bishops, who not long ago would have shunned such a service." According to a report of the Ecumenical Press Service on August 4th, during the Archbishop of Canterbury's celebration of the Lima liturgy, the Orthodox and the Catholics did not receive communion, but did participate in common prayer. Archbishop Kirill (of the Moscow Patriarchate) pronounced a prayer that "we might soon attain visible unity in the Body of Christ by blessing the bread and cup on this same altar."

The Greek Archbishop Iakovos served a separate liturgy on the day of the Transfiguration (N.S.) at which, according to reports we have received, Communion was given out without sufficient discrimination not only to the Orthodox, but also to others who approached the chalice. Thus we see with grief that the process of the increase in practice of the heresy of Ecumenism among Orthodox Christians, of which we warned our brethren in our Sorrowful Epistles, has not stopped, but is even growing. The development of an interdenominational understanding of Baptism, the Eucharist, and the Priesthood in recent years has been manifested in various so-called ecumenical services and was especially clearly expressed in the Lima Accord and now in Vancouver. Our Council has decisively condemned this manifestation and has ordered that an anathema of the heresy of Ecumenism be added to the Rite of Orthodoxy.

In addition, any sort of participation by Orthodox in prayer with non-Orthodox, and in particular participation in common prayer

Synod in New York City picturing Bishop Constantine (Essensky) on the day of consecration for Brisbane, with Metropolitan Philaret

at the so-called ecumenical Lima liturgy, is strictly forbidden for Orthodox according to the 45th and 46th canons of the Holy Apostles, and subjects them to excommunication from the Church. The 32nd and 33rd canons of the Council of Laodicea particularly forbid the reception of bread and wine blessed by non-Orthodox clerics and joint prayer with them. The famous Russian canonist, Bishop John of Smolensk, writes in his commentary on the 46th canon of the Holy Apostles, "In general the Apostolic Canons indicate one basis for rejecting heretical religious rites the fact that in a heresy there cannot be true priesthood, but only pseudo-priesthood. This is so because with the separation of the heterodox from the Church, the apostolic succession of their holy orders ceases, for one thing, and along with this the succession of the gifts of grace from the Holy Spirit in the mystery of orders is also cut off; and consequently the ministers of a heresy, as ones not having grace in themselves, cannot convey it to others, and as they have not received a lawful right to perform the mysteries, so they cannot make true and salvific the rites performed by them."

In all the activities of the Vancouver Assembly a lively part was played by a very large delegation of the Moscow Patriarchate, which extensively uses the World Council of Churches for Soviet propaganda. The latter directs its efforts toward spreading lies about a supposed freedom of the Church in the USSR and, under the guise of defending peace, to hindering the arming of those countries which might be able to prevent the spread of Communism in the West. Moscow church delegates speak out on a large scale in defense of pro-Communist movements, but in no way permit anyone to accuse the Soviets of persecuting religion. Thus, as a consequence of the opposition of the Moscow delegation, the petition from Deacon Vladimir Rusak, who has written a book about the difficult position of the persecuted Church in the USSR, was not allowed to be read to the Assembly. For his book he was dismissed from Church service and called to account by the KGB. In vain did he hope to call the attention of the Assembly to the persecution of the Church in his homeland. While speaking long and loud about the defense of the interests of various leftist political groups, these Assemblies from year to year have remained deaf to the cries of the real and most numerous victims of atheism.

There is no doubt that this occurs in large measure as a result of the fact that they do not want to hear any voice from Russia but that of the Moscow Patriarchate, which, however, says only what it is told to say by the enemies of all religion through the organs of the KGB. A special resolution of the Council of Bishops was also issued on this subject, referring to a scandalous incident the directions of the Moscow Synod to serve panikhidas for the atheist and persecutor of the Church, Brezhnev, who died last year, and whose actions Patriarch Pimen blasphemously called "pleasing to God." In the prescription for serving panikhidas for him it was indicated that he should not be called "servant of God," which he most certainly was not.

However, everyone must have felt uncomfortable in offering any sort of prayers for the repose in the Kingdom of Heaven of a person who denied the very existence of that Kingdom. Thus, violation of Church canons to please the atheists unavoidably leads to hypocrisy. This Council observed that whatever Brezhnev might be called, panikhidas for him contain an internal contradiction, hypocrisy, and falsehood. They are an unforgivable blasphemy. It would seem that the whole world, especially the Orthodox world, should have trembled with indignation in view of such blasphemy, but, alas, everyone is silent, while an unconditional statement of protest has come only from our Council.

In view of such indifference to the truth and of increasing modernism, a significant number of Orthodox pastors and faithful have turned to our hierarchs in order to preserve genuine Orthodoxy and the course of Church life, sanctified by age-old tradition, in accordance with the Orthodox calendar established by the First Ecumenical Council. Thus our Church has been enriched by new children and continues to be enriched not only by Greeks devoted to the faith, but also by parishes torn away from the Russian Church in recent decades into the unlawful American autocephaly and now returning to its bosom. For many of them this decision was not easily made and has been associated with great sacrifices. We rejoice in their love for the truth and how we wish that all the children of our Church would conduct their religious life with as much zeal as these new ones who quite recently have come to know the truth and have attached themselves to it.

While those of different nationality and previous culture who have joined our Church may sometimes pose one pastoral problem or another, we view this calmly, remembering that before the face of God there is neither Greek nor Jew, Russian, American, or any other sort of distinction according to origin. All are felt to be our beloved children who have a common goal: to preserve unharmed the faith of the Holy Fathers and to save their souls, whatever might be the external conditions surrounding us. We live in the same world, and for all of us there are the same dangers and temptations from the apostasy that has engulfed the whole world, i.e. turning away from God and the Church, about which the Apostle Paul warned the faithful in his Second Epistle to the Thessalonians.

Many now note signs of the approaching end of the world. Some scientists already are viewing this as a likely possibility for the worn-out and so-to-say "aging" world, guessing when it might happen. Others are studying the prophecies of the Sacred Scriptures and, applying them to the course of current political life, foresee the imminent occurrence of worldwide crises and of the last days. However, the times and seasons are not yet revealed to us. The Lord only warned us about certain manifestations in the world which would precede its end, telling us, "Take heed that no man deceive you. For many shall come in My name, saying, I am Christ; and shall deceive many" (Matthew 24:4-5).

Now to various obvious false messiahs there are added reports of the birth and preparation of a more serious claimant to the position of Universal King and False Messiah. We still cannot affirm anything positively except that the signs have appeared according to which one can anticipate the appearance of the "Son of Perdition" in a period of history that is very near or even in the next few years, after the unification of the whole world under one world government. But it is not without cause that in the ways of His Providence the Lord does not reveal them fully to us. For us it is enough to know that we have already entered a period of history when the relatively imminent appearance of the Antichrist is very probable. And this means that we must be spiritually prepared for it.

What does such readiness mean? It means working to strengthen one's spiritual powers so as to develop the capability of resisting the Antichrist's temptations. Many of these temptations — in the sense of a [weakening] of faith, divinization of mankind, betrayal of faith in the one, true Church for the sake of a humanistic religious unity in a pseudo-church — are already before us, preparing even Orthodox Christians for a readiness to follow the ways of the Antichrist. But what can we do besides just observing the signs of the times? We must develop in ourselves, in our flocks, in all Orthodox families a firm faith in the fact that the Lord has given us the good fortune to belong to the one, true Church, which, as at the very beginning of its existence, is not defined by being a minority of the believers on earth, but which, although a minority, is made up only of people who are faithful and devoted to this true Church. This is not an easy task, and it demands firm faith, spiritual strength, and devotion to the truth in the midst of a surrounding world which is alien to Christ.

In the face of the temptations which already exist and confront us, we must direct all our spiritual and mental powers to being ready for any trials. We are helped in this preparation by the expectation of the imminent (in five years) celebration of the thousandth anniversary of the Baptism of Russia. By renewing in our minds and hearts those principles of piety which Prince St. Vladimir planted in Russia, we will try to restore them in our daily lives, with the hope that the Lord will permit us to take them back to our homeland so that we can be reunited with that portion of Holy Russia which, despite all deceit and persecution, has continued to exist there in however small a number.

The Lord has granted us so far to live in freedom, in no way externally constrained and in no way restricted in our spiritual life, except by our lack of faith and our laziness. To avoid being contaminated by the swamp of sin and vice which surrounds us, we must spiritually rouse ourselves. In an inspired and ardent report to the Council on the necessity of a spiritual rebirth, the Most Reverend Archbishop Vitaly wrote: "Our whole flock is already in communion with the grace of the Holy Spirit through all the Mysteries; we need only stir that fire into flame by all the means available for pastoral work, and do everything we possibly can to be, in the words of the Apostle Paul, all things to all men, so that some might be saved. As concrete measures we must persuade the faithful to abandon the old practice of communing of the Holy Mysteries only once a year, if any are still holding to that less-than-praiseworthy custom. We must convince all our pastors themselves to pray before performing the Mystery of Holy Confession that the Lord might grant them the gift of love, wisdom, compassion, and mercy. We must show all our flock the necessity of praying, too, before coming to confession that the Lord would grant them the gift of the Holy Spirit, true repentance, the gift of emotion and contrition for their sins, the gift of tears which wash our souls with the water of a second Baptism, which is what confession should be, and not a passing recitation of one's sins."

Along with this, we ask all our spiritual children to refrain from being easily attracted into the sin of judging each other, and especially their pastors. The latter action is often provoked by the many enemies of our Church, who long ago chose the center of our Church Administration — the Synod of Bishops selected by the whole Council of Bishops — as the object of their especially bitter attacks. In doing this they do not quibble at any sort of falsehood and slander, hoping thereby to undermine the authority and importance of our center which they hate. Do not believe false rumors, remembering that they are often circulated, sometimes even under the appearance of a defense of the truth, by enemies of the Orthodox Church, behind whom stand Soviet agents and secret supporters of the Moscow Patriarchate.

In encouraging us and reminding us of His love and care for us, the Lord has recently sent us a miraculous manifestation: the myrrh-streaming Iveron Icon of the Mother of God, before which we also prayed during the Council, observing the miraculous manifestation of an abundant flow of fragrant myrrh from it. Thus the All-Pure Theotokos again manifests her care for us, which we have seen in the course of all these years through our marvelous Odigitria as well — her wonder-working Kursk Root Icon. We recognize that the world stands before an historically unprecedented danger of unbelievable upheavals and misfortunes, and shall draw strength and encouragement for ourselves from this marvelous manifestation and, along with this, prepare ourselves by means of the penitent labor of piety for the joys or trials which it may please God to send us.

Above all, though, let us labor not to let ourselves be swallowed by the evil which is growing in the world around us. The question now is ever more frequently and sharply posed before each person. To whom does he wish to belong, to Christ or to the devil? According to which principles will he live Christian or anti-Christian? We ask you, our spiritual children, without wavering or fearing anything, to give within yourselves an Orthodox answer to these questions and to choose the bright way of a virtuous life: and having chosen it, bravely to follow it, so that we might all freely attain the Kingdom of God. May God's grace and the prayers and examples of the valiant Russian New-Martyrs help us all in this!

Chairman of the Council of Bishops
+ Metropolitan Philaret

MEMBERS OF THE COUNCIL:

Seraphim, Archbishop of Chicago-Detroit and Middle America
Athanasius, Archbishop of Buenos-Aires and Argentina-Paraguay
Vitaly, Archbishop of Montreal and Canada
Anthony, Archbishop of Los Angeles and Southern California
Anthony, Archbishop of Geneva and Western Europe
Anthony, Archbishop of San Francisco and Western America
Seraphim, Archbishop of Caracas and Venezuela
Paul, Archbishop of Sydney and Australia-New Zealand
Laurus, Archbishop of Syracuse and Holy Trinity Monastery
Constantine, Bishop of Richmond and Britain
Gregory, Bishop of Washington and Florida
Mark, Bishop of Berlin and Germany
Alypy, Bishop of Cleveland

An Encyclical Letter of the Chairman of the Council of Bishops of the Russian Orthodox Church Outside Russia[60]

Our beloved spiritual children:

In recent days we have addressed to you the words of the Council of Bishops on general matters in the life of our Church. However, the same Council directed us in addition to write you instructions on how we ought to "struggle for the faith delivered to the saints from the Lord" in our present life. For if in the days of the apostles' preaching there already was an abundance of those who, in the words of the Apostle Jude, "are godless men, who change the grace of our God into a license for immorality and deny Jesus Christ our only Sovereign and Lord" (Jude 4), then now this evil is many times more prevalent, and it is becoming harder and harder for us to struggle against it.

---

60 Metropolitan Philaret of New York, "An Encyclical Letter of the Chairman of the Council of Bishops of the Russian Orthodox Church Outside Russia," *Orthodox Life* 33, no. 6 (November-December 1983): 19-24.

When we look at the society which surrounds us in the world, we could often repeat the words the Apostle Paul wrote about the pagans. In speaking of the unnatural vices of men and women (prevalent among and approved of by the unbelieving in our days), the Apostle explained that "since they did not think it worthwhile to retain the knowledge of God, He gave them over to a depraved mind, to do what ought not to be done. They have become filled with every kind of wickedness, evil, greed, and depravity. They are full of envy, murder, strife, deceit, and malice. They are gossips, slanderers, God-haters, insolent, arrogant, and boastful; they invent ways of doing evil; they disobey their parents; they are senseless, faithless, heartless, ruthless" (Romans 1:28-31). In various forms and to various degrees we see an abundant manifestation of these sins around us. As the Apostle Paul further observed, when people fall into them, they often know what God's judgment should be on those who perform such acts of unrighteousness. "However," he writes, "they not only continue to do these very things, but also approve of those who do them" (Romans 1:32).

It does not surprise us when in the anti-Christian kingdom of Soviet lies, the whole structure of life is directed towards punishing faith and virtue and encouraging evil. But is there any justification for us when in free conditions we prefer evil and vice, rather than good and sanctity? In many cases when we ask why certain Orthodox Christians live according to the customs of sin, rather than according to the law of God, we receive the answer that everyone lives that way now. However, being Christians, we should not consider ourselves in this world like "everyone," but like the "Chosen People" to whom the Apostle Peter wrote that they are "a people belonging to God, that [they] may declare the praises of Him Who called [them] out of darkness into His wonderful light" (1 Peter 2:9). Are we permitted to measure our responsibility before God with the same measure as the unbelieving and those who have no hope of Heaven?

Look at what is happening around us among people who have no concern for faith, who live not according to God's law, but according to the laws of sin, in opposition to the natural order established by the Creator. Look at the countless rapes of women and even of children, at child prostitution, at murders of parents by children, and of children by parents, at murders of many people on the spur of the moment without any sort of sense or point, at mass suicides, at indifference to depravity, and at the demonstrations of thousands shamelessly proclaiming the manifestation of unnatural vices to be lawful. With horror we read of the insanity of people who have enslaved themselves to drugs to a greater extent than when only drunkenness was widespread. What could be more horrible than the case which has now happened of the birth of infant narcotics addicts, poisoned by narcotics or alcohol while still in their mothers' wombs'?

According to the laws of existence, people do not immediately become totally subject to sins, nor vice versa, to virtue and sanctity. In the one case and in the other, their development is gradual along the path of good or evil they have chosen. Each one chooses his path according to his own free will, but the conditions of one's training from childhood on are very significant for the correct choice of this path from one's early years. And the choice of path which is correct is that which leads us to God's Kingdom, taking us away from the gloomy realm of the tortures of hell, which is chosen by those who act lawlessly. Each of us knows how joyful and comforting it is for us to come into contact with people who are living according to God's law of love. On this law the world created by God is built, and it alone is the pledge of unity.

Sin came into the world and immediately introduced divisions when the first people violated the law of love for God. While they had up until then felt themselves to be one being, after their fall into sin they immediately felt themselves divided. "Then the eyes of both of them were opened, and they realized they were naked; so they sewed fig leaves together and made coverings for themselves" (Genesis 3:7). They were alienated from God (Genesis 3:10). Adam began explaining his sin as the woman's fault (Genesis 3:12). Up until then they had been even more innocent than a newborn baby is now. After sinning, Adam ceased to be the master of everything created on earth and remained such only in his own family. Now it is often forgotten that the woman was created as a helper for Adam, like unto him (Genesis 2:20). Only after she first gave herself over to the devil's temptation and led Adam into it, was God's judgment pronounced on her, "I will greatly increase thy pains in childbearing with pain wilt thou give birth to children. Thy desire will be for thy husband, and he will rule over thee" (Genesis 3:16).

Thus the supremacy of Adam and of all his male descendants is not the result of arbitrariness, but is the law of the hierarchical structure of human nature, about which spouses are reminded by the Epistle reading during the marriage ceremony, "Wives, submit to your husbands as to the Lord. For the husband is the head of the wife as Christ is the head of the Church, his Body, of which He is the Saviour. Now as the Church submits to Christ, so also wives should submit to their husbands in everything" (Ephesians 5:22-24). However, this is not just man's predominance over woman in the sense of rights, for Christian relations between husband and wife are not defined by their rights, but by their different kinds of service in the Church and family, and by their boundless love for each other. Therefore, the Apostle further commands that men should love their wives "as their own bodies. He that loveth his wife loveth himself. For no man ever yet hated his own flesh; but nourisheth and cherisheth it, even as the Lord the Church" (Ephesians 5:28-29).

The female nature is chiefly endowed with tenderness and the capacity for compassion, as a consequence of which female Christian nurses are so precious. This quality is especially important in the raising of children by the mother in the early childhood years. To instill in children faith in God, love, respect for their father, and the other Christian virtues is the most important aspect of the service of an Orthodox wife and mother. Orthodox marriage, thus, resembles the Church, i.e. an organism in which, under the headship of Christ, the members are united, but have different functions. We are all united in the Church, the Body of Christ, but Bishops, clergymen of various levels, laymen, and monastics serve God in different ways. In the same way the husband, wife, and children occupy different positions in the family, the Church of the home, as the Apostle Paul called it (Romans 16:5).

It has a very destructive effect on the whole of society when such an understanding of each person's position and service in hierarchical dependence on each other, based on love of God and each other, is replaced by the idea of rights and the struggle for these rights. Many misfortunes and disorders are produced by the fact that the principle of struggling for rights (instead of a consciousness of obligations taken upon oneself and of responsibility) is now being introduced into all levels of society and even into families. Misunderstandings in the family, which often lead to divorce when they are intensified, very often begin right here. Psychological separation, which develops in such soil, is capable of growing and intensifying until, beginning with intimate relations between the spouses, it destroys love and shatters the family.

A. S. Khomiakov, the great Russian theologian, defines the relations of Orthodox spouses in this way, "in the person of the first human couple, 'husband and wife,' holy and perfect laws were given for the earthly life of mankind. The image of that same earthly life of all mankind, of that holy and perfect law, is also renewed by each Christian couple in the Sacrament of Marriage. For the husband, his companion is not just one of many women, but the woman; her mate is not one of many men, but the man; for both of them, the rest of the human race has no sex. Bound by the noble bonds of spiritual brotherhood with all creatures like themselves, the Christian husband and wife, the Adam and Eve of all ages, alone receive a blessing to taste of the joys of that most intimate cohabitation because of the physical and moral law placed at the basis of the earthly life of the human race. And so," Khomiakov concludes, "marriage is not a contract, not an obligation, and not legal slavery; it is a reproduction of the image established by divine law; it is the organic, and consequently, mutual union of two of God's children" (Vol. 11, edition 5, Moscow, 1907, p. 138).

The different functions in the family of the husband and wife, father, mother, and children imply also a different position in the family and Church, with which are associated differences in external matters. Men are directed to pray and stand in Church with uncovered heads, while women should have covered heads. The

Apostle Paul explains that this symbolizes the family hierarchy, "Now I want you to realize that the head of every man is Christ, and the head of the woman is man" (1 Corinthians 11:3). Similarly, male monastics are supposed to go about with covered heads and not only in Church, while clergymen are directed to distinguish themselves from the rest of the faithful by both clothes and hair (6th Ecumenical Council 21; Gangr. 21, et al.). Even in worldly life, many kinds of service and position are distinguished by style of clothing. Thus, when the Church instructs women to have covered heads in Church, this is not done for any sort of humiliation, but only to remind them of their position and the necessity of obeying the Church.

The latter is required of all — of clergymen and laymen, men and women — so that everything might be done decently and in order (1 Corinthians 14:40). Consider it yourselves, is it proper for us to come to God's temple to pray for God's help and to approach the Mysteries and at the same time, break the rules given us by the Church? Among those rules is also included one that men should not dress in women's clothing, nor women in men's. If women sometimes dress that way at home for convenience in housework, that is a lesser departure from good order, but to come thus to Church or to a celebration is not decent and in order, and therefore is sinful. As is well known, both in the Old Testament and in the canons of the 6th Ecumenical Council, the wearing of clothing inappropriate to one's sex is strictly forbidden (Deuteronomy 22:5; 62nd Canon of the Fifth Ecumenical Council).

We would also like to warn our children about the necessity of being careful to protect their feelings and bodies from any sort of moral impurity, which is so abundantly widespread in the society around us. Before the fall of the Tsarist government in Russia, anti-Christian revolutionary organizations carried out deliberate efforts aimed at the moral corruption of youth in order to break down society. Propaganda was conducted for so-called "free love" and for the spread of shamelessness and vice. Now such propaganda is being conducted in the West many times more extensively and successfully than at that time, and sometimes it is even supported by the civil authorities in the name of a falsely understood freedom. In this there is a manifestation of rebellion against God and the order established by Him in the world.

After creating man and the animal world, the Lord commanded Adam and Eve to be fruitful and multiply, to fill the earth and subdue it (Genesis 1:28). For this purpose the nature of man and woman was created different, with one fulfilling and attracting the other. Just as man was given an appetite for food to bring about the nourishment necessary in life, similarly the attraction of one sex for the other was placed in human nature for fulfilling the commandment to be fruitful and to multiply. But as in healthful eating the appetite must be limited by rational restraint, so also sexual attraction, which in marriage leads to the union of the man and woman "into one flesh," is limited by certain laws. Inasmuch as man consists not just of a body, but also a soul, in marriage both of these parts of the human being are united.

In marriage, as A. S. Khomiakov explained in the words cited above, the husband and wife are two beings singled out from the rest of mankind, whose intimate, shared life, motivated by mutual love and physical attraction, is an area hidden from other people. Therefore also, those parts of the female body through which the attraction of a husband to his wife especially comes about should not be revealed to outsiders, and from the days of Adam have been covered by clothing, in contradistinction to senseless animals and certain wild people. The now widespread nudism profanes the human body, and in the end undermines the exclusive union of husband and wife. No less, if no more, does this depravity affect young women, undermining their innocence which nothing can replace for them when they marry and come together with their chosen husband. For this reason, from of old, Christian parents have protected the youth of their children from those sorts of impressions which might give rise to desire. "Then desire gives birth to sin and sin, when it is full grown, gives birth to death" (James 1:15).

These impressions include immodest spectacles, any sort of nakedness in the presence of representatives of the other sex, and especially pornography, whether written, or on the stage and television. If it is poison for adults, then how much more does it serve to destroy the moral purity and spiritual health of young people. Man is so made that his perception of the world enters him and develops by means of the sense organs: sight, hearing, touch, smell and taste. They are all extraordinarily important and serve as a means of contact with those like oneself, particularly with members of the opposite sex. When these elements are harmoniously connected in peoples' lives, they lead them to sensible, beneficial contacts with others.

The sin of the first human beings caused a division in the whole created world which affects all of us. Since that time, whenever disharmony — caused by sinful thoughts and actions — has developed in individuals, then bitter feelings, dissatisfaction, and irritability appear, which may lead to accidie (now called despondency) and, in some cases, to aggressive and even criminal tendencies. This has repeatedly been established by different investigations. Only prayer, repentance, and love wipe out the consequences of sin. If sin is a symptom of spiritual sickness, then the means of repelling the temptations it produces are prayer, fasting, and living according to the laws of the Church. These are the sort of preventive measures which protect us from moral falls.

This is why, in our concern for the moral purity of our spiritual children, we ask them to refrain from mixed bathing in places where tempting nakedness is now allowed, and from other amusements which might lead them into temptation. While warning our children of the necessity of protecting themselves from social phenomena and habits which might attract them into the sins of our times, we beg them to look for direction in their lives not to the evil of perverted, faithless humanity, but to that Light of the World which we have in the Holy Church. The stronger the evil surrounding us, the more we must oppose to it the power of good by strengthening and developing our life in the Church and by practicing acts of love. Orthodox families must make an effort to form circles of acquaintances and friends from among people of their own faith and culture, united around their parish church and the grace-filled life of the Church.

Thus, beloved ones, we have tried to show you the danger of the surrounding temptations and to warn you, so that you will see and recognize them. "Beware lest ye also, being led away with the error of the wicked, fall from your steadfastness. But grow in grace, and in the knowledge of our Lord and Saviour Jesus Christ. To Him be glory now and forever. Amen" (2 Peter 3:17-18).

Chairman of the Council of Bishops
+ *Metropolitan Philaret*
September 1983

Resolution of the Council of Bishops of the Russian Orthodox Church Abroad 15/28 September 1971[61]

On the question of the baptism of heretics who accept Orthodoxy the following resolution was passed:

The Holy Church has from old believed that there can be but one true baptism, namely that which is performed within her bosom, "One Lord, one faith, one baptism" (Ephesians 4:5). In the Symbol of Faith "one baptism" is also confessed, while Canon 46 of the Holy Apostles decrees, "we order any Bishop, or Presbyter, that has accepted any heretics' baptism, or sacrifice, to be deposed." However, when the zeal of any of the heretics weakened in their battle with the Church, or when the question of their mass conversion to Orthodoxy arose, the Church, to facilitate their union, received them into her bosom through another form. In his first canon, which was incorporated into the decrees of the Sixth Ecumenical Council, St. Basil the Great indicates the existence of various practices in the reception of heretics in different countries. He explains that every separation from the Church deprives one of grace and writes concerning schismatics, "the beginning, true enough, of the separation resulted through a schism, but those who

---

61 Translated from The Council of Bishops of the Russian Orthodox Church Outside of Russia, "Resolution of the Council of Bishops of the Russian Orthodox Church Abroad," *Orthodox Russia* 42, no. 20 (November 1971): 12.

seceded from the Church had not the grace of Holy Spirit upon them; for the impartation thereof ceased with the interruption of the service.

For although the ones who were the first to depart had been ordained by the Fathers and with the impartation of their hands had obtained the gracious gift of the Spirit, yet after breaking away they became laymen, and had no authority either to baptize or to ordain anyone, nor could they impart the grace of the Spirit to others, after they themselves had forfeited it. Wherefore, they [the ancient partisans of Sts. Cyprian and Firmilian] bade that those baptized by them [the heretics] should be regarded as baptized by laymen, and that, when they came to join the Church, they should have to be repurified by the true baptism as prescribed by the Church." However, "for the sake of the edification of many," St. Basil does not object to the use of another form of reception for the schismatic Cathari in Asia. Concerning the Encratites he writes, "if, however, this is to become an obstacle in the general economy" [of the Church], another practice may be employed, explaining it in this way, "for I am inclined to suspect that we may, by the severity of the prescription, actually prevent men from being saved."

Thus, St. Basil the Great, and through his words the Ecumenical Council, while confirming the principle that outside the Holy Orthodox Church there is no true Baptism, allows through pastoral condescension the reception, called economy, of certain heretics and schismatics without a new baptism. In conformity with such a principle, the Ecumenical Councils permitted the reception of heretics in various ways, corresponding to the weakening of their embitterment against the Orthodox Church. The *Kormchaya Kniga* (The Slavonic Rudder) cites an explanation of this by Timothy of Alexandria. To the question: "Why do we not baptize heretics who have converted to the Catholic Church?" he replies, "if this were not so, man would not readily turn away from heresy, being ashamed of baptism [i.e. a second baptism], knowing moreover that the Holy Spirit comes even through the laying on of a priest's hands and through prayers, as the Acts of the Holy Apostles testify."

With regard to Roman Catholics and Protestants who claim to have preserved baptism as a mystery (e.g. the Lutherans), in Russia since the time of Peter I the practice has been followed of receiving them without baptism, through the renunciation of their heresy and by the chrismation of Protestants and unconfirmed Catholics. Until Peter's reign, Catholics were baptized in Russia. In Greece the practice also varied, but for the past almost 300 years, after a certain interval, the practice of baptizing those converting from Catholicism and Protestantism was again introduced. Those received in another manner are not recognized as Orthodox in Greece. There have been many cases in which such members of our Russian Church have not been admitted to Holy Communion.

Having in mind this circumstance and the growth today of the heresy of Ecumenism, which attempts to eradicate completely the distinction between Orthodoxy and all the heresies, so that the Moscow Patriarchate, in violation of the sacred canons, has even issued a resolution permitting Roman Catholics to receive Communion in certain cases, the Council of Bishops recognizes the necessity of introducing a stricter practice, i.e. that baptism be performed on all heretics who come to the Church, excepting only as the necessity arises and with permission of the Bishop, for reasons of economy or pastoral condescension, another practice of reception in the case of certain persons (i.e., the reception into the Church of Roman Catholics and those Protestants who perform their baptism in the name of the Holy Trinity) through the renunciation of their heresy and by chrismation.

The Russian Orthodox Church Outside of Russia's Anathema Against Ecumenism (1983)[62]

"Those who attack the Church of Christ by teaching that Christ's Church is divided into so-called 'branches' which differ in doctrine and way of life or that the Church does not exist visibly,

---

62 Synod of the Russian Orthodox Church, Outside of Russia, "ROCOR's Anathema Against Ecumenism (1983)," *Orthodox Life* 37, no. 2 (March-April 1987): 13.

but will be formed in the future when all 'branches' or sects or denominations and even religions will be united into one body; and who do not distinguish the priesthood and mysteries of the Church from those of the heretics [Latin Papists, Monophysites, Protestants, etc.], but say that the baptism and eucharist of heretics is effectual for salvation; therefore, to those who knowingly have communion with these aforementioned heretics or who advocate, disseminate, or defend their new heresy of Ecumenism under the pretext of brotherly love or the supposed unification of separated Christians, Anathema!"

APPENDIX A

Ecumenical Doxology with Archbishop Iakovos, Sunday, January 26, 1969[63]

To the Faithful Orthodox Reader:

The event transcribed below is the Heretical Ecumenist event that was the subject and reaction of Metropolitan Philaret of New York's Letter to the Greek Orthodox Archdiocese Archbishop Iakovos in his letter, "An Open Letter to His Eminence Archbishop Iakovos (Koukouzis)." In this transcription of this Ecumenist gathering performed by Archbishop Iakovos can be seen a clear disregard of the Holy Canons. "Let any Bishop, or Presbyter, or deacon that merely joins in prayer with heretics be suspended, but if he had permitted them to perform any service as Clergymen, let him be deposed. Canon XLV of the Holy Apostles."

Doxologia

ARCHBISHOP IAKOVOS:

Blessed art Thou our God, always, now and ever, and unto ages of ages.

---

63 "Ecumenical Doxology with Archbishop Iakovos, Sunday, January 26, 1969," Orthodox Christian Information Center, accessed July 25th, 2022, http://orthodoxinfo.com/ecumenism/doxology.pdf

CATHEDRAL CHOIR:
Amen.

CHOIR OF HOLY CROSS SEMINARY:

Blessed art Thou, Christ our God; Thou who hast into sages the fisherman turned, and hast the world captivated thereby as in a fisher's net. Glory to Thee, O Merciful One. When He descended from on High, the tongues He confused, the people He divided; but when the tongue of fire He distributed, to unity He called all thereby. Wherefore, we, with no voice of discord, the All-Holy Spirit glorify. The grantor of all that is good the Holy Spirit is: the source of prophecy, the perfecter of priests; illiterates it taught wisdom, fishermen it made theologians; the Church is created and holds together. Glory to Thee, of the same power and of the same substance with the Father and with the Son, O Paraclete.

THE MOST REV. METROPOLITAN PHILIP, SYRIAN ANTIOCHIAN ARCH-DIOCESE OF NEW YORK AND NORTH AMERICA:

Psalm 111

Praise ye the Lord. I will praise the Lord with my whole heart, in the assembly of the upright, and in the congregation. The works of the Lord are great, sought out of all of them and have pleasure therein. His work is honourable and glorious: and his righteousness endureth forever. He hath made his wonderful works to be remembered, the Lord is gracious and full of compassion. He hath given meat unto them that hear him: we will ever be mindful of his covenant. He hath shewed his people the power of his works, that he may give them the heritage of the heathen. The works of his hands are verity and judgment: all his commandments are sure. They stand fast for ever and ever, and are done in truth and uprightness. He sent redemption unto his people: he hath commanded his covenant forever: holy and reverend is his name. The fear of the Lord is the beginning of wisdom: a good understanding have all they that do his commandments: his praise endureth forever.

Photos taken from secular coverage of the heretical Ecumenist event.

THE CHANCELLOR:

Have mercy on us, O God, according to Thy abundant mercy; we pray hear us with favour and have mercy.

CATHEDRAL CHOIR:

Lord Have Mercy. (Thrice)

THE CHANCELLOR:

Let us Pray for the Pious and Orthodox Christians.

CATHEDRAL CHOIR:

Lord Have Mercy. (Thrice)

THE CHANCELLOR:

Let us pray for our Archbishop and Patriarch Athenagoras.

CATHEDRAL CHOIR:

Lord Have Mercy. (Thrice)

HIS EXCELLENCY TERENCE COOKE: ROMAN CATHOLIC ARCHBISHOP OF NEW YORK:

Be mindful, O lord, of all the Church leaders who preach correctly the Word of Thy Truth and of Thy servant Patriarch Athenagoras. Be mindful, O Lord, of the Presbytery in the diaconate of Christ and of all priestly and monastic

Orders. Do not, we pray, reject anyone of us who now stand before Thy Holy Altar. Visit and strengthen us in Thy Goodness, our Lord. Become manifest to us by Thy many favours; make the seasons temperate and let Thy rain gently fall for our land to fruit. Bless this anniversary that in Thy goodness Thou hast allowed to be reached. Cease divisions among the Churches; stifle the rage of those who are against us; disturbances of heresies quickly dispel by the power of Thy Holy Spirit. Illumine us with Thy light, and receive us in Thy kingdom. Grant unto us Thy peace and Thy love, Lord our God; Thou hast given us so much. Amen.

CATHEDRAL CHOIR:

Glory to Thee who hast shown forth the Light. Glory be to God on High, and peace on earth, goodwill among men. We praise Thee, we bless Thee, we worship Thee, we glorify Thee, we thank Thee for Thy great glory. Blessed art Thou, Lord, God of our Fathers, and praised and glorified is Thy name for ever. Amen. Extend Thy mercy unto those who have come to Thy knowledge. Holy God, Holy Mighty, Holy Immortal, have mercy upon us.

READER:

The reading is from the Epistle of St. Paul to the Hebrews chapter 7, verses 15-28

Brethren, this becomes even more evident when another priest arises in the likeness of Melchizedek, who has become a priest, not according to a legal requirement concerning bodily descent but by the power of an indestructible life. For it is witnessed of him, Thou art a priest forever, after the order of Melchizedek." On the one hand, a former commandment is set aside because of its weakness and uselessness (for the law made nothing perfect); on the other hand, a better hope is introduced, through which we draw near to God. And it was not without an oath. Those who formerly became priests took their office without an oath, but this one was addressed with an oath, "The Lord has sworn and will not change his mind, 'Thou art a priest forever.'" This makes Jesus the surety of a better covenant. The former priests were many in number, because they were prevented by death from continuing in office; but he holds his priesthood permanently, because he continues for ever. Consequently he is able for all time to save those who draw near to God through him, since he always lives to make intercession for them. For it was fitting that we should have such a high priest, holy, blameless, unstained, separated from sinners, exalted above the heavens. He has no need, like those high priests, to offer sacrifices daily, first for his own sins and then for those of the people; he did this once for all when he offered up himself. Indeed, the law appoints men in their weakness as high priests, but the word of the oath, which came later than the law, appoints a Son who has been made perfect for ever.

CATHEDRAL CHOIR:
Alleluia, Alleluia, Alleluia.

PRIEST:
Wisdom; let us stand up and attend to the Holy Gospel.

BISHOP:
Peace be to you all.

CATHEDRAL CHOIR:
And with thy Spirit.

HIS GRACE EPISCOPAL BISHOP STEPHEN BAYNE, JR.:
The reading is from St. John's Gospel
chapter 10, verses 1-16
"Truly, truly, I say to you, he who does not enter the sheep-fold by the door but climbs in another way, that man is a thief and a robber; but he who enters by the door is the shepherd of the sheep. To him the gatekeeper opens; the

sheep hear his voice, and he calls his own sheep by name and lead them out. When he has brought out all his own, he goes before them, and the sheep follow him, for they know his voice. A stranger they will not follow, but they will flee from him, for they do not know the voice of strangers." This figure Jesus used with them, but they did not understand what he was saying to them. So Jesus again said to them, "Truly, truly, I say to you, I am the door of the sheep. All who came before me are thieves and robbers; but they sheep did not heed them. I am the door, if anyone enters by me, he will be saved and will go in and out and will find pasture. The thief comes only to steal and kill and destroy; I came that they may have life, and have it abundantly. I am the good shepherd. The good shepherd lays down his life for the sheep. He who is a hireling and not a shepherd, whose own the sheep are not, sees the wolf coming and leaves the sheep and flees; and the wolf snatches them and scatters them. He flees because he is a hireling and cares nothing for the sheep. I am the good shepherd; I know my own and my own know me, as the Father knows me and I know the Father; and I lay down my life for the sheep."

CATHEDRAL CHOIR:
Glory to Thee, O Lord, glory to Thee.

DR. R.H. EDWIN ESPY, GENERAL SECRETARY OF THE NATIONAL COUNCIL OF CHURCHES:
SERMON (was not available for transcription)

DEAN OF THE CATHEDRAL:
In peace let us beseech the Lord.

SEMINARY CHOIR:
Lord have Mercy.

THE DEAN:
For heavenly peace and for the salvation of our souls let us beseech the Lord.

SEMINARY CHOIR:
   Lord have Mercy.

THE DEAN:
   For the peace of the whole world, for the stability of the Holy
Churches of God, and for the union of all people, let us beseech
the Lord.

SEMINARY CHOIR:
   Lord have mercy. Let us pray.

THE REV. DR. ROBERT J. MARSHALL, PRESIDENT OF THE LUTHERAN
CHURCH OF AMERICA:
   Thou, Christ our God, who do not shun from receiving a
sacrifice of praise and a worship to Thy pleasure offered by those
who call upon Thee from the depths of their hearts; Thou who in
prayer Thyself asked the heavenly Father: Holy Father, keep these
my disciples united into one as thou and I are. Preserve, we pray, the
Ecumenical Patriarch Athenagoras the First, in the service of Thy
will that all the Holy Churches of God be united; also preserve in
sanctification our people present here and now. And strengthen us at
all times and under all circumstances so that we may attend to Thy
righteousness, be guided to Thy will, and after having done all that
is pleasing to Thee be rendered worthy of standing on Thy right
when Thou come to judge the living and the dead. Those of our
brothers who are in captivity, we pray, free; those in sickness, visit;
those in danger at sea, steer safely; all the souls that have departed
this life in the hope of life everlasting lay to rest under the light of
Thy countenance; grant a favourable ear, we pray to all those who
are in need of Thy help. For Thou art the granter of all that is good,
and to Thee we ascribe the glory together with Thy Father without
beginning, and Thy all-Holy, Good, and life-giving Spirit, now and
forever and ever.

CATHEDRAL CHOIR:
   Amen.

CATHEDRAL CHOIR:

The Patriarch's Anthem Grant a long life, Lord our God, to our holy divine master, and Archbishop, the Ecumenical Patriarch Athenagoras the First. Preserve him, our Lord, for many, many years to come (thrice).

CATHEDRAL CHOIR:

The Dismissal (While Archbishop Iakovos is giving the Dismissal, the choir prays to God to grant him, in return for his blessing the people, a long and spiritually fruitful life.) Our Master and Archbishop preserve, our Lord, for many years to come.

+ + +

The above Ecumenical Doxology was offered at the Greek Orthodox Archepiscopal Cathedral of the Holy Trinity in New York City on January the 26th, at eleven o'clock, to celebrate the Twentieth Anniversary of His Holiness Athenagoras I, the Ecumenical Patriarch, on the Throne of St. Andrew.

The following church leaders participated (alphabetically):
- His Grace Stephen F. Bayne, Jr. Episcopal Bishop
- His Excellency Terence Cooke, Roman Catholic Archbishop of New York
- Dr. R. H. Edwin Esby, General Secretary of the National Council of Churches
- Dr. R. H. Robert J. Marshall, President of the Lutheran Church in America
- The Most Rev Metropolitan Philip, Archbishop of the Syrian Antiochian Church of New York and North America

APPENDIX B

A Brief Word from Metropolitan Philaret on the Soviet church.[64]
Translated from an Audio Recording.

"Here is what I wanted to bring to your attention, a fact that many of you may not have realized. Archimandrite Constantine, editor of the journal 'Orthodox Russia,' a man with a deep Christian mind, now deceased, whom many of you probably knew, considered the creation of the Soviet church to have been the most dangerous of all the communist achievements. That is where the unfortunate people were sent instead of the True Church that was hidden in the catacombs beneath the surface. Do not think that I exaggerated Fr. Constantine's words. At the time of the All-Russian Orthodox Church Council (Sobor) in 1918, Patriarch Tikhon, head of the Russian Church, anathematized and excommunicated not only the atheists and radical revolutionaries, but also all collaborators with them."

---

64   "On the Soviet Church," Metropolitan Philaret (Voznesensky) Audio Recording, accessed July 27th, 2022, https://app.box.com/s/ki1x0vx8obex3kszzor13idqj5d40yj2

Above: St. John of San Francisco, Metropolitan Philaret, and
Bishop Sava of Edmonton in San Francisco, California.
Below: Metropolitan Philaret at Holy Trinity Seminary, with Protodeacon
Nikita Chakirov, and future Fr. Serge Lukianov (in background).

BIBLIOGRAPHY

IN CHRONOLOGICAL ORDER OF CITATION:

Brotherhood of Saint Herman of Alaska. "Our Living Links with the Holy Fathers: Metropolitan Philaret of New York." *Orthodox Word* 12, no.1 (January-February 1976): 3-5.

Official Website of the Eastern American Diocese of the Russian Orthodox Church Outside of Russia. "Biography of Metropolitan Philaret (Voznesensky)."Accessed July 8th, 2017. http://archive.eadiocese.org/History/metphilaret.en.htm

Holy Trinity Russian Orthodox Monastery. "A Short Biography of the Late Metropolitan Philaret." *Orthodox Life* 35, no. 6 (November-December 1985): 3-5.

Holy Trinity Russian Orthodox Monastery. "New Primate of the Russian Orthodox Church Abroad." *Orthodox Life* 87, no. 3 (May-June 1964): 15-17.

Holy Trinity Russian Orthodox Monastery. "The Enthronement of Metropolitan Philaret." *Orthodox Life* 87, no. 3 (May-June 1964): 6-15.

Holy Trinity Russian Orthodox Monastery. "The Repose and Funeral Service of Metropolitan Philaret First-Hierarch of the Russian Orthodox Church Abroad." *Orthodox Life* 35, no. 6 (November-December 1985): 5-9.

Holy Trinity Russian Orthodox Monastery. "Sermon at the Burial of His Eminence The Most Reverend Philaret First-Hierarch of the Russian Orthodox Church Abroad by Archbishop Vitaly of Montreal & Canada." *Orthodox Life* 35, no. 6 (November-December 1985): 10-11.

Holy Trinity Russian Orthodox Monastery. "Eulogy on the Late Metropolitan Philaret from the Hermitage of Our Lady of Kursk." *Orthodox Life* 35, no. 6 (November-December 1985): 21-22.

Official Website of the Eastern American Diocese of the Russian Orthodox Church Outside of Russia. "Protopresbyter Alexander Kiselev's Eulo-

gy at the Funeral of Metropolitan Philaret." Accessed July 8th, 2017.
http://archive.eadiocese.org/History/metphilaret/eulogy.en.htm

Brotherhood of Saint Herman of Alaska. "Our Living Links with the Holy
Fathers: Metropolitan Philaret of New York." *Orthodox Word* 12, no.1
(January-February 1976): 3-5.

Metropolitan Philaret of New York. "Paschal Epistle of the Primate of
the Russian Orthodox Church Outside of Russia." *Orthodox Life*, no. 2
(March-April 1969): 3-4.

Metropolitan Philaret of New York. "Christmas Message of the President
of the Synod of Bishops of the Russian Orthodox Church Outside of
Russia." *Orthodox Life*, no.1 (January-February 1970): 3-4.

Metropolitan Philaret of New York. "Paschal Epistle by Metropolitan Philaret (1982)." *Orthodox Heritage* 17, no. 03-04 (March-April 2019): 28-29.

Metropolitan Philaret of New York. "Speech Made by the First-Hierarch,
His Eminence, Metropolitan Philaret, On Handing the Hierarchal Staff
to His Grace, Bishop Hilarion of Manhattan." *Orthodox Life* 35, no. 1
(January-February 1985): 39-40.

Metropolitan Philaret of New York. "On the Canonization of our Holy and
God-Bearing Father Saint Herman of Alaska." *Orthodox Word* 6, no.3
(May-June 1970): 111-114.

Metropolitan Philaret of New York. "The Glorification of Blessed Xenia."
Orthodox Word 14, no. 4 (July-August 1978): 148-150 & 199.

Metropolitan Philaret of New York. "Metropolitan Philaret on Blessed
Father Herman." *Orthodox Word* 6, no. 1 (January-February 1970): 3.

Official Diocese of the Eastern American Diocese ROCOR, translated by
Reader Gregory Levitsky. "He Who Believeth and is Baptized Shall be
Saved." Accessed July 13, 2022. http://archive.eadiocese.org/History/
metphilaret/01believeth.en.htm

Official Diocese of the Eastern American Diocese ROCOR, translated
by Reader Gregory Levitsky. "Refresher for a Russian Orthodox
Pastor." Accessed July 13, 2022. http://archive.eadiocese.org/History/
metphilaret/02orthodoxpastors.en.htm

Official Diocese of the Eastern American Diocese ROCOR, translated by Reader Gregory Levitsky. "Epistle to Titus by Metropolitan Philaret." Accessed July 13, 2022. http://archive.eadiocese.org/History/metphilaret/03titus.en.htm

Official Diocese of the Eastern American Diocese ROCOR, translated by Reader Gregory Levitsky. "Discussion with a Youth Group about the Vespers Service." Accessed July 13, 2022. http://archive.eadiocese.org/History/metphilaret/04vespers.en.htm

Official Diocese of the Eastern American Diocese ROCOR, translated by Reader Gregory Levitsky. "Saint Nicholas the Wonderworker." Accessed July 13, 2022. http://archive.eadiocese.org/History/metphilaret/05stnicholas.en.htm

Official Diocese of the Eastern American Diocese ROCOR, translated by Reader Gregory Levitsky. "Necessity of Fulfilling the Church's Commandments." Accessed July 13. 2022, http://archive.eadiocese.org/History/metphilaret/06commandments.en.htm

Official Diocese of the Eastern American Diocese ROCOR, translated by Reader Gregory Levitsky. "Every Christian Must Bear His Cross." Accessed July 13, 2022. http://archive.eadiocese.org/History/metphilaret/bearcross.en.htm

Official Diocese of the Eastern American Diocese ROCOR, translated by Reader Gregory Levitsky. "Christ is the Conqueror of the World." Accessed July 13, 2022. http://archive.eadiocese.org/History/metphilaret/christconqueror.en.htm

Official Diocese of the Eastern American Diocese ROCOR, translated by Reader Gregory Levitsky. "Sermon on the Fourth Sunday of Great Lent." Accessed July 13, 2022. http://archive.eadiocese.org/History/metphilaret/4sungtlent.en.htm

YouTube. "Sermon of Saint Metropolitan Philaret of ROCOR 1981." Accessed. July 29th, 2022. https://youtu.be/IBk7IA7-jCM

Metropolitan Philaret of New York. "A Sorrowful Epistle." *Orthodox Life*, no. 4 (July-August 1969): 3-14.

St. Herman of Alaska Brotherhood. "Second Sorrowful Epistle of Metropolitan Philaret," *Orthodox Word* 8, no. 2 (March-April 1972): 42.

Orthodox Christian Information Center. "The Second Sorrowful Epistle of Metropolitan Philaret." Accessed July 9, 2022. http://orthodoxinfo. com/ecumenism/sorrow2.aspx

Metropolitan Philaret of New York. "On the Thyateira Confession." *Orthodox Life* 26, no. 2 (March-April 1976): 21-25.

Metropolitan Philaret of New York. "The Triumph of Orthodoxy." *Orthodox Life* 45, no. 1 (January-February 1995): 2-4.

Metropolitan Philaret of New York. "A Conversation with His Eminence Metropolitan Philaret: With Students of Holy Trinity Theological Seminary in Jordanville, New York." *Orthodox Life* 49, no. 6 (November-December 1999): 39-48.

Metropolitan Philaret of New York. "Address of Metropolitan Philaret before the Memorial Service for Vladika John." *Orthodox Life* 100, no. 4 (July-August 1966): 3-5.

Metropolitan Philaret of New York. "Metropolitan Philaret on Archbishop John." *Orthodox Life* 101, no. 5 (September-October 1966): 3-4.

Archimandrite Philaret (Voznesensky). "Will the Heterodox Be Saved." *Orthodox Life* 34, no. 6 (November-December 1984): 33-35.

Metropolitan Philaret of New York. "Concerning the Old Ritual." *Orthodox Life* 33, no. 5 (September-October 1983): 39-41.

Metropolitan Philaret of New York. "Declaration to the Bishops, Clergy and Laity Assembly at St. Tikhon's Monastery." *Orthodox Life*, no. 5 (September-October 1970): 3-7.

Metropolitan Philaret of New York. "An Epistle to All the Faithful Children of the Russian Orthodox Church Abroad Concerning the Approaching Glorification of the New-Martyrs of Russia." *Orthodox Life* 31, no. 4 (July-August 1981): 11-14.

Metropolitan Philaret of New York. "The Catacomb Church: The Epistle of Metropolitan Philaret." *Orthodox Word* 2, no. 2 (April-June 1966): 63-69.

Metropolitan Philaret of New York. "First Statement of Metropolitan Philaret on the American Metropolia." *Orthodox Word* 1, no. 3 (May-June 1965): 117-118.

Metropolitan Philaret of New York. "An Open Letter to His Eminence Archbishop Iakovos." *Orthodox Life*, no. 2 (March-April 1969): 21-24.

Metropolitan Philaret of New York. "In Defense of Orthodoxy: Epistle of Metropolitan Philaret to Metropolitan Ireney." *Orthodox Word* 11, no. 1 (January-February 1975): 3-5.

Metropolitan Philaret & Bishop Gregory. "The Announcement of the Extraordinary Joint Conference of the Sacred Community of the Holy Mount Athos & An Epistle Response to Mount Athos & An Epistle." *Orthodox Life* 30, no. 3 (May-June1980): 8-13.

Metropolitan Philaret of New York. "An Appeal to His Holiness Athenagoras of Constantinople, New Rome, and Ecumenical Patriarch," *Orthodox Word* 2, no. 1 (January-March 1966): 27-30.

Ostroumoff, Ivan N. *The History of the Council of Florence*. Boston: Holy Transfiguration Monastery, 1971.

Metropolitan Philaret of New York. "Epistle of the Sobor of Bishops of the Russian Orthodox Church Abroad to the Faithful." *Orthodox Life* 87, no. 3 (May-June 1964): 3-5.

Metropolitan Philaret of New York. "Archpastoral Encyclical of the Synod of Bishops of the Russian Orthodox Church Outside of Russia to the Orthodox Russian People in Diaspora." *Orthodox Life*, no. 1 (January-February1970): 14-18.

Synod of Bishops of the Russian Orthodox Church Outside of Russia. "Epistle of the Council of Bishops of the Russian Orthodox Church Abroad to the Russian People." *Orthodox Life* 28, no. 6 (November-December 1978): 15-18.

Synod of Bishops of the Russian Orthodox Church Outside of Russia. "Epistle to the Flock of the Russian Church Abroad, Beloved of God." *Orthodox Life* 28, no. 6 (November-December 1978): 19-22.

Synod of the Russian Orthodox Church Outside of Russia. "Encyclical Letter of the Council of Bishops of the Russian Orthodox Church Outside Russia." *Orthodox Life* 33, no. 6 (November-December 1983): 11-19.

Metropolitan Philaret of New York. "An Encyclical Letter of the Chairman of the Council of Bishops of the Russian Orthodox Church Outside Russia." *Orthodox Life* 33, no. 6 (November-December 1983): 19-24.

Translated from The Council of Bishops of the Russian Orthodox Church Outside of Russia. "Resolution of the Council of Bishops of the Russian Orthodox Church Abroad." *Orthodox Russia* 42, no. 20 (November 1971): 12.

Synod of the Russian Orthodox Church, Outside of Russia. "ROCOR's Anathema Against Ecumenism (1983)." *Orthodox Life* 37, no 2 (March-April 1987): 13.

Orthodox Christian Information Center. "Ecumenical Doxology with Archbishop Iakovos, Sunday. January 26, 1969." Accessed July 25th, 2022. http://orthodoxinfo.com/ecumenism/doxology.pdf.

Metropolitan Philaret (Voznesensky) Audio Recording. "On the Soviet Church." Accessed July 27th, 2022. https://app.box.com/s/ki1x0vx8obex3kszzor13idqj5d40yj2

Graced with an Apostolic Mind, Enthroned with the Hierarchs of the Russian Church Abroad, Divinely Wise Cultivator of the Russian Diaspora, Confessor of the Love of Christ, Zealot of Orthodoxy, Holy Father Philaret our Hierarch, Entreat Christ our God, to establish spiritual unity in the Church of our Fathers and to save our souls!

Metropolitan Philaret of New York
at Holy Transfiguration Monastery
in Boston, Massachusetts (1970s)

UNCUT MOUNTAIN PRESS TITLES

Books by Archpriest Peter Heers

Fr. Peter Heers, *The Ecclesiological Renovation of Vatican II: An Orthodox Examination of Rome's Ecumenical Theology Regarding Baptism and the Church*, 2015

Fr. Peter Heers, *The Missionary Origins of Modern Ecumenism: Milestones Leading up to 1920*, 2007

The Works of our Father Among the Saints, Nikodemos the Hagiorite

Vol. 1: *Exomologetarion: A Manual of Confession*

Vol. 2: *Concerning Frequent Communion of the Immaculate Mysteries of Christ*

Vol. 3: *Confession of Faith*

Other Available Titles

Elder Cleopa of Romania, *The Truth of our Faith, Vol. I: Discourses from Holy Scripture on the Tenants of Christian Orthodoxy*

Elder Cleopa of Romania, *The Truth of our Faith, Vol. II: Discourses from Holy Scripture on the Holy Mysteries*

Fr. John Romanides, *Patristic Theology: The University Lectures of Fr. John Romanides*

Demetrios Aslanidis and Monk Damascene Grigoriatis, *Apostle to Zaire: The Life and Legacy of Blessed Father Cosmas of Grigoriou*

Protopresbyter Anastasios Gotsopoulos, *On Common Prayer with the Heterodox According to the Canons of the Church*

Robert Spencer, *The Church and the Pope*

G. M. Davis, *Antichrist: The Fulfillment of Globalization*

Athonite Fathers of the 20th Century, Vol. I

St. Gregory Palamas, *Apodictic Treatises on the Procession of the Holy Spirit*

St. Hilarion Troitsky, *On the Dogma of the Church: An Historical Overview of the Sources of Ecclesiology*

Fr. Alexander Webster and Fr. Peter Heers, Editors, *Let No One Fear Death*

Elder George of Grigoriou, *Catholicism in the Light of Orthodoxy*

Archimandrite Ephraim Triandaphillopoulos, *Noetic Prayer as the Basis of Mission and the Struggle Against Heresy*

Select Forthcoming Titles

Nicholas Baldimtsis, *Life and Witness of St. Iakovos of Evia*

Georgio, *Errors of the Latins*

Fr. Peter Heers, *Going Deeper in the Spiritual Life*

Abbe Guette, *The Papacy*

Athonite Fathers of the 20th Century, Vol. II

This 1ˢᵗ Edition of

METROPOLITAN PHILARET OF NEW YORK

ZEALOUS CONFESSOR FOR THE FAITH

edited by Subdeacon Nektarios Harrison, M.A. with a cover design by George Weis, typeset in Baskerville, and printed in this two thousand and twenty second year of our Lord's Holy Incarnation is one of the many fine titles available from Uncut Mountain Press, translators and publishers of Orthodox Christian theological and spiritual literature. Find the book you are looking for at

u n c u t m o u n t a i n p r e s s . c o m

**GLORY BE TO GOD
FOR ALL THINGS**

AMEN.